Folklore, Literature, and Cultural Theory

NEW PERSPECTIVES IN FOLKLORE
VOLUME 2
GARLAND REFERENCE LIBRARY OF THE HUMANITIES
VOLUME 1395

DRESSING THE DRAGON.

From Juliana Horatia Ewing's *The Peace Egg and a Christmas Mumming Play*

Folklore, Literature, and Cultural Theory
Collected Essays

Edited by
Cathy Lynn Preston

New York and London

First published 1995 by Garland Publishing, Inc.

This edition published 2013 by Routledge

Routledge
Taylor & Francis Group
711 Third Avenue,
New York, NY 10017, USA

Routledge
Taylor & Francis Group
2 Park Square, Milton Park,
Abingdon, Oxfordshire OX14 4RN

First issued in paperback 2016

Routledge is an imprint of the Taylor and Francis Group, an informa business

Copyright © 1995 by Cathy Lynn Preston
All rights reserved

Library of Congress Cataloging-in-Publication Data

Folklore, literature, and cultural theory : collected essays / edited by
 Cathy Lynn Preston.
       p.   cm. — (Garland reference library of the humanities ; vol.
 1395. New perspectives in folklore ; vol. 2)
   Includes bibliographical references.
   ISBN 0-8240-7271-5 (alk. paper)
     1. Literature and folklore.   2. Folklore in literature.   3. Folklore.
 I. Preston, Cathy Lynn.   II. Series: Garland reference library of the humani-
 ties. New perspectives in folklore ; vol. 2.
 GR41.3.F65   1995
 809—dc20   95-13920
                                                                        CIP

ISBN 13: 978-1-138-97443-2 (pbk)
ISBN 13: 978-0-8240-7271-1 (hbk)

Contents

Acknowledgments vii
Introduction
    Cathy Lynn Preston   ix

PART I: THE LITERARY

1. Politics and Indigenous Theory in Leslie Marmon Silko's "Yellow Woman" and Sandra Cisneros' "Woman Hollering Creek"
    Alesia García   3

2. Graffiti as Story and Act
    Danielle M. Roemer   22

3. Folklore and the Literature of Exile
    Mark E. Workman   29

4. Writing the Hybrid Body: Thomas Hardy and the Ethnographic "Money Shot"
    Cathy Lynn Preston   43

5. "Writing" and "Voice": The Articulations of Gender in Folklore and Literature
    Cristina Bacchilega   83

6. Social Protest, Folklore, and Feminist Ideology in Chicana Prose and Poetry
    María Herrera-Sobek   102

PART II: THE TRADITIONAL, VERNACULAR, AND LOCAL

7. "Sidebar Excursions to Nowhere": The Vernacular Storytelling of Errol Morris and Spalding Gray
    John D. Dorst   119

8. Shakespeare's Step-Sisters: Romance Novels and the Community of Women
    Clover Williams and *Jean R. Freedman*   135

9. Chuck Berry as Postmodern Composer-Performer
    Peter Narváez   169

10. Pieces for a Shabby Hut
    Lee Haring   187

11. Slave Spirituals: Allegories of the Recovery from Pain
    Laura O'Connor   204

12. Re-presentations of (Im)moral Behavior in the Middle English Non-Cycle Play "Mankind"
    Michael J. Preston   214

13. Oralities (and Literacies): Comments on the Relationships of Contemporary Folkloristics and Literary Studies
    Eric L. Montenyohl   240

Notes on Contributors   257

Acknowledgments

Because this collection of essays took considerably longer to produce than I had anticipated, I would like to thank the contributors to the collection for their patience. I would also like to thank Garland Publishing, and Gary Kuris in particular, for its continuing support of folklorists' work. And I would like to thank Mike, Theresa, and Stephanie for coping through my disappearing acts when I am writing.

Introduction

Cathy Lynn Preston

Placing questions concerning the politics of culture at the center of literary and vernacular performances and of our readings of those performances, the contributors to *Folklore, Literature, and Cultural Theory* attempt to extend and, in some cases, to rethink current discussions of cultural production. Focussing on the construction of community and disjunctures within community and on questions concerning identity politics and the possibility of "voice," contesting boundaries previously drawn between the traditional and the contemporary and between the oral and the written (and oralities and literacies), exploring the negotiated and mutually appropriative domains of local and larger-than-local cultural production as well as questions concerning the politics of the authentic and the touristic—the following essays seek to establish a cross-disciplinary dialogue between folklore and literature and among folklorists, literary scholars, and cultural theorists.

Such a collection of essays has been made possible and, indeed, is necessitated by the disciplinary critiques that both folklore and literature have undergone. Critique has, in large part, been instigated by the field of cultural studies which, on the one hand, has forced disclosures of the ways in which academic disciplines (as ways of knowing) are embedded in socio-cultural power-relations and which, on the other hand, has provided a meeting ground for cross-disciplinary studies of variously situated performances by arguing that all forms of cultural production—"the entire range of society's arts, beliefs, institutions, and communicative practices" (Grossberg 1992:4)—need to be theorized in relation to each other. As a result of critique, English departments, for example, have "opened up" the traditionalized, privileged literary canon in order to include literary performances of people variously situated by gender, class, ethnicity, race, nationality, and sexuality, as well as to include discussions of popular and variously situated traditional, local, and vernacular performances ("vernacular" is used here to designate that mixed field of mutual appropriations among popular, traditional, and local communicative registers in their negotiations of situated meaning and their productions and reproductions of culture). Doing so, English departments have begun to make space for indigenous theories of literature and "up from under" theories of cultural production in general.

Still, all is not as open as it might be, for while there has been an increased interest in theorizing variously situated performances of what de Certeau (1984) refers to as "everyday life," folklorists, who have spent considerable time and effort documenting and analyzing its (everyday life's) traditional, vernacular, and local forms have been increasingly marginalized by hegemonic academic discourse. To some extent, this seems due to a dated understanding among literary and social theorists as to what folklorists study and what they do when they study it—a misunderstanding (in part created in the past by folklorists themselves) that associates folklore with 19th-century notions of "peasants" and "antiquities" and that has consequently, for discussions of modern industrialized society, resituated folklore and folk life, through an appropriative rhetorical move, under the catch-all rubric of popular culture. Such a move seems a bit awkward given most scholars' general recognition of a need to distinguish carefully between peoples' life-practices and academic constructions of those practices. In everyday life, appropriation is a *mutual* process and, as a two-way street, may signify a continuity of tradition as long as continuity includes the concepts of change and emergence. Although marginalized to the extent of erasure within dominant academic discourse, folklore is not dead in the modern (or postmodern) world, just subject to manipulation by situated group-politics as it always has been. Thus, insomuch as that which is marginalized by any group may actually be quite central to it, the contributors to this collection of essays, in a counter-move, attempt to reclaim folklore as an important site of contestation in the production and re-production of culture.

On the other hand, although folklorists perhaps rightfully claim a more extensive disciplinary history than, for example, many of their literary-minded counterparts, in the documentation and study of variously situated peoples' public and private, emergent and traditional, everyday, artistic, communicative performances, disciplinary critique has meant that, contrary to older practices, folklorists have had to acknowledge that the nature of traditional and local performances is not and never has been a pure, flowing stream untouched by larger-than-local discourse. Furthermore, as in the field of anthropology, folklorists have had to rethink the politics of their methods of collection and documentation, as well as that of their analytical models. In particular, folklorists have had to rethink their use and definition of the term "folk." In the past, folklorists have not only participated in but actively shaped a construction of the "folk" as "traditional, peasant, working class, rural, poor, self-trained, or marginal," a construction that, as Shuman and Briggs note, "invents its opposites, whether named as elite, mainstream, popular, academic, or modern," and that is enmeshed within "romantic conceptions that essentialize particular groups" thereby perpetuating stereotypes of them (1993:123). Thus, folklorists have shifted their gaze to include "*any group of people whatsoever* [including themselves] who share at least one common factor. It does not matter what the linking factor is...what is important is that a group formed for whatever reason will have some traditions which it calls its own...traditions which help the group have a sense of group identity" (Dundes 1980 [1965]:6-7). But if, as Dundes's definition suggests, folklorists have foregrounded "group identity" and its affect on situated performances as the locus of meaning, they have not been unaware of the "multiple identities" which differentiate one member of a group from another and which may be respectively intensified for an individual in different life experiences and performance contexts (Nicolaisen 1980; Mills 1993). Thus, while folklore "as a discipline is concerned with the study of traditional, vernacular, and local cultural productions" (Shuman and Briggs 1993:109) and the ways in which cultural production is theorized from within situated communities (whether through embodied performance or through overt commentary), folklorists have increasingly addressed the ways in which the traditional, the vernacular, and the local, as well as folkloristic inscriptions of those domains, are enmeshed within broader sociocultural relations.

The politics of inscription (the writing, engraving, or printing, and, by extension, the making of an audio and/or visual record) and its equally political, reciprocal, and embedded process, that of reading (as in interpreting and thereby rewriting), is, thus, a meeting ground for folklorists, literary scholars, and cultural theorists. While ethnographic inscription, whether folkloric or anthropological, has recently been heavily critiqued for its naive belief in the "objectivity" of its "scientific" methods (Clifford and Marcus 1986; Collins 1990), thereby causing a crisis in ethics among its practitioners, that critique, disclosing as it has the extent to which ethnographic inscription is itself a form of rhetoric (a situated argument for the order of things) has, in a positive way, complicated our thinking about what it is we do when we "decontextualize" and "recontextualize" performances by lifting them from their primary sites, with their situated ways of knowing, for inclusion in our secondary sites with their equally situated ways of knowing (on decontextualization and recontextualization, see Bauman and Briggs 1990 and the various essays in Briggs and Shuman 1993). It has also shortened the distance between folkloristic concerns and those of literary scholars and social theorists whose readings of literary and other forms of cultural texts need equally to be informed by an understanding of the politics of ethnographic inscription, particularly when those texts self-consciously incorporate ethnographic detail— whether for the purpose of naturalizing the self by marking the other as "other," for the purpose, as "other," of naturalizing one's own discourse, or, in either case, for the purposes of estrangement and defamiliarization.

Furthermore, although the politics of the participant-observation method that underlies academic ethnography may be criticized, there is still something to its claim of "I was there, so I should know," even when one recognizes such a claim as a rhetorical strategy for naturalizing folkloristic discourse. To be there is to experience gradually people's everyday lives in a variety which, once documented (even granting the mixed-politics of that documentation) provides folklorists (as well as literary scholars and cultural theorists) with models through which to read the politics of literary and popular inscriptions of everyday life. In other words, folkloristic ethnographic inscription provides access to traditional ways of knowing otherwise frequently unavailable to the literary scholar and social and cultural theorist, just as the self-conscious literary text or pop-culture performance, particularly when auto-ethnographic, might provide the folklorist with performances akin (though, perhaps, not identical) to the "up from under" or "experience near" or "low" (Mills 1990, 1993) theorizing (and its situated politics) that has been argued for in the discipline of folklore. In short, folklorists, literary scholars, and cultural theorists might, through cross-disciplinary dialogue, learn better how to listen to and for the multiplicity of voices embodied in variously situated performances by listening better to each other. And it is with this in mind that I initially decided to edit this collection of essays; it is also with this in mind that I determined the somewhat eclectic nature of the collection.

In Part I of the collection, the contributors address literary constructions of traditional and emergent cultures, those of Leslie Marmon Silko, Sandra Cisneros, Pat Mora, Carmen Tafolla, Julio Cortázar, Milan Kundera, Franz Kafka, Philip Roth, Thomas Hardy, and Dacia Maraini. The contributors to Part II of the collection offer readings of a variety of traditional, vernacular, and local performances: the postmodernist storytelling of documentary filmmaker Errol Morris and performance artist Spalding Gray; the construction of community among female readers of popular romance novels; the method-acting of Chuck Berry; the interview-situation in the collection of Madagascar and Mauritius cosmogonic tales published for 19th-century French readers; the merger of voice and body in performances of slave spirituals; the performance politics of conflicting registers in the medieval play, *Mankind*; and the possibilities engendered through a renegotiated postmodern understanding of oralities (and literacies).

Although I have divided the collection of essays into two parts, there are points of similarity among the essays that cross this divide. To begin with, one might note that a number of essays explore the function of storytelling in the construction, maintenance, and healing of community. For example, drawing on selected contemporary theories by folkloristic and anthropological ethnographers and Native American writers as they coincide with the Laguna Pueblo theories outlined by Leslie Marmon Silko, Alesia García shows how indigenous theories emerge in "Yellow Woman," Silko's version of the well known Pueblo myth. García then compares and contrasts Pueblo theories with Chicano theories of language and literature in order to explore a Chicano theory of storytelling as it emerges in Sandra Cisneros' recent version of the well-known legend of La Llorona in "Woman Hollering Creek." In both she foregrounds the function, for subordinated peoples, of storytelling (its weaving of new stories with old, its constructing of the emergent even as it preserves the past) as a form of "political as well as personal resistance to continuing oppression by an assimilationist dominant culture." María Herrera-Sobek (drawing on and yet contesting the writings of social theorist Antonio Gramsci 1978) extends García's discussion of the politics of indigenous storytelling by focussing on the writings of Chicana intellectuals in order to demonstrate the role of those writings as "mediators between folk and literary genres" and the function of their authors as "mediators or 'hinge intellectuals' between the ruling-class elites and the pueblo or Chicano working-class. Laura O'Connor draws on Elaine Scarry's *The Body in Pain* (1985) to explore slave spiritual performances as a movement towards an integration of body and voice in the individual and communal articulation of and recovery from pain. And Clover Williams and Jean R. Freedman—having conducted extensive interviews with middle-class Anglo women who, as readers and writers of romance novels, are frequently scorned and marginalized—couple "experience near" theorizing with reader-response theory as they work towards an explanation of the breadth of the genre's appeal among women and the ways in which women negotiate and re-vision the genre's seeming paradoxes so that the genre functions as a positive force in women's lives, stimulating both reflexivity and community among its readers.

Another group of essays explores the problematics of individual "identity" and "voice" when the sense of belonging to a particular community is ruptured. Although, as Mark Workman explains, folklore is generated within groups and the inevitable predilection of the discipline of folklore has been for performances which are communal reaffirmations, not all performances are such. Instead, for many, performance enables the voicing of rupture and contestation. Exiles, for example, Workman notes, exist by definition in a state of tension with the groups from which they stand apart, and their expressions reveal a variety of attitudes towards those communities from which they have been excluded. Thus, Workman's readings of novels by Milan Kundera, Franz Kafka, and Philip Roth consider the bases of what those novels reveal about the dynamic that exists between insiders and outsiders and the ways in which this tension informs folklore itself. In turn, Cathy Preston, Cristina Bacchilega, Lee Haring, and Michael Preston—drawing on the work of Bakhtin (1981, 1984), Derrida (1976, 1978), Cixous (1986), de Man (1983), Benjamin (1969), and others—respectively explore the politics of identity and the problematics of "voice" in relation to the hybrid caught between communities, the ways in which a woman rewrites the fragmentation and hybridization that are "written" into a her body by community, the metaphorical "shabby hut" created during interviews between disparate communities, and the situated performance of competing formal structures within community.

Also addressed by the contributors to this collection is our inherited modernist tendency towards setting up dichotomies, as, for example, when thinking about oral and written performances, the relationship between the folk and the popular, and the defining of the authentic and the inauthentic. Such a tendency functions, in part, as a strategy for privileging one means of cultural production over another and, therefore, is itself embedded in socio-cultural politics. Thus, Bacchilega reminds us that, "In spite of folklore's reputed oral nature, its ties with writing have been strong in a variety of ways," and Eric Montenyohl argues for a resituating of our thinking to take into account a wholly different concept of orality and literacy—something more along the lines of McLuhan's (1962) and Ong's (1977, 1982) understandings—than we have generally been working under. Noting that not all folklore is oral, one might, as does Danielle Roemer, turn to an examination of graffiti as story and act in an examination of the ways in which the walls written on become "sites of contention" where authority and the individual compete for the right to expression, a site of contestation that, once inscribed within a Julio Cortázar story, opens the notion of text to the constitutive and yet, simultaneously, dominating potential of context. Or one might decenter the overly simplistic dichotomies between the oral and the written by foregrounding French feminist theory, as Bacchilega does, and turn to Hélèn Cixous's "rethinking of 'voice' in contestation with Jacques Derrida's redefinition of 'writing'" as offering a possible contribution to "a dual feminist project of reconstruction and deconstruction in folklore and literary studies."

The need to write, particularly in pre-cassette and pre-video recording days, in order to preserve and to analyze has, as Bacchilega explains, lain at "the heart of the discipline of folklore studies" and yet to write means to change the medium in which much folk communication and art actually took and takes place. In particular, as Bacchilega notes, "a great deal of folklore from premodern cultures comes to us mediated through written sources." If folklorists are not to follow what has sometimes been the model in the sciences of marking old data as obsolete and metaphorically dumping it in the trash-can in preference for the continuous flow of new (and supposedly better because of technologically advanced forms of collection and documentation) data, then we must become more complicated readers of written texts. Thus, folklorists might ask, along with Bacchilega, how contemporary critical theory might be used to enable better readings of older textualized data. And this is the question that Haring, M. Preston, and C. Preston, in particular, begin to address. Focussing on questions concerning the inscription of oral performances and questions concerning authentic and the touristic, Haring turns to an analysis of 19th-century tale collections in which inauthenticity is less obvious than it is in, for example, decontextualized and re-contextualized colorful dance performances, although in both cases, "artistic behavior leaves one audience and performance context for another." When cosmogonic tales ("myths") were collected in Madagascar and Mauritius and published for French readers in the 19th-century, they became examples of the kind of decontextualization now called folklorism—the cultivation of attractive elements of traditional culture for the pleasure of tourists. Thus, drawing on contemporary theories of cultural production as well as on contemporary ethnographic work in Madagascar (his own and that of others), Haring attempts to read and to think through 19th-century French collections of Madagascar and Mauritius tales in order to theorize the site of their initial inscription, the decontextualized performance called an interview, thereby disclosing the ways in which the politics of the interview situation are embedded in the texts. Analogously, M. Preston draws on contemporary theory and contemporary folkloric performances in order to explain the esoteric-exoteric politics inscribed within (and which have been part of subsequent readings of) the medieval play, *Mankind*, while C. Preston explores the sexual politics of eroticized writerly-readerly negotiations of touristic moments embedded within Hardy's narratives.

    Finally, John Dorst and Peter Narváez, respectively move to analyze postmodernist (Lyotard 1984) performances which, as Dorst explains, cannot be fully explained by our current use of such terms as "folk, popular, elite, mass, vernacular, industrial, official, unofficial, etc." To do so, Narváez turns to the "shifting imagery of method acting" in order to explain Chuck Berry's successful synthesis of "specific musical influences into a variety of social roles for different audiences." Similarly, Dorst focuses on a local children's narrative playground game (called by the children "Super Mario Five") and the vernacular storytelling of Spalding Gray and Errol Morris in order to describe forms of cultural production which enact a "blending of roles and narrative positions." Such performances not only disclose a "consumer culture in which performance spectacles are the very substance of experience" thereby making "any easy distinction between the natural and the artificial" or the authentic and the inauthentic "more misleading than illuminating," but they also, as Dorst argues, break down "the old stabilities of teller/tale/told to" as well as old ideas of "natural storytelling situations" and of seeming dichotomies between the collector/ethnographer and the folk performer and among "the folk artist, the folklorist, and the fine arts user of folk material."

Addressing folklorists, Shuman and Briggs have recently noted that

> The process of cultural representation has received deep and wide-ranging criticism of late; the authority of all established scholarly perspectives has accordingly come under attack. Numerous critiques, from Derrida's (19[76], 197[8]) technique of deconstruction, Foucault's (1972, 1979) method of excavating institutional discourses, Said's (1978) account of Orientalism, the feminist critiques presented by Cixous (1976), Haraway (1989, 1992), Kristeva (1984), Spivak (1981), and others have challenged the authority of any nation, group, gender, or class to represent the experience of an-Other. The right to place scholarly concepts, theories, and methodologies in a privileged position, one in which their interpretive powers are seemingly not constrained contextually by their positional provenience in particular nations, classes, genders, ideologies, and races, has been withdrawn. The growing centrality of these concerns in a range of fields can provide folklorists with a deeper appreciation of Américo Paredes' challenge to place questions of the politics of culture at the heart of the discipline of folklore (see 1970, 1978, and the essays recently collected in 1993). (1993:114-115)

In turn, while seeking to further Shuman and Briggs's agenda among folklorists, the project of *Folklore, Literature, and Cultural Theory* is simultaneously to argue that the politics of folklore (variously situated traditional, vernacular, and local forms of artistic and everyday communicative performance) should become more central to literary and cultural theorists' understandings of cultural production.

References

Bakhtin, Mikhail. 1981. *The Dialogic Imagination*, ed. Michael Holquist. Trans. Caryl Emerson and Michael Holquist. Austin: University of Texas Press.
———. 1984. *Rabelais and His World*. Trans. Hélène Iswolsky. Bloomington: Indiana University Press.
Bauman, Richard and Charles Briggs. 1990. Poetics and Performance as Critical Perspectives on Language and Social Life. *Annual Review of Anthropology* 19:58-88.
Benjamin, Walter. 1969. *Illuminations*, ed. Hannah Arendt. Trans. Harry Zohn. New York: Schocken.
Briggs, Charles and Amy Shuman, eds. 1993. Theorizing Folklore: Toward New Perspectives on the Politics of Culture. *Western Folklore* Special Issue 52:2,3,4.
Cixous, Hélèn. 1976. The Laugh of the Medusa. *Signs* 1:875-893.
———. 1986. Sorties. In *The Newly Born Woman*, ed. Hélèn Cixous, Hélèn and Catherine Clément, pp. 63-132. Translated by Betsy Wing. Minneapolis: University of Minnesota Press.
Clifford, James and George E. Marcus, eds. 1986. *Writing Culture: The Poetics and Politics of Ethnography*. Berkeley: University of California Press.
Collins, Camilla, ed. 1990. Folklore Fieldwork: Sex, Sexuality and Gender. *Southern Folklore Quarterly* Special Issue 47:1.
de Certeau, Michel. 1984. *The Practice of Everyday Life*. Berkeley: University of California Press.
de Man, Paul. 1983 [1971]. *Blindness and Insight: Essays in the Rhetoric of Contemporary Criticism*. Intro. by Wald Godzich. Theory and History of Literature 7. Minneapolis: University of Minnesota Press.
Derrida, Jacques. 1976. *Of Grammatology*. Trans. Gayatri Chakravorty Spivak. Baltimore: Johns Hopkins University Press.
———. 1978. *Writing and Difference*. Trans. Alan Bass. Chicago: University of Chicago.
Dundes, Alan. 1980 [1965]. Who Are the Folk? In *Interpreting Folklore*, ed. Alan Dundes, pp. 1-19. Bloomington: Indiana University Press.
Foucault, Michel. 1972. *The Archaeology of Knowledge*. Trans. A. M. Sheridan Smith. New York: Harper Colophon.
———. 1979. *Discipline and Punish: the Birth of the Prison*. Trans. A. M. Sheridan Smith. New York: Harper Colophon.
Gramsci, Antonio. 1978. *Prison Notebooks*. New York: International Publishers.
Grossberg, Lawrence, Cary Nelson, and Paula Treichler. 1992. Cultural Studies: An Introduction. In *Cultural Studies*, eds. Lawrence Grossberg, et al., pp. 1-22. New York: Routledge.

Haraway, Donna. 1989. *Primate Visions: Gender, Race, and Nature in the World of Modern Science*. New York: Routledge.

Kristeva, Julia. 1984. *Revolution in Poetic Language*. Trans. Margaret Waller. New York: Columbia University Press.

Lyotard, Jean-Francois. 1984 [1979]. *The Postmodern Condition: A Report on Knowledge*. Trans. Geoff Bennington and Brian Massumi. Minneapolis: University of Minnesota Press.

McLuhan, Marshall. 1962. *The Gutenberg Galaxy: The Making of Typographic Man*. Toronto: University of Toronto Press.

Mills, Margaret A. 1990. Critical Theory and the Folklorists: Performance, Interpretative Authority, and Gender. *Southern Folklore* 47:5-16.

_____. 1993. Feminist Theory and the Study of Folklore: A Twenty Year Trajectory. *Western Folklore* 52:173-192.

Nicolaisen, W. F. H. 1980. Variant, Dialect, and Region: An Exploration in the Geography of Tradition. *New York Folklore* 6:137-149.

Ong, Walter J. 1977. *Interfaces of the Word: Studies in the Evolution of Consciousness and Culture*. Ithaca: Cornell University Press.

_____. 1982. *Orality and Literacy: The Technologizing of the Word*. New Accents. New York: Methuen.

Paredes, Américo. 1970. Proverbs and Ethnic Stereotypes. *Proverbium* 15:511-513.

_____. 1978. On Ethnographic Work Among Minority Groups: A Folklorist's Perspective. *New Scholar* 7:1-32.

_____. 1993. *Folklore and Culture on the Texas-Mexican Border*, ed. Richard Bauman. Austin: Center for Mexican American Studies.

Said, Edward W. 1978. *Orientalism*. New York: Vintage/Random House.

Scarry, Elaine. 1985. *The Body in Pain*. Oxford: Oxford University Press.

Shuman, Amy and Charles L. Briggs. 1993. Introduction. In Theorizing Folklore: Toward New Perspectives on the Politics of Culture. *Western Folklore* Special Issue 52:109-134.

Spivak, Gayatri Chakravorty. 1981. Can the Subaltern Speak? In *Marxism and the Interpretation of Culture*, ed. Cary Nelson and Lawrence Grossberg, pp. 271-313. Houndmills, Basingstoke, Hampshire: Macmillan Education.

_____. 1988. *In Other Words: Essays in Cultural Politics*. New York: Routledge.

＃ Part I: The Literary

1

Politics and Indigenous Theory in Leslie Marmon Silko's "Yellow Woman" and Sandra Cisneros' "Woman Hollering Creek"

Alesia García

> As with any generation
> the oral tradition depends upon each person
> listening and remembering a portion
> and it is together—
> all of us remembering what we have heard together—
> that creates the whole story
> the long story of people.
>
> I remember only a small part.
> But this is what I remember.
> —Leslie Marmon Silko (1981)

> In my writing as well as that of other Chicanas . . . there is the necessary phase of dealing with those ghosts and voices most urgently haunting us, day by day.
> —Sandra Cisneros (1987)

One of the most important functions of Native American storytelling is its preservation of indigenous cultural traditions. In any given narrative or story, there is always a direct or implied reference to indigenous ancestors and beliefs, and as the storyteller weaves new stories with old, tribal histories and identities are reaffirmed while new traditions are created. Leslie Marmon Silko's "Yellow Woman" (in *Storyteller*, 1981) and Sandra Cisneros' "Woman Hollering Creek" (in *Woman Hollering Creek*, 1991) are two contemporary stories in which these writers recognize the importance of their indigenous heritage in relation to their thinking, writing, and identity as Native women in the 20th century. Preservation of Native American languages and stories, according to N. Scott Momaday, "represents the only chance . . . [one] has for survival" (1983:415). Maintaining native cultures and traditions, therefore, is a form of political as well as personal resistance to continuing oppression by an assimilationist dominant culture; Native American literature is a constant challenge to the threat of what Acoma poet Simon J. Ortiz calls "cultural ethnocide" (1987:192).

Historically, indigenous oral narratives collected by anthropologists and others have been considered "authentic" or "traditional" representations of native verbal art; however, until recently, transcriptions of these oral stories rarely acknowledged the continuing tradition of storytelling within the on-going performative contexts of these cultures. The aim of current scholars is to show that indigenous oral narratives resist closure and stasis, for each generation of storytellers continues to sing the songs and tell the stories; they incorporate new experiences, and thus continually recontextualize the stories. Referring specifically to performance of oral literature, folklorist Richard Bauman asserts that

> The concept of *emergence* is necessary to the study of performance as a means toward comprehending the uniqueness of particular performances within the context of performance as a generalized cultural system in a community. The ethnographic construction of the structured, conventionalized performance system standardizes and homogenizes description, but all performances are not the same, and one wants to be able to appreciate the individuality of each, as well as the community-wide patterning of the overall domain. (1977:37; my emphasis)

"Emergence" in oral tradition has several implications. Bauman indicates that the contexts of oral performances are as diverse as cultures and languages themselves. And as cultures shift and change with time, so do the content and context of many traditional narratives. For example, one of the coyote trickster stories Leslie Marmon Silko tells depicts coyote as a male member of Laguna Pueblo at Hopi pretending to be a Medicine Man. This story has all the humor of "traditional" coyote stories, but through its characters and descriptions, it also shows how the contemporary Pueblo Indian community has been affected by social and historical changes within and around the culture, such as the infusion of popular culture, technology, and the cultural interchange with Mexicans and Mexican-Americans.

Anthropologist James Clifford's theories illuminate the dynamism in Native American storytelling and also recognize a need for contextualizing indigenous oral literatures. In *The Predicament of Culture*, Clifford states that

> Twentieth-century identities no longer presuppose continuous cultures or traditions. Everywhere individuals and groups improvise local performances from (re)collected pasts, drawing on foreign media, symbols, and languages. (1988:14)

> Throughout the world indigenous populations have had to reckon with the forces of "progress" and "national" unification. The results have been both destructive and inventive. Many traditions, languages, cosmologies, and values are lost, some literally murdered; but much has simultaneously been invented and revived in complex oppositional contexts. If the victims of progress and empire are weak, they are seldom passive. (1988:16)

Clifford's theories, echoing Momaday, imply that emergent Native traditions have allowed, through language, the assertion of political opposition to Western cultural hierarchies. Indigenous stories give voice to conquered Native cultures, and with each generation, particularly the current generation of contemporary Native writers, the voices gain prominence and, in many contexts, spark controversy. By "politics," I am not referring to a specific political ideology, but the idea of resistance through language. As Ortiz suggests, the very existence of Native language and storytelling in this sense becomes political because it defies the idea of an homegeneous America or an "American" language and literature. Native American literature need not express an overt political statement or position to be counter-hegemonic and counter-discursive. Native American cultures, therefore, become powerfully resistant to the interpretive modes of Western-European literary discourses and theories.

Specifically resisting ethnographic authority and, by association, Western-European literary authority, Chicano anthropologist Renato Rosaldo argues that

> a sea change in cultural studies has eroded once-dominant conceptions of truth and objectivity. The truth of objectivism—absolute, universal, and timeless—has lost its monopoly status. It now competes, on more nearly equal terms, with

> the truths of case studies that are embedded in local contexts, shaped by local interests, and colored by local perceptions. The agenda for social analysis has shifted to include not only eternal verities and lawlike generalizations but also political processes, social changes, and human differences. Such terms as *objectivity*, *neutrality*, and *impartiality* refer to subject positions once endowed with great institutional authority, but they are arguably neither more nor less valid than those of more engaged, yet equally perceptive, knowledgeable social actors. Social analysis must now grapple with the realization that its objects of analysis are also analyzing subjects who critically interrogate ethnographers—their writings, their ethics, and their politics. (1989:21)

Rosaldo argues for analyses of culture and literature through "subjective" rather than "objective" positions. Similar to Ortiz and, as will be discussed later, Silko, Rosaldo's theory points to the necessity of seeking cultural meaning from *within* rather than imposing dominant ideologies onto Native cultures. The key point reverberating in Rosaldo's theories as well as those of other scholars is that native cultures, particularly verbal art, are not simply something to be transcribed, catalogued, and archived, but are continually evolving and reasserting their difference.

In an essay, entitled "Song/Poetry and Language—Expression and Perception," Ortiz describes Acoma Pueblo language as "perception[s] of experience as well as expression" (1983:401). He focuses on the relationship between language and experience, which, he suggests, emphasizes the importance of understanding Native American literature from a Native American perspective and within Native American historical and socio-political contexts. Ortiz describes Pueblo expression as

> A song . . . made substantial by its context—that is its reality, both that which is there and what is brought by the song. The context in which the song is sung or that a prayer song makes possible is what makes a song substantial, gives it that quality of realness. The emotional, cultural, spiritual context in which we thrive—in that, the song is meaningful. The context has to do not only with your being physically present but it has to do also with the context of the mind, how receptive it is, and that usually means *familiarity with the culture in which the song is sung*. (1983:403; my emphasis)

The necessity of using a contextualized and indigenous approach to understanding Native American culture could not be more directly expressed. However, to argue that an indigenous theoretical approach should replace dominant theories, or that it is more valid, would simply result in shifting the hierarchy. Rather than replacing one ethnocentric theory for another, the key is to recognize how Native cultures have always had their own theories about language and storytelling already woven into their traditions. As scholars, we must not devalue these indigenous theories; neither should we erase the historical affects of colonization upon the traditions of indigenous cultures by continuing to privilege theories of the dominant culture that reduce our understanding of native cultures. The radical aspect of indigenous theory is that, unlike other theoretical frameworks, it cannot be easily categorized or defined; it is not static and unchanging. Like the Native oral texts it critiques, indigenous theory is itself emergent and must shift and change in different contexts.

Laguna Pueblo Culture and Indigenous Theory

As has been demonstrated here, Native American culture and language has been explored by many scholars, both Native and non-Native, but Leslie Marmon Silko perhaps best articulates a theory of storytelling based on oral tradition within the context of the Laguna Pueblo Indian community in New Mexico in her 1979 essay, "Language and Literature from a Pueblo Indian Perspective." Pueblo Indian theories, as Silko explains, focus on the dynamic process of oral literature whose structure demands interpretations that resist distorting Pueblo Indian cultural codes and contexts. Silko introduces an indigenous literary theory which is coterminous with the theories of many contemporary anthropologists, ethnographers, and folklorists who have rallied against "classic" modes of cultural and literary interpretations that misappropriate and decontextualize Native rituals and texts.

In her essay, Silko shows that Pueblo language and storytelling is emergent and appears in many forms. The stories all have distinct patterns. Pueblo language is

> English in a nontraditional structure, a structure that follows patterns from the oral tradition. . . . the structure of Pueblo expression resembles something like a spider's web with many little threads radiating from a center, criss-crossing each other. As with the web, the structure will emerge as it is made and you must simply listen and trust. (1979:54)

Literary critic Linda L. Danielson has outlined how Silko has patterned her book, *Storyteller* (1981), to resist Western-European, linear narrative formats and has, instead, woven the book like a spider's web with interconnected stories emerging from a center. Danielson points out that although the book has a cover, title page and prominently displays the author's name, the

> non-linear structure of the book provides the reader with the principle subtext. This structure, which may appear baffling and haphazard at first glance, makes sense when one looks hard at it, as one sometimes has to do in morning light to recognize a spider web. (1988:332)

Using such metaphors as "radiating spokes" (1988:333), "filament" (1988:333), "lateral connections" (1988:341), and "strand" (1988:343) to describe Silko's narrative strategy, Danielson, theorizing from a Pueblo Indian perspective, deftly explains how Silko's writing is an extension of Pueblo thought. As Silko has noted:

> each version [of the story] is true and . . . correct and what matters is to have as many of the stories as possible and to have them together and to understand the emergence, keeping all the stories in mind at the same time. (Silko and Wright 1986:87)

Even as individual stories converge and diverge, Pueblo storytellers are conscious of a center, or the "original thought" myth of "Tseitsinako, Thought Woman" (Silko 1979:55); therefore, keeping the concept of original thought in mind, Pueblo storytellers weave their stories like Grandmother Spider.

Another important characteristic of Pueblo oral tradition is that the culture is linked to a specific geographic location: the individual pueblos in New Mexico. Silko has pointed out that

> one of the . . . advantages that . . . [Pueblos] have enjoyed is that .

> . . [we] have always been able to stay with the land. The stories cannot be separated from geographical locations, from actual physical places within the land. [Pueblos] . . . were not relocated like so many Native American groups who were torn away from . . . [their] ancestral land. And the stories are so much a part of these places that it is almost impossible for future generations to lose the stories. (1979:69)

Laguna stories frequently mention landscapes and locations in and around their actual geographic setting. The stories, according to Silko, are like maps that teach generations about the history of their ancestral homeland. "So long as the human consciousness remains within the hills, canyons, cliffs, and the plants, clouds, and sky," says Silko, "the term *landscape* as it has entered the English language, is misleading" (1986:84); therefore, Pueblo consciousness is synonymous with Pueblo landscape.

The Pueblo culture was originally an oral culture. Commenting on Pueblo orality, Silko refers to the "ancient Pueblo people" who

> depended upon collective memory through successive generations to maintain and transmit an entire culture, a world view complete with proven strategies for survival. The oral narrative or "story," became the medium in which the complex of Pueblo knowledge and belief was maintained. (1986:87)

Silko has shown, that even though Laguna Pueblo stories are often handed down through the generations in English as well as Laguna, it is more important that the stories are told rather than insisting on recreating stories in their original tribal language:

> if you begin to look at the core of the importance of the language and how it fits in with the culture, it is the *story* and the feeling of the story which matters more that what language it's told in. (1979:69)

Laguna Pueblos learn about who they are through the stories they tell; a sense of cultural identity and community is passed on. Story structures, the Pueblo origin myth, the idea of an ancestral homeland, and the continuity of the stories are all ideas embodied in the Pueblo theory of language and literature, and all of these elements of thought and language can be found in Yellow Woman stories. Many variations of the Yellow Woman myth have been recorded by anthropologists and ethnographers over the past century. In *The Sacred Hoop*, Laguna Pueblo writer Paula Gunn Allen states that

> Yellow Woman stories are about all sorts of things—abduction, meeting with happy powerful spirits, birth of twins, getting power from the spirit worlds and returning it to the people, refusing to marry, weaving, grinding corn, getting water, outsmarting witches, eluding or escaping from malintentioned spirits, and more. (1986:226-227)

Joan Thompson points out that Silko includes "six versions" (1989:22) of the Yellow Woman myth in *Storyteller*; however, according to Gunn Allen, Yellow Woman is also associated with Mother Corn Woman, and her sister Corn Mother (sacred corn-ear bundle) (1986:226); therefore, theorizing from a Pueblo Indian perspective, I suggest that there are actually two more versions of Yellow Woman in *Storyteller*: Aunt Susie's story of "the little girl who ran away" in which the mother prepares Yashtoah, the hardened crust of corn meal mush (1981:7-5), and the story of Reed Woman, Corn Woman, and the drought (1981:158-159). With eight emergent versions or representations of Yellow Woman, Silko uses stories to represent the eight legs of Grandmother Spider.

Within the narrative of "Yellow Woman," Silko again enacts Pueblo theories of storytelling. This story is emergent in its inclusion of many socio-historical changes which have affected the Pueblo culture. Abduction by Kat'sinas becomes abduction by invading cultures. Gunn Allen has suggested that

> ... abduction and captivity by spirit people preoccupied earlier tribal women, and, after the coming of the white man, narratives of that sort proliferated because abduction by Spaniards, Mexicans, Frenchmen, and Anglos, as well as by other Native people, became a relatively frequent occurence. The narrator's confusion in "Yellow Woman" reflects the *confusion* in the tradition, as spiritual and historical events blend into one another in American Indian life and consciousness. (1989:219; my emphasis)

"Confusion" is a misleading term. Rather, Silko's story represents an emergent, contextualized version of Yellow Woman—an oppositional text which resists hegemonic structural and temporal linearity. Even though Silko's version has been framed like a short story, she includes many Yellow Woman stories within the larger framework of the *Storyteller* text.

In "Yellow Woman," a married Pueblo woman is abducted by a stranger named Silva, a cattle rustler who wears Levi's and carries a .30-30. In many "traditional" versions, Yellow Woman is rescued; but in Silko's version, she escapes from her captor and returns to her pueblo on her own. Replacing mythic characters such as Whirlwind Man and Buffalo Man are characters who are "real" people who live in contemporary communities, talk about places like Concha Valley and Marquez, and refer to such things as tribal police and Jell-O. With these themes, Silko recontextualizes the entire story within a 20th century setting, showing that, though "progress" and "national" unification have affected the lifestyles of Laguna Pueblos, Yellow Woman remains a part of their oral tradition. Silko's story represents an emergent, oppositional text which resists containment by more conventional theories.

Another important aspect of Pueblo storytelling is what Silko refers to as "stories within stories" (1979:56), an emergent quality that also subverts a linear form. Silko's Yellow Woman, much like Thought Woman, thinks about creation and identity. On several occasions, Silko's Yellow Woman protagonist ponders the Yellow Woman myth:

> I was wondering if Yellow Woman had known who she was—if she knew that she would become part of the stories. Maybe she'd had another name that her husband and relatives called her so that only the kat'sina from the north and the storytellers would know her as Yellow Woman. (1981:55)

At first, Yellow Woman is not able to "simply listen and trust" that she is a part of the tradition of Yellow Woman stories although she accepts their existence in "time immemorial" (1981:55):

> I will see someone, eventually I will see someone, and then I will be certain that he [Silva] is only a man—some man from nearby—and I will be sure that I am not Yellow Woman. Because she is from out of time past and I live now and I've been to school and there are highways and pickup trucks that Yellow Woman never saw. (1981:56)

With this expression of ambivalence that a native person may feel when confronting indigenous traditions and cosmological beliefs that colonizing cultures have denied her—Silko echoes one of the themes addressed in *Ceremony*, her novel which shows how storytelling works to heal this ambivalence. Colonization has historically attempted to purge indigenous beliefs and practices of their value for Native Americans, replacing them with "education" and "technology." Silko addresses this political issue directly by telling a story about a people who have resisted these attempts of cultural ethnocide.

Yellow Woman finally does trust in the stories; however, as the story "ends," she has a new dilemma; feeling ambivalent about which world she would rather inhabit, the spiritual or the "real." She thinks:

> I came back to the place on the river bank where he [Silva] had been sitting the first time I saw him. The green willow leaves that he had trimmed from the branch were still lying there, wilted in the sand. I saw the leaves and I wanted to go back to him—to kiss him and to touch him—but the mountains were too far away now. And I told myself, because I believe it, he will come back sometime and be waiting again by the river.
>
> I followed the path up from the river into the village. The sun was setting low, and I could smell supper cooking when I got to the screen door of my house. I could hear their voices inside—my mother was telling my grandmother how to fix the Jell-O and my husband, Al, was playing with the baby. I decided to tell them that some Navajo had kidnaped me, but I was sorry that old Grandpa wasn't alive to hear my story because it was the Yellow Woman stories he liked to tell best. (1981:62)

In "Yellow Woman," Silko enacts emergent Pueblo theories of storytelling, or the theory of the web, which in its criss-cross pattern represents a literary tradition that is just as important and complex as dominant literary theories. Like Pueblo oral tradition, Chicano oral and literary tradition is emergent, but there are several distinct differences between the two cultures. Most profoundly, Chicanos vary in their particular awareness of and identification with indigenous myths and an ancestral homeland.

Chicano Culture and the Reclaiming of Indigenous Theory

Although there is no single text outlining Chicano oral tradition the way Silko has for Laguna Pueblos, many Chicano and Chicana scholars have theorized about their culture's language and literature. As Ortiz does in his discussion of Pueblo expression, Chicano literary critic Juan Bruce-Novoa recognizes that "Chicano literature is a ritual of communal cohesion and transcendance in the face of constant threats to existence" (1990a:81). Furthermore, although there have been attempts by dominant culture to categorize Chicanos into one homogeneous group, Bruce-Novoa argues that Chicanos

> refuse to fit these patterns. We [Chicanos] insist on being, not those who have crossed an absolute boundary, but the active producers of interchange and synthesis between the would-be binary opposites. We construct the alternative, if nothing else on the ideal plane, of transcendance. . . . Chicanismo calls for a definition of culture as process, open ended process, not a static code of permanent characteristics. (1990b:68-69)

Bruce-Novoa shows that, unlike Laguna Pueblo Indian culture, Chicanos live in an "intercultural space" (1990b:71) and are comprised of diverse groups of people. "In contrast with the classic view, which posits culture as a self-contained whole made up of coherent patterns," states Rosaldo in *Culture and Truth*, "[Chicano] culture can arguably be conceived as a more porous array of intersections where distinct processes criss-cross from within and beyond its borders" (1989:20). The idea of crossing borders is imperative to the understanding of Chicano oral tradition because transculturation has not only affected where Chicanos make their homes, but also how they choose to identify themselves in relation to Mexico and their indigenous heritage, and has determined the ways they tell their stories about La Llorona. Because the scope of this essay does not allow for a complete analysis of the vast range of Chicano verbal art, I must limit my theoretical exploration to the legend of La Llorona as transmitted among Chicanos, people of Mexican descent in the United States.

Chicanos do not usually associate La Llorona stories with the beliefs of their indigenous ancestors as do Laguna Pueblos. La Llorona stories, as many Chicanos tell them, are fragmented from a deliberate

Mexican Indian perspective. Emergence and origin myths did exist in pre-Columbian cultures and have been recorded by many historians and anthropologists, such as Mexican scholar Miguel León-Portilla whose works were among those consulted by members of the Chicano Movement when reclaiming their indigenous heritage (Bruce-Novoa 1990a:81) in a formal act of resistance to assimilation of dominant culture. A recent example of this reclamation of indigenous heritage can be seen in *Borderlands/La Frontera: The New Mestiza* (1987). In this text, Gloria Anzaldúa positions herself within a pre-Columbian, specifically Aztec, world view and fuses it with a Western-European world view, which culminates in her New Mestiza theory. Working through her theories, she attributes pre-Columbian origins to La Llorona. Folkorist Américo Paredes is another Chicano scholar who unequivically assumes an Aztec origin of the legend (1970:xvi). It would be false, however, to assume that all Chicanos in the United States acknowledge connections between contemporary La Llorona stories and the beliefs of their indigenous ancestors. For most Chicanos growing up in the United States, indigenous myths are not commonly introduced as part of cultural traditions. However, since the turn of the century, and specifically within the last thirty years, these myths have been rediscovered, reappropriated, and recontextualized by many Chicano poets, writers, and scholars in an effort to reclaim an indigenous, Native American link between all Chicanos.

In an essay, entitled "Aztlán: A Homeland Without Boundaries," Rudolpho Anaya explains that

> two crucial decisions were made during [the Chicano Movement]: one was the naming of the Chicano community and the second was the declaration of Aztlán as the ancestral homeland. . . . By using this term the Chicano community consciously and publicly acknowledged its Native American heritage, and thus opened new avenues of exploration by which we could more clearly define the Mestizo who is the synthesis of European and Indian ancestry. . . . (1989:232)

> Part of the Movement's work was to revive our connection with our Indian past, and to seek a truer definition of that past. This meant reviving the history, myths, spiritual thought, legends, and symbols from Native America which were part of the Chicano's collective history. The search found the umbilical cord which led to Indian Mesoamerica and the Pueblos of the Rio Grande; that is, in

> the act of declaring our identity and nationality, we acknowledged our American Indian heritage. (1989:234)

This "rebirth" of indigenous heritage can itself be considered a contemporary creation myth, a reference for Chicano consciousness which points to a pre-Columbian past.[1]

The language in which La Llorona stories are told vary according to the predominant language and geographic location of the storyteller. Sometimes the story is told only in Spanish, sometimes only in English, and sometimes the story represents a linguistic synthesis and is told in a mixture of both languages or various dialects. The languages within Chicano culture are themselves emergent and are created differently within each Chicano context. Bruce-Novoa agrees that Chicano texts and languages have at times emerged as "interlingual . . . a blend of Spanish and English" (1990c:49) and that the

> instinctual use of one's personal native idiom is . . . much more complex than a simple preference for English over Spanish. It is interlingualism—not bilingualism. Chicanos blend Spanish and English, at times in obvious ways, such as juxtaposing words from both languages, but more often in such subtle fusions of grammar, syntax or cross-cultural allusions . . . . Interlingualism is a linquistic practice highly sensitive to the context of speech acts, able to shift add-mixtures of languages according to situational needs or affects desired.
> This interlingual form of expression is the true native language of Chicano communities. (1990c:50)

Therefore, like Pueblo stories, Chicano versions of La Llorona depend more upon the preservation of the stories rather than upon an original tribal language.

Within Chicano culture, La Llorona emerges in many forms. Descriptions of both her behavior and appearance vary according to the landscapes and socio-historical contexts within each Chicano community. In some contexts, La Llorona is represented as a malevolent child murderer; in others, she appears as a warning to those who see her; still in others, she transforms into a benevolent protectress. Some storytellers always associate her with water; others only hear her wailing in the wind. There is no single description or composite variant that would serve as a justifiable text of La Llorona;

she is many things to many people.

There are many origin theories about La Llorona. In the scholarship conducted in the past several decades, she has been attributed to actual women from Mexico City (Janvier 1910:162); La Malínche, Hernan Cortés' translator and mistress (Anaya 1984); the Medusa (Anzaldúa 1987:47); and the Germanic floating legend of "The White Lady" (Kirtley 1960:157). Using historical documents such as Bernardino Sahagún's 1585 *General History of the Things of New Spain*, Chicano scholars, such as Anzaldúa and others, have most often attributed her origins to the pre-Columbian goddesses Cihuacóatl and Coatlicue primarily because Sahagun's descriptions are strikingly similar to variant descriptions and representations of La Llorona that appear in both Mexicano and Chicano culture.

Sandra Cisneros is one Chicana who has recently reappropriated the legend of La Llorona. In "Woman Hollering Creek," Cisneros alludes to a pre-Columbian origin for La Llorona, weaves in existing versions of the legend, such as the major motifs of La Llorona as she is associated with water, El Borracho, and her depiction as both a mother and a betrayed lover, and shows how Chicano culture has responded to ongoing socio-historical events by recontextualizing the legend and placing La Llorona in a contemporary setting much like Silko does in "Yellow Woman."

The protagonist, Cleófilas Enriqueta De León Hernandez, is a young, inexperienced Mexicana who is married off by her father to a young Chicano who brings her across the border to Seguín, Texas. Like Silko's reference to the negative aftermath of colonization, Cisneros addresses the plight that some Mexicanas and Chicanas face in a patriarchal system, which makes "Woman Hollering Creek" an oppositional text. Ramón Saldívar asserts that contemporary Chicano narratives

> embody new ways of perceiving social reality and significant changes in ideology. As resistant ideological forces in their own right, their function is to shape modes of perception in order to effect new ways of interpreting social reality and to produce in turn a general social, spiritual, and literary revaluation of values. (1990:7)

Cisneros' narrator comments on Cleófilas' identity as a married woman:

> But what Cleófilas has been waiting for, has been whispering and sighing and giggling for, has been anticipating since she was old enough to lean against the window displays of gauze and butterflies and lace, is passion. (1991:44)

Cleófilas has been raised in a Mexican Catholic culture which expects women to suppress their sexuality and bear many children at the same time. Anzaldúa points out that after the Conquest, the Catholic Church desexualized indigenous goddesses, thereby enforcing a new model for Mestizo women in the form of La Virgen de Guadalupe (1987:27). José E. Limón corroborates Anzaldúa's analyses of Mexicano and Chicano culture. He argues that the image of La Virgen has also been politically appropriated by the Mexican "masculinized official church and the Partido Revoluccionario Institucional (PRI)" (1990:405-6). In an article entitled: "La Llorona, the Third Legend of Greater Mexico: Cultural Symbols and the Political Unconscious," Limón states that La Virgen in Mexicano and Chicano culture has come to represent "a pure, maternal yet virginal figure [who] sets the ideological standard by which real ordinary women are judged and controlled" (1990:404). Limón, as well as Anzaldúa, has shown that among the symbols most associated with women in Mexicano and Chicano culture—La Malínche and La Virgen de Guadalupe—La Llorona is often overlooked as an essential part of an interchangable triad of representations of Mexicanas/Chicanas, a figure who, if contextualized historically, may be understood "as a positive, contestative symbol" (1990:400).

While deciding whether to leave her husband, Cleófilas realizes the consequences she confronts when faced with the ideological standards that juxtaposes real women against icons of purity and contamination:

> Sometimes she thinks of her father's house. But how could she go back there? What a disgrace? What would the neighbors say? Coming home like that with one baby on her hip and one in the oven. Where's your husband? (1991:50)

While her husband spends time at the cantina, Cleófilas and her male child spend their days sitting on the edge of a creek that runs through her backyard. Here, she is like La Llorona who often roams the waterways; however, Cleófilas is not a malevolent child murderer. Instead, as a representation of La Llorona, Cleófilas is a positive mother figure who is leaning toward independence as she and the other women in the story create a woman-centered community. But rather than sentimentalizing female bonding and the theme of motherhood, Cisneros empowers the story with a Chicana feminism, a resistant ideology anchored in working class origins and the Mexicana/Chicana community.

In a passage that parallels Silko's "Yellow Woman," Cisneros' story exemplifies how Chicano storytelling tradition has also begun weaving stories within stories similar to Laguna Pueblo tradition. And at the same time, Cisneros alludes to a indigenous link to La Llorona:

> La Gritona. Such a funny name for such a lovely arroyo. But that's what they called the creek that ran behind her house. Though no one could say whether the woman had hollered from anger or pain. The natives only knew the arroyo one crossed on the way to San António, and then once again on the way back, was called Woman Hollering, a name no one from these parts questioned, little less understood. *Pues, allá de los indios, quién sabe*—who knows, the townspeople shrugged, because it was of no concern to their lives how this trickle of water received its curious name. (1991:46)

The reference to los indios is ironic. The "natives" do not question or understand La Llorona's origins because years of colonization and pressures to assimilate into dominant culture have conditioned them *not* to know. Their ignorance of indigenous origins resembles Yellow Woman's ambivalence toward her native history.

Many Lloronas exist in "Woman Hollering Creek." Female characters who represent negative aspects of La Llorona include Cleófilas, for the first seven pages; Dolores ("the pains"); and Soledad ("lonely" or "grieving"). Soledad and Dolores each live alone—the result of either being a widow or of abandonment by a husband. Both are childless, Dolores' sons having died in "the last war" (1991:47), which, because of the contemporary setting of the story, is presumably Viet Nam.

Cleófilas, as a battered woman, is in the midst of a war herself:

> The first time she had been so surprised she didn't cry or try to defend herself. She had always said she would strike back if a man, any man, were to strike her. . . .
> In her home her parents had never raised a hand to each

> other or to their children. Although she admitted she may have been brought up a little leniently as an only daughter—*la consentida*, the princess—there were some things she would never tolerate. Ever.
>
> Instead, when it happened the first time . . . she had done nothing but reach up to the heat on her mouth and stare at the blood on her hand as if even then she didn't understand.
>
> She could think of nothing to say, said nothing. Just stroked the dark curls of the man who wept and would weep like a child, his tears of repentance and shame, this time and each. (1991:47-8)

Cleófilas' husband cannot decide whether he should worship her or abuse her. His weeping is a sign of the unstable position Chicanos occupy because of ambiguous and unrealistic gender roles constructed by the male-centered Catholic Church. Women are at once pure and impure; men become "father, rival, keeper, lord, master, and husband" (1991:49).

Positive aspects of La Llorona are represented by the female characters Graciela (grace) and Felice (happiness). While she is pregnant with her second child, Cleófilas' husband physically beats her. One day as she is waiting in her doctor's office, a Chicana nurse, Graciela, and her friend Felice, a Chicana who drives a pickup which she owns and has paid for herself, notice the signs of physical abuse on Cleófilas' body. They then conspire to help her leave her abusive husband. Felice offers to drive Cleófilas to the Greyhound Bus Station; and as she drives over the arroyo, Felice "let[s] out a yell as loud as any mariachi" (1991:55)—La Llorona self-fashioned.

These strong women, whom Chicana feminist Sonia Saldivar-Hull calls "mujeres de fuerza" (women of strength) (1991), have a profound affect on Cleófilas because from them she learns that women in her culture have more choices than she has been lead to believe. Cleófilas, as an aspect of La Llorona, aligns herself with a community of women, which includes Cisneros, who have recontextualized the story of La Llorona and have reappropriated her from the misappropriated texts and contexts of dominant culture.

Sandra Cisneros and Leslie Marmon Silko represent Native women writers who have participated in the emergent storytelling traditions of their cultures. As women who have consciously reappropriated "traditional" oral narratives, they have recognized the implicit responsibility to sustain their indigenous heritage; to practice resistance through language and literature. Momaday reminds us that "language involves the elements of risk and responsibility, and in this it seeks to confirm itself. In a word, everything is a risk. That may be true, and it may also be that the whole of literature rests upon that truth" (1983:415).

Notes

1. It should be emphasized as well that not all Americans of Mexican descent identify themselves as "Chicano," and in identifying myself as a Chicana, I am both privileging this term and aligning myself with other scholars whose goal is to reclaim our indigenous heritage. In addition, in this essay, I initially adopt the position of "objective" Western-European literary critic; however, my position shifts to the "subjective" when I identify myself as a Chicana who is privileging an emergent, intercultural theoretical point of view. In doing so it is my intention to intersect theory and practice.

References

Anaya, Rudolfo A. 1984. *The Legend of La Llorona*. Berkeley: Quinto Sol.
_____. 1989. A Homeland Without Boundaries. In *Aztlán: Essays on the Chicano Homeland*, ed. Rudolfo A. Anaya and Francisco Lomelí, pp. 230-241. Albuquerque: University of New Mexico Press.
Anzaldúa, Gloria. 1987. *Borderlands/La Frontera: The New Mestiza*. San Francisco: Spinsters/Aunt Lute.
Bauman, Richard. 1977. *Verbal Art as Performance*. Illinois: Waveland.
Bruce-Novoa, Juan. 1990a. Chicano Literary Production. In *Retrospace*, by Juan Bruce-Novoa, pp. 75-90. Houston: Arte Público.
_____. 1990b. Chicanos in Mexican Literature. In *Retrospace*, by Juan Bruce-Novoa, pp. 63-74. Houston: Arte Público.
_____. 1990c. Spanish-language Loyalty and Literature. In *Retrospace*, by Juan Bruce-Novoa, pp. 49-50. Houston: Arte Público.
Brundage, Burr Cartwright. 1979. *The Fifth Sun: Aztec Gods, Aztec World*. Austin: University of Texas Press.
Cisneros, Sandra. 1987. Ghosts and Voices: Writing from Obsession. *The Americas Review* 15,1:69-73.
_____. 1991. *Woman Hollering Creek*. New York: Random House.
Clifford, James. 1988. *The Predicament of Culture: Twentieth-Century Ethnography, Literature, and Art*. Cambridge: Harvard University Press.
Danielson, Linda L. 1988. Storyteller: Grandmother Spider's Web. *Journal of the Southwest* 30:325-355.

Gunn Allen, Paula. 1986. *The Sacred Hoop: Recovering the Feminine in American Indian Traditions*. Boston: Beacon Press.
_____, ed. 1989. *Spider Woman's Granddaughters*. New York: Fawcett.
Janvier, Thomas A. 1910. *Legends of The City of Mexico*. New York: Harper.
Kirtley, Bacil F. 1960. La Llorona and Related Themes. *Western Folklore* 19:155-168.
León-Portilla, Miguel. 1986. *Pre-Columbian Literatures of Mexico*. Translated by Grace Lobano and Miguel León-Portilla. Norman: University of Oklahoma Press.
Limón, José E. 1990. La Llorona, The Third Legend of Greater Mexico: Cultural Symbols, Women, and the Political Unconsciousness. In *Between Borders: Essays on Mexicana/Chicana History*, ed. Adelaida R. Del Castíllo, pp. 399-431. Encino: Floricanto Press.
N. Scott Momaday. 1983. The Man Made of Words. In *Symposium of the Whole: A Range of Discourse on the Study of Ethnopoetics*, ed. Jerome Rothenberg and Diane Rothenberg, pp. 414-416. Berkeley: University of California Press.
Ortiz, Simon J. 1983. Song/Poetry and Language—Expression and Perception. In *Symposium of the Whole: A Range of Discourse on the Study of Ethnopoetics*, ed. Jerome Rothenberg and Diane Rothenberg, 399-407. Berkeley: University of California Press.
_____. 1987. The Language We Know. In *I Tell You Now: Autobiographical Essays by Native Americans*, ed. Brian Swann and Arnold Krupat, pp. 185-194. Lincoln: University of Nebraska Press.
Paredes, Américo, ed. 1970. *The Folktales of Mexico*. Chicago: University of Chicago Press.
Rosaldo, Renato. 1989. *Culture and Truth: The Remaking of Social Analysis*. Boston: Beacon Press.
Sahagún, Bernardino de. 1950-1968. *Florentine Codex: General History of the Things of New Spain*, 12 Vols. Edited and Translated by Arthur J.O Anderson and Charles E. Dibble. Santa Fe: School of American Research, and Salt Lake City: University of Utah Press.
Saldívar, Ramón. 1990. *Chicano Narrative: The Dialectics of Difference*. Madison: University of Wisconsin Press.
Saldívar-Hull, Sonia. 1991. Mujeres de Fuerza/Women of Strength in Sandra Cisneros' "Woman Hollering Creek." Lecture. Arizona Quarterly Symposium. Tucson.
Silko, Leslie Marmon. 1979. Language and Literature from a Pueblo Indian Perspective. *Selected Papers from the English Institute*, pp. 54-72. Baltimore: Johns Hopkins Press.
_____. 1981. *Storyteller*. New York: Little Brown.
_____. 1986. Landscape, History, and the Pueblo Imagination. *Antaeus* 51: 83-94.
_____. 1988. *Ceremony*. New York: Penquin.
_____ and James Wright. 1986. *The Delicacy and Strength of Lace*, ed. Anne Wright, pp. 87. Saint Paul: Graywolf.
Thompson, Joan. 1989. Yellow Woman, Old and New: Oral Tradition and Leslie Marmon Silko's *Storyteller*. *Wicaso Sa Review* 5(Fall):22-25.

2

Graffiti as Story and Act

Danielle M. Roemer

My focus here is both literary and folkloristic. I draw on the premises of graffiti as folk practice in considering a short story, "Graffiti," by Julio Cortázar (1983).[1] At the same time, I look to the shape and voicing of that story in an attempt to contribute to our understanding of the folk practice.

At the level of the story's plot, this intertextual tension is centered in issues of access. Living in a repressive police state, one in which personal expression is deemed a threat to those in power, a young man and woman begin a conversation whose utterances are the marks of graffiti. Drawing sketches at night and in alternative and clandestine spurts, they try to avoid the police patrols. They never meet, although the man does catch a glimpse of the woman on the night she is arrested, beaten, and shoved into a police wagon. At some later time, she returns to the site and draws a sketch of her battered face next to a recent drawing of the man's:

> you saw the orange oval and the violet splotches where a swollen face seemed to leap out, a hanging eye, a mouth smashed with fists. I know. I know, but what could I have sketched for you? What message would have made any sense now? In some way I had to say farewell to you and at the same time ask you to continue. (1983:38)

The couple's inscriptions to each other are not political in content and never verbal. But the government has banned all wall writing: "the prohibition covered everything, and if some child had dared draw a house or a dog it would have been erased in just the same way" (1983:33). Nevertheless, the young man and woman have access to each other only through their graffiti—a practice which, not coincidentally, is one of deferred response. Typically, there are no co-present exchanges in graffiti writing. Each writer is separated from the other by temporal and other coordinates of social event. The couple's own communicative separation serves as an analogue to the situation of the non-graffiti-writing citizens of the town. Denied the right to signal publically their feelings about the government, passers-by are afraid even to pay obvious attention to the drawn signs of those who would risk governmental retribution: "Looking at your sketch from a distance you could see people casting a glance at it as they passed, no one stopped of course" (1983:33).

In this context of separation, wall writing comes to stand for the exercise of rights of expression and assembly, rights denied the citizens of this police state. There is no encompassing paradigm here bringing the government and its citizens into ameliorative focus. In literary terms, there is no metanarrative; Cortázar brings this point into relief with his selection of a narrator, or, better said, perhaps, a speaker. The words of the story are the woman's and her's alone. She is talking to the man, but only she serves as audience to what is said. In effect, she is talking to herself, imagining her partner's motivations, actions, and reactions. Her stance is appropriate in a story about the political repression of community. In such a context, the self turns inward, seeking company with itself. Her stance is also appropriate in a story that takes graffiti as one of its referents. Here, a solitary speaker carves out an expressive space of her own. Mute though it is, graffiti offers an empirically perceivable sign of individualistic intent, one that will remain noticeable for some period of time, staining the barrier of silence.

Nevertheless, as with the practice of graffiti, we should also notice that meaning in the story is structural, positional. It is defined through interfacings with an other. We can notice these interfacings readily: the citizens and the government, the couple and the government, the man and the woman separately against the government, and the man and the woman as a couple. These interfacings form sites of meaning that life in the city fosters and intimidates. The first three of these are increasingly more specific localizations of unilateral access to the power to make meaning. In each case, it is the government that exercises that power most effectively. The force of its power characterizes the story as a whole. The fourth interfacing offers a rebuttal to the authoritative assertion of meaning. Here, meaning is attempted in a pairing of communion, one that tries out the give and take of significance between equal partners. It is this sense of emergent and dialogic meaning that is ultimately frustrated by the powers of authority.

"So many things begin and perhaps end as a game" (1983:32). So the story itself begins. In "real" life, as well as in a game, what occurs between perceptual parentheses is involvement. "Graffiti" is in part a story about responses, of middles and what occurs in them and by means of them.

The story begins with the young women hypothesizing that her partner found amusing her first response to his graffiti. She supposes that his own drawings began as a game, growing out of simple boredom, rather than as "a protest against the state of things in the city" (1983:32). She imagines him as a spectator, surreptitiously reviewing not only his own graffiti the next morning but the clean-up crews' erasing of the sketches. The insults of the crews were "useless" at these times because, though present, the young man was sheathed in the conventional anonymity of the graffiti artist. Indeed, she imagines that the man never ran any risk at all because he "knew how to choose well" (1983:34). Supposedly the game was between the man and the government, a sort of artistic version of tag in which the representatives of authority always arrived too late to nab their counterpart.

Typically, wall writing is an activity of resurfacing. We give the name "graffiti" to the uppermost layer(s). The quickest way to "erase" graffiti (the term Cortázar chooses) is to paint over it, to resurface it with a seemingly neutral layer. Although it is not made clear in the story, we might guess that that is the method chosen by the state's clean-up crews. If so, we can say that the man and the government compete in terms of surface, the one of marks, the other, of blanked out areas. Competition is emphasized because both kinds of sign matter concurrently: the statement and the achieved silence, the trace and its covering over. The involvement of the man and the government is polarized. The two "write" from the perspective of differing ideologies.

This simple polarity alters, though, when the woman responds a second time to the man's sketches. Only then, she guesses, does he realize that her own sketch was an intentional response to his. The women's involvement mediates and complicates the interaction, extending the situation into the level of deep play (Geertz 1973). The buffering parentheses of play become jeopardized while the quality of play is intensified: "suddenly the danger had become double, someone like you had been moved to have some fun on the brink of imprisonment or something worse" (1983:33). As the couple continues to respond to each other, the implication is of a romantic trist, one layered (as the woman sees it) upon a political base. For her, surfaces have become especially double voiced—both romantic and political. Interaction in a public sphere now attempts privacy. Context becomes ambivalent. The couple sheds the implications of context in trying to communicate with each other through play; yet, the "realistic fact" is that they are operating within an ideological environment that cannot be safely ignored.

Conventionally, play makes the mark subject to reversal and erasure. In play, actions and reactions don't necessarily "count" (Stewart 1978). In Cortázar's story, however, the ambivalence of context allows these conditions themselves to be reversed. To the government, a clean wall is a safe wall. To the woman, graffiti creates the "very clean space where there [is] almost room for hope" (1983:33). She experiences quite literally the consequences of her belief when she is arrested. The reversibility of play is itself reversed. Acts of graffiti are turned back on the woman as she is beaten. The government's "marks," no longer those solely of erasure, become the bruises and lacerations on her face. This reversal localizes and thus emphasizes the power of the police state. As symbolic of citizens' rights, play is forcefully negated—denied the capacity to achieve its own kind of erasure. The women herself becomes someone who doesn't "count," someone who can't be allowed to matter because of her threat to authority. The one possibility for hope (from her point of view) comes with her final appeal to her partner. Though spoken only within her own imagination, she appeals to him not only to continue with his sketches but, by implication, to continue them with political motives: "imagining that you were going out at night to make other sketches" (1983:38).

Graffiti is always a compromised activity because it is a writing against authority. Simultaneously, though, it is an externalization of the writer's sense of individuality: "graffiti promises and indeed depends upon a dream of the individualized masses" (Stewart 1987:174). As the inappropriate display of self, a crime of signature, graffiti can be considered a form of pollution. Like "garbage, noise, dirt, and broken doors" (Castleman 1982), it is a mark that interrupts the seamless sense of experience promoted by authority. The walls written on are not mere concrete or brick supports for expressive display. They are sites of contention (Grider 1979:145-146). In the competition for expressive space, the "winner" will be the one that can exercise the most potent control over materiality. The couple inscribes themselves on the body of the city. So does the government. As well, though, the government can and does inscribe its signs of power on the bodies of its citizens—those they catch writing graffiti.

Even more basic to the theme of materiality than the "what's" of inscription are the "how's" of those acts—the dimension of representation. We know the world and express our interpretations of it through socially re-invented and ratified meaning systems. There is no direct and nonarbitrary link between signifier and signified, between sign and referent in this process. Instead, all communication is biased: all ordering systems are suspect and all discourse systems are problematic (Hutcheon 1989:24): Cortázar emphasizes these issues by setting the story's events in a context in which authority and subversion, the social and the individual, play off one another.

It is appropriate that the artists of the story should work singly and in darkness. They manage briefly a sense of community but that sense becomes possible only in the light of day when the drawings become visible yet, at the same time, vulnerable to the government's own response. The public and the private become supplements to each other here, each defining yet provisional to the other. The privatized autonomy of the graffiti is bracketed by occasions of disclosure, and its social display is parenthesized by occasions of solitary execution.

With these contingencies, Cortázar seems to be pointing to the constitutive capacity of environment. The authoritative actions of the government illustrate this capacity in blatant ways. A more subtle and localized example comes with the woman's situating of her drawings. Like graffiti artists in our own world, the woman intentionally incorporates features of the environment into her sketches: "One night you saw her first sketch all by itself; she'd done it in red and blue chalk on a garage door, taking advantage of the worm-eaten wood and the nail heads" (1983:35). Yet, her simple act of opening the artistic work to the outside world has political implications. It presages the government's encroachment upon any graffiti display. She opens herself and her art to an other. The government moves into that space of the other, displacing the man as her partner. He is saved in a later situation by mere chance, by the buffer of unexpected context:

> There was a confused crowding by the wall, you ran, in the face of all good sense, and all that helped you was the good luck to have a car turn the corner and put on its brakes when the driver saw the patrol wagon, its bulk protected you and you saw the struggle, black hair pulled by gloved hands, the kicks and the screams, the cut-off glimpse of blue slacks before they threw her into the wagon and took her away. (1983:36)

He is saved, in other words, by the luck of the "amateur" graffitist, the one who has yet to acknowledge the political implications of his art. Environment is a highly charged dimension in this story. As the woman hopes the man learns, there is no safe corner, no value-free mark, no stance that will allow commitment without the threat of a heavy price.

Authority and individuality, context and text, come into uneasy dialogue in Cortázar's story. So too can they in the folk practice of graffiti. Rarely though (in American society at least) does graffiti prompt such stern consequences as Cortázar depicts. Yet, the capacity of graffiti to expose relationships of power serves as a critique of all situated discourse—its vulnerability to both the surges and the seeming securities of context. Contextualization is interpretation, and therein lies the threat of acts of erasure as much as of the graffiti they cover. The one is the negation of individuality; the other, its herald.

Notes

1. Belgium born of Argentenian heritage, Julio Cortázar situates many of his stories in fictional versions of the Buenos Aires suburb where he spent his adolescence and early childhood. From the 1950's on, Cortazar published over eighty short stories, five novels, four miscellanies, two books of poetry, two plays, and many essays, prose poems, and travelogues. He has been called one of the most important authors of the "new narrative" in Spanish America (Peavler 1990).

References

Castleman, Craig. 1982. *Getting Up. Subway Graffiti in New York*. Cambridge, Mass.: MIT Press.
Cortázar, Julio. 1983. Graffiti. In *We Love Glenda So Much and Other Tales*. Trans. by Gregory Rabassa. New York: Alfred A. Knopf.
Geertz, Clifford. 1973. Deep Play: Notes on the Balinese Cockfight. In *The Interpretation of Cultures*, by Clifford Geertz, pp. 412-453. New York: Basic Books.
Grider, Sylvia. 1979. *Con Safos*: Mexican-Americans, Names and Graffiti. In *Readings in American Folklore*, ed. Jan Harold Brunvand, pp. 138-151. New York: W.W. Norton Co.
Hutcheon, Linda. 1989. *Politics of Postmodernism*. London: Routledge.
Peavler, Terry J. 1990. *Julio Cortazar*. Boston: Twayne Publishers.
Stewart, Susan. 1978. *Nonsense. Aspects of Intertextuality in Folklore and Literature*. Baltimore: The Johns Hopkins Press.
_____. 1987. *Ceci Tuera Cela*: Graffiti as Crime and Art. In *Life after Postmodernism: Essays on Value and Culture*, ed. John Fekete, pp. 161-180. New York: St. Martin's Press.

3

Folklore and the Literature of Exile

Mark E. Workman

Milan Kundera tells us in his novel, *The Book of Laughter and Forgetting* (1981), that historians typically concern themselves with events of apparent human significance: the resettlement of Palestine by Jews, the successive occupations of Bohemia or Bessarabia by Celts, Slavs, Romanians, or Russians. In the meanwhile, little or no attention has been given to an ongoing phenomenon of potentially much greater and lasting impact, the migration of blackbirds from countryside to city. And yet, says Kundera,

> nobody dares to interpret the last two centuries as the history of the blackbird's invasion of the city of man. We are all prisoners of a rigid conception of what is important and what is not. We anxiously follow what we suppose to be important, while what we suppose to be unimportant wages guerilla warfare behind our backs, transforming the world without our knowledge and eventually mounting a surprise attack on us. (1981:197)

Folklorists, too, can be accused of recording those things which seem almost to be marked a priori for recognition. Furthermore, like historians, they construct accounts which instill additional order and consequence, while life's residue remains disordered and trivial, outside the realm of notice and narrative.

Nor is it surprising that this is the case. At the center of the discipline of folklore—providing, to turn the terminology of the field upon itself, one of its root metaphors—is the concept of community. Community is that which binds, which unites the many into the one through the production of a localized language. Such a language is fluid, of course; it is open to revision as its speakers employ it in new ways and in new situations. But its primary orientation is toward the past, for it is precisely the authority of the past, commemorated in ritual and tradition, which gives ongoing legitimacy to the present and future.

Any number of studies reflect this celebration of community. To name but a few: a parable is analyzed to determine how it restores order to a destabilized situation; occupational narratives are seen as a device for establishing and maintaining dignity within an oppressed group; Sea Island basketry is used as a measure of the implantation of African customs in the New World (Kirshenblatt-Gimblett 1975; Santino 1983; and Vlach 1978). The prevailing attitude in all these studies is a comic one, as communities are observed in integration rather than disintegration.

There is nothing wrong with such an attitude, and the three studies just alluded to are all noteworthy for their especial quality and insight. But there is a countercurrent at work in culture as well as a centripetal one, waging guerilla warfare on the very communities whose coherence draws us to them in the first place, and we ignore it at our own scholarly peril. This countercurrent is the force of exile. Where community merges, exile splits apart; where the former produces a "progressive knotting into,"[1] the latter unties such knots. Clearly the two processes require one another. According to medievalist David Williams, "COUNSEL is the etymological opposite in English of exile, the root of each being 'salire,' to leap, thus: ex-salire—to leap out of/con-silare—to jump (in) with, together" (1975:1). So an exile always calls to mind the place from which he departs, and community always carries within it a negative image of itself, what it means to be "outside." Beyond the protective wall of Troy, split off by his own defiance from family and friends, Hektor learns at the cost of his life just how difficult it can sometimes be to traverse this tantalizingly narrow distance.

To speak of exile as a force is to acknowledge that community is not a fixed entity but something in-the-making, a process whose termination, like life's, means death. This is as true of folk communities as of any other, and awareness of this counterforce must form a part of their proper study. But again, it is here that folklorists seem to be caught in paradox. For even equipped with knowledge of the processual nature of culture, we are led by our discipline to focus on groups, and groups are defined by and inconceivable apart from the traditions which enable them to persist over time. A group, in fact, only emerges as patterns of expectations come to be shared amongst its potential members. In cases of small groups whose members interact frequently, these patterns are relatively quickly formed and quickly become pervasive throughout the full range of the group's behavior. Thereafter, it is in the group's best self-interest to sacralize at least some of these patterns or traditions to provide a permanent reference by which ongoing behavior may be periodically sanctioned and properly guided.

The entire thrust of tradition, therefore, is towards the past, towards permanence, towards inscription. Memory is its servant; epic is its vehicle. The ultimate culmination of this movement is a discourse always fully cognizant of itself, informing a world totally known, whole, and complete. This epic past, according to Mikhail Bakhtin,

> is as closed as a circle; inside it everything is finished, already over. There is no place in the epic world for any openmindedness, indecision, indeterminacy.... Everything incorporated into this past was simultaneously incorporated into a condition of authentic essence and significance. . . . By its very nature the epic world of the absolute past is . . . sacred and sacrosanct, evaluated in the same way by all and demanding a pious attitude toward itself. (1981:20)

We no longer occupy an all-encompassing epic world such as that described by Bakhtin. However, moments occur when we do achieve a vision of fullness and plenitude, captivated by the authority of some potent mythology. When this happens, it is for one of two reasons: either, as Michael Holquist says, "intimacy with our own voice conduces to the illusion of presence"(1981:xxi); or such an intimacy is thrust upon us, often in violation of the democracy of speech. In both instances, desired or not, it is again the image of the circle, the many bodies joined in holy communion as one, which comes to the fore. The phenomenon is acutely described by Kundera who, like Hektor, has experienced both sides of the wall:

> I too once danced in a ring. It was the spring of 1948. The Communists had just taken power in my country, the Socialist and Christian Democrat ministers had fled abroad, and I took other Communist students by the hand, I put my arm around their shoulders, and we took two steps in place, one step forward, lifted first one leg than the other, and we did it just about every month, there being always something to celebrate, an anniversary here, a special event there, old wrongs were righted, new wrongs

perpetrated, factories were nationalized, thousands of people went to jail, medical care became free of charge, small shopkeepers lost their shops, aged workers took their first vacations ever in confiscated country houses, and we smiled the smile of happiness. Then one day I said something I would better have left unsaid. I was expelled from the Party and had to leave the circle.

  That is when I became aware of the magic qualities of the circle. Leave a row and you can always go back to it. The row is an open formation. But once a circle closes, there is no return. It is no accident that the planets move in a circle and when a stone breaks loose from one of them it is drawn inexorably away by centrifugal force. Like a meteorite broken loose from a planet, I too fell from the circle and have been falling ever since. Some people remain in the circle until they die, others smash to pieces at the end of a long fall. The latter (my group) always retain a muted nostalgia for the circle dance. After all, we are everyone of us inhabitants of a universe where everything turns in circles. (1981:65-66)

  Folklorists, of course, perceive neither themselves nor their subject matter as utterly enclosed. Indeed, thirty years ago formal declaration was made by Richard Bauman, the editor of *Toward New Perspectives in Folklore* (1972), that professional interest once and for all had shifted from the products to the processes of folklore. Implicit in this claim is the notion that, while they are animated by the past, folk performances are not mere replications of immutable scripts but dynamic recreations which modify the very traditions they invoke. Nevertheless, for the reasons I have already explained, even such continuous modifications are usually viewed as contributing to the ideational heritage, the *raison d'etre* of the community. We are, to a large degree, what we remember, and most people expend great effort in accumulating and safeguarding a storehouse of memorabilia as a bulwark against forgetting just what that is.

  Against this tendency folklorists must strive to keep the concept of exile before them; they must strive, in Kundera's configuration, to be alert to the excursion of the row from the circle. The effects could prove to be exhilarating. The exile is he for whom nothing is sacred. Liberated from his bondage to the monologic past, he is free to examine up close, to scrutinize, to "uncrown" the most privileged of icons. The exile, to adapt Bakhtin's formulation, is the supreme epistemologist: outside the boundaries of conventional thinking, he is in the ideal position to reflect upon the grounds of knowledge from a perspective which, by virtue of his isolation, can never be compromised. To incorporate this subversive concept into the epistemology of folklore would assure a discipline sufficiently self-reflexive to guard against its own intellectual closure. It would remain unfettered, that is, by the very institutionalization which it studies.

Incorporating exile into the language of the discipline would have another salutary effect: it would provide guarantee against closure of the canon of folklore. Now it is true that this is open to begin with, given that new folk groups will continue to form as long as people enter into new alliances with one another, and new folk groups will continue to produce new folklore. But what I refer to is something more subtle. I alluded above to the distinction between the consciousness presumed by the epic past and that of the modern world. In the former, one voice is elevated above all others; according to the Gospel of John, for instance, "In the beginning was the Word, and the Word was with God, and the word was God." Life is lived according to the dictates of this authoritative voice, and the language of everyday life is regarded as a manifestation of a perfect code which man can imitate, in his fallible way, only imperfectly.[2] All action in such a world is designed ultimately to lead back to reunification with the eternal being—whether it be state, a deity, a matriarch or patriarch—whose undeniable presence infuses the world with order and meaning.[3]

Such a presence, pervasive and encompassing, is lacking in the modern world. Certainly it is not lacking entirely, for in the absence of a past language itself is unthinkable. But we no longer live totally filled by presence, either, arrested by its reductive charm. Instead, many voices and the ideologies they represent compete with one another. Like other forms of competition, this one too can be friendly or hostile, sincere or sarcastic, supplementary or detractive, complimentary or derisive. Since no voice possesses absolute power, none can be spoken without acknowledging, even if implicitly, the conflicting claims of those other voices which seek to dominate it. Nothing remains sacred for long in this world, for that which previously had been remote and inviolable is, as Bakhtin notes, now familiar and laughable. The result, he says, is that the reality which each of these voices posits itself becomes suspect: "The present is something transitory, it is flow, it is an eternal continuation without beginning or end; it is denied an authentic conclusiveness and consequently lacks an essence as well (1981:20)." From this point of view literature provides a repository not only for meaning but also, in some cases, a decentering commentary on meaning, thereby undermining the ground of any mimetic pretensions it might affect. Herein lies the distinction between what Barthes calls "work" and "text": the former, monologic, ultimately is decipherable; the latter, dialogic, ultimately is not. "Every text," according to Barthes,

> being itself the intertext of another text, belongs to the intertextual, which must not be confused with a text's origins: to search for the "sources of" and "influences upon" a work is to satisfy the myth of filiation. The quotations from which a text is constructed are anonymous, irrevocable, and yet *already read*: they are quotations without quotation marks. The work does not upset monistic philosophies, for which plurality is evil. Thus, when it is compared with the work, the text might well take as its motto the words of the man possessed by devils: "My name is legion, for we are many" (Mark 5:9). (1979:77)

Folklore represents a reaffirmation of the possibility for meaning and authority. But even here, in this modern world of radically shifting contexts and—welcome or not—unsettling intrusions, impermanence makes itself felt. The community, in other words, is more permeable and fragile than it once was, and consequently its folklore echoes more loudly than ever before with the voices impinging from without. Thus conceived, folklore presents a battleground on which the demands of community, the memorialization of the past, come into direct conflict with the forces of irreverence and revision. Folklore is a manifestation of a dialectic between language and babel, sense and non-sense, constraint and freedom. Against the imperiousness of tradition is waged the impertinence of the exile.

Framed in these terms, the canon of folklore is opened up in two ways. First, any performance of folklore—even those which appear to "belong" to one particularly gifted and acclaimed master—represents a confluence of voices, many from within the community and perhaps some from without, some from the past and some from the present. The boundaries of folklore are thus considerably extended, beyond the immediate context, the immediate group, the immediate moment (Barthes 1979:77). Second, the boundaries must also be extended by inclusion into the canon of those texts which articulate this dialectic between community and exile—however variously it may be phrased—for it is on the border between the two that folklore carries on its vigorous existence.

One text among the many which are brought into the purview of the folklorist as a result of this reconceptualization of the field is Franz Kafka's *The Castle* (1974). Kafka himself, without ever going far from home—or at least its malign influence—experienced exile as intensively as any writer ever has. "I am literature," Kafka wrote to his sister Felice and, as Erich Heller informs us, this was particularly problematic in a city (Prague) in which "the homelessness of the artist was superimposed upon the estrangement felt by the Jews among gentiles, of German-speaking Jews among Czechs" (1982:2). Nor did it help matters that his own father, a strongwilled, aggressive, and narrow-minded man where Franz was "shy, subtle, and self-doubting," had only scorn for the literary identity of his son (Heller 1982:2). All of these forces which haunted Kafka throughout his life appear to be given ghostlike voice in the pages of *The Castle* where K., engaged in what Bakhtin describes as a "hidden polemic"[4] with an enemy he can rarely see and never comprehend, seeks desperately to make himself heard. Ordered by Erlanger to return Frieda to her position in the Herrenhof, K. is

> "confronted . . . with . . . the futility of all his endeavors. The orders, the unfavorable and the favorable, disregarded him, and even the most favorable probably had an ultimate unfavorable core, but in any case they all disregarded him, and he was in much too lowly a position to be able to intervene or, far less, to silence them and to gain a hearing for his own voice. (1974:349)

Like the author who conceived him, K. is an exile who has left his home, the nature of which is never clearly defined, in order to assume duties as a land-surveyor in a village whose identity is equally enigmatic. K.'s mission, as he perceives it, is to gain entry into the castle which towers over yet remains strangely remote from the village below. Once there, his intention is to speak with Klamm, the person K. regards as the omnipotent figure of authority to whom he is responsible and who K. believes can justify his existence and make it purposeful. But Klamm is elusive. Once K. peeks at him through a hole in a door, but afterwards it is uncertain whether it is really Klamm he has seen. In the course of his efforts, meanwhile, K. becomes engaged, is assigned a position as a janitor—not his ultimate goal, certainly, but at least steps towards achieving it. K. depicts his accomplishments spatially, as he views himself no longer as an isolated individual but within a communal network:

> . . . how much more complicated the game is now that I have, so to speak, a larger circumference—which means something, it may not be much—yet I have already a home, a position, and real work to do, I have a fiancee who takes her share of my professional duties when I have other business, I'm going to marry her and become a member of the community, and besides my official connection I have also a personal connection with Klamm, though as yet I haven't been able to make use of it. That's surely quite a lot? (1974:254-255)

K. is wrong of course, his accomplishment merely delusion. For in this novel, which Kafka left incomplete and which never could really conclude, the past—the world built upon traditions, shared assumptions and expectations—recedes from K. almost as quickly as he attains it. K.'s frustrated efforts thus provide bitter evidence for his discovery that identity is socially constituted. After waiting interminably and in vain for Klamm (just as his descendents Vladimir and Estragon will wait for Godot), K. produces a haunted and haunting meditation on what it means to be a stranger:

> . . . it seemed to K. . . . as if now in reality he were freer than he had ever been, and at liberty to wait here in this place, usually forbidden to him, as long as he desired, and had won a freedom such as hardly anybody else had ever succeeded in winning, and as if nobody could dare to touch him or drive him away, or even speak to him; but—this conviction was at least equally strong—as if at the same time there was nothing more senseless, nothing more hopeless, than this freedom, than waiting, this inviolability. (1974:136)

Kafka's fiction has been described by Austin Warren as "spiritual picaresque." This claim is valid up to a point. Like the exile, according to Ulrich Wicks, "Exclusion—from society, from God, from himself—characterizes the picaro's essential situation" (1975:22). When he does encounter society, the result is likely to be destructive, for the picaro, for society, or for both. Unlike K., however, the picaro can sometimes retrospectively subject his acts to memory to produce a narrative ordering of his tumultuous experiences. This is hardly true of *The Castle*, whose prose is as labyrinthine as the perplexity of relationships it depicts, and which tantalizingly plays on a border of opacity through which the reader can no longer pierce. The one truth to emerge in Kafka's universe, where the castle is perceived merely in shadow—reality's negation—is that no community or language can exist in the absence of such a presence.

The shadow of the castle is insubstantial, but it is by no means short. It stretches, on the contrary, across the decades of modern literature to fall upon the widely-read pages authored by Milan Kundera. Like Kafka, whom he refers to as "the prophet of a world without memory" (1981:158), Kundera is a Czech; his books were banned from his native country, and he himself continues to live even now as an exile in France. Unlike Kafka, whose prose (despite its simple elegance) is opaque, Kundera's is translucent, but it yields access to a vision of life which rivals Kafka's in bleakness. For Kundera, the problem is not the impossibility of accumulating a past, but the horrific consequences of being forcibly severed from it. As he says in an interview with Philip Roth, "the self . . . is the sum of everything we remember" (1981:234), and thus the most terrifying prospect in life is the loss of this past through forgetting. This is Kundera's own dilemma as an exile, it is the dilemma of his native country whose customs were systematically destroyed through a process of "organized forgetting" and replaced with official Soviet ideology, and it is the dilemma of Tamina, the heroine about and for whom *The Book of Laughter and Forgetting* is written.

Just as K. mirrors the plight of his creator, so too does Tamina's life bear resemblance to Kundera's. Like him, Tamina is an exile from Czechoslovakia. She fled with her husband to avoid persecution and betrayal and, since his death a short time later, has struggled to keep intact her memory of him and thereby her own self-integrity. To facilitate this dialogue with the past—very private and increasingly difficulty to sustain—Tamina fervently wishes to repossess the diaries chronicling her years of marriage which were left behind when she and her husband left their country illegally. These diaries are all that she has left of the communal tradition she created with her husband, the language of which they were the only two speakers in the world.⁵ When confronted with the likelihood that these notebooks have been read by her mother-in-law and father,

> ... it seemed to her that the outsiders' eyes were like rain washing away inscriptions on a stone wall. ...
> She realized that what gave her written memories value, meaning, was that they were meant for *her alone*. As soon as they lost that quality, the intimate chain binding her to them would be broken and instead of reading them with her own eyes, she would be forced to read them from the point of view of an audience perusing an impersonal document. Then the woman who wrote them would lose her identity, and the striking similarity that would nonetheless remain between her and the author of the notes would be nothing but a parody, a mockery. No, she could never read her notes once they had been read by someone else. (Kundera 1981:100-101)

Folklore, I have argued, is dynamic: each time it is given voice the way is opened for change. The community established by Tamina and her husband, however, open only towards the past and not towards the future, is particularly vulnerable to such change. With only one member—and she a silent one—left to defend and lovingly resurrect their mutual heritage, any revision of their memories will transform them entirely. Clearly in such a volatile world no voicing of inscriptions is merely passive and innocuous; instead, the act of articulation "leaves no language safe or untouched" (Barthes 1979:81) from its mocking tone. The result of such mockery is the violation and destruction of the numinous order which binds together the past and the present and instills the world with meaning. Tamina and her lost letters suffer the same fate: both are polluted, defiled—they by foreign eyes, she by a man who has dehumanized her in order to inflate himself. Having given herself to him on the condition that he retrieve the letters for her, she discovers that memory of him has come to supplant memory of her husband:

> Before her eyes was the image of that boy's balls, prick and pubic hair. She could smell the sour breath from his mouth, feel the pressure of his thighs on her backside. It occurred to her that she was no longer able to remember what her husband's genitals looked like—in other words, the memory of revulsion was stronger than the memory of tenderness (God yes, the memory of revulsion is stronger than the memory of tenderness!)—and that soon all she'd have left

> in her miserable head was this boy with bad breath. And she vomited, writhed and shook, and vomited. (1981:114)

Tamina eventually swims out to the middle of a lake and blissfully drowns, delivered at last from her oppressors. Kundera in some ways seems more fortunate, in other ways not. He lives, but not at home. Apart from his memories, his folklore, his community, his self, he has maintained a voice but cannot safeguard its purity, its humanity, or its mythic power. This is why Kundera calls *The Book of Laughter and Forgetting* "a novel in the form of variations" (1981:165). It has but one theme, yet each time it is sounded it is slightly metamorphosed. The result, ultimately, is a world without essence. Such, too, is the vision expressed in Kundera's earlier novel, *The Joke* (1982), whose publication contributed to the liberalization culminating in the Prague Spring of 1968. The novel centers on a centuries old Moravian folk custom called the Ride of the Kings. Originally a reenactment of revelation, the tradition has come to be debased to the point where it reveals not fullness but hollowness. It provides, therefore, a barometer for measuring the disintegration of a culture which no amount of folk-revivalism can counter:

> For many centuries young men have been riding forth from Moravian villages like this one today with strange messages whose incomprehensible words they spell out with touching fidelity. At some point far in the past a group of people had something important to say, and they come alive again today in their descendents like deaf and dumb orators holding forth by means of beautiful and incomprehensible gestures. Their message will never be deciphered not only because there is no key, but because people lack the patience to listen in an age when an accumulation of messages old and new is such that their voices cancel one another out. By now history is nothing more than a thin thread of what is remembered stretched out over the ocean of what has been forgotten; but time moves on, and new eras will arise, eras the limited memory of the individual will be unable to grasp; centuries, millennia, will therefore fall away, centuries of paintings and music, centuries of discoveries, battles, books, and the consequences will be dire: man will lose all insight into himself, and his history—unfathomable, inscrutable—will shrink into a handful of senseless schematic signs. Thousands of deaf-and-dumb Rides will set out to deliver their messages to far-off descendents of ours, and none of them will have the time to listen. (1982:244)

Kundera and Kafka are both exiles, the one literally, the other figuratively, from their native land. Each seeks to hold onto a language or tradition which for one reason or another eludes him. For them, therefore, the dialectic of continuity and change is an unequal one, with change occurring at an ever more accelerated rate. This is not always the case. Lest the concept of exile be perceived as a simple one, it is worthwhile juxtaposing with Kafka and Kundera an author for whom the dialectic is weighted in the other direction, Philip Roth. The basis of Alexander Portnoy's complaint is that he is so burdened by the past that he can never enjoy the present with spontaneity or envision the future with hope. I have analyzed Portnoy's situation elsewhere as being the predicament of enslavement to a reductive ethnicity.[6] Here it is appropriate simply to ask what it is about exile that Portnoy finds so alluring. That is the state he repeatedly attempts to enter into as he flees his parents, his job, his country, his lover. What Portnoy apparently believes he will discover there is the freedom to be himself. For just as no man wishes to be utterly unknown, so too does no man wish to be known in his entirety, and under the relentless scrutiny of his mother and father, Portnoy is only able to preserve his wildest fantasies for himself. Portnoy is thus in no danger of forgetting; on the contrary, he is "impaled upon the long ago" by the endless memories, the endless childhood which he won't relinquish—or which won't relinquish him (1980:306).

So the anonymity which threatens K. and the loss of memory which haunts Tamina are both welcomed by Portnoy. It is ironic, then, but not in any way surprising, that when he seeks his liberation it is to Israel, the "promised land," that he flies; or further, that he runs directly away from his past smack into a reincarnation of his mother. When he attempts to force himself upon her, the Oedipal implications are not lost upon this most psychologically preoccupied of characters:

> But what a battle she gave me, this big farm cunt! this ex-G.I.! This mother-substitute! Look, can that be so? Oh please, it can't be as simplistic as that! *Not me*! Or with a case like mine, is it actually that you can't be simplistic enough! Because she wore red hair and freckles, this makes her, according to my unconscious one-track mind, my mother? Just because she and the lady of my past are off-spring of the same pale Polish strain of Jews? This then is the culmination of the Oedipal drama, Doctor? More farce, my friend? Too much to swallow, I'm afraid! Oedipus Rex is a famous

> tragedy, schmuck, not another joke. You're a sadist, you're a quack and a lousy comedian! I mean this is maybe going too far for a laugh, Doctor Spielvogel, Doctor Freud, Doctor Kronkite! How about a little homage, you bastards, to The Dignity of Man! *Oedipus Rex* is the most horrendous and *serious* play in the history of literature—it is not a gag! (1980:300-301)

Portnoy need not be concerned, as it turns out, for unlike Oedipus, who emerges from his incestuous encounter with wisdom and ample justification for guilt, Portnoy is unable to consummate his ultimate fantasy: he is instead impotent in Israel. Appropriately, he turns to a language of the past, invented by another repressed Jewish man, to explain his failures, thereby assuring that he will never escape the circle which encloses him.

Portnoy cannot depart from his castle, K. cannot enter his, and Tamina cannot return to hers. Locked within is a reservoir of memory, language, and ritual; while outside there exist disparate voices, disparate acts, disparate people. Life lived exclusively within—in community—and life lived exclusively without—in exile—are equally intolerable and equally sterile. It is on the interface between the two where traditions evolve, absence mingles with presence, ideologies are "valorized" and then "uncrowned" (Bakhtin 1981). This replenishment of culture—sometimes quickened, sometimes leisurely—is a continuous process. It is in this area of most intense destructive and creative activity that folklore flourishes, a language at once responsive to the moment yet enduring over time. When the folklorist directs his attention here, it will be to discover a world of texts—like the novels I have discussed, or the forms with which he is already familiar—in which a multitude of voices beckon him playfully to an infinity of dialogue.

Notes

1. The phrase is taken from Thomas Pynchon, *Gravity's Rainbow* (New York: Viking, 1973), p. 3.

2. There is a comparison to be drawn here to the linguist's distinction between "langue" and "parole."

3. Eugene Vance makes this same point with reference to the *Chanson de Roland* in his essay "Roland and the Poetics of Memory" (1979).

4. This concept is elaborated upon in Bakhtin's book, *Problems of Dostoevsky's Poetics* (1973), Chap. 5, "The Word in Dostoevsky."

5. Compare Pynchon's *Gravity's Rainbow* (1973), p. 351.
6. For a more extended consideration of this novel see Workman, 1987.

References

Bakhtin, M. M. 1973. *Problems of Dostoevsky's Poetics*. Ann Arbor: Ardis.

———. 1981. *The Dialogic Imagination*. Austin: University of Texas Press.

Barthes, Roland. 1979. From Work to Text. In *Textual Strategies: Perspectives in Post-Structuralist Criticism*. ed. Josue V. Harari, pp. 73-81. Ithaca: Cornell University Press.

Bauman, Richard. 1972. Introduction. In *Toward New Perspectives in Folklore*, ed. Américo Paredes and Richard Bauman, pp. vi-ix. Austin: University of Texas Press.

Heller, Erich. 1982. *Franz Kafka*. Princeton: Princeton University Press.

Holquist, Michael. 1981. Introduction. In Bakhtin, *The Dialogic Imagination*. Austin: University of Texas Press.

Kafka, Franz. 1974. *The Castle*. New York: Viking.

Kirshenblatt-Gimblett, Barbara. 1975. A Parable in Context: A Social Interactional Analysis of Storytelling Performance. In *Folklore: Performance and Communication*, eds. D. Ben-Amos and K. S. Goldstein, pp. 105-130. Hague: Mouton.

Kundera, Milan 1981. *The Book of Laughter and Forgetting*. New York: Penguin.

———. 1982. *The Joke*. New York: Harper and Row.

Pynchon, Thomas. 1973. *Gravity's Rainbow*. New York: Viking.

Roth, Philip. 1980. *Portnoy's Complaint*. New York: Bantam.

Santino, Jack. 1983. Miles of Smiles, Years of Struggle: The Negotiation of Black Occupational Identity Through Personal Experience Narrative. *Journal of American Folklore* 96:393-411.

Vance, Eugene. 1979. Roland and the Poetics of Memory. In *Textual Strategies: Perspectives in Post-Structuralist Criticism*, ed. Josue V. Harari, pp. 374-403. Ithaca: Cornell University Press.

Vlach, John Michael. 1978. *The Afro-American Tradition in Decorative Arts*. Cleveland: The Cleveland Museum of Arts.

Wicks, Ulrich. 1975. Onlyman. *Mosaic* 8:47-54.

Williams, David. 1975. The Exile as Uncreator. *Mosaic* 8:1-14.

Workman, Mark E. 1987. The Serious Consequences of Ethnic Humor in *Portnoy's Complaint*. *Midwestern Folklore* 13:16-26.

4

Writing the Hybrid Body: Thomas Hardy and the Ethnographic "Money Shot"

Cathy Lynn Preston

> Hardy country is of course Wessex: that is to say mainly Dorset and its neighbouring counties. But the real Hardy country, we soon come to see, is that border country so many of us have been living in: between custom and education, between work and ideas, between love of place and an experience of change. (Williams 1973:197)

As Raymond Williams's somewhat solipsistically romanticized yet cogent emphasis on "betweenness" suggests, Hardy country is the liminal domain of emergent hybrid identity.[1] As such, Hardy country is inherently reflexive, mirroring that which is without and within and, thus, providing cultural critique while seeking to construct a space in which to imagine cultural alternatives.[2] In this chapter, I will read particular Hardy narratives in relation to the politics of ethnographic inscription. Specifically, I am interested in the extent to which certain of Hardy's narratives (*Tess of the d'Urbervilles*, *The Woodlanders*, and "The Dark-Eyed Gentleman") are enmeshed in the phallocentric and ethnocentric subject-object relations inherent in what eventually developed as the participant-observer ethnographic method (a method developed to study cultural groups other than one's own) and the extent to which those narratives simultaneously encode a form of auto-ethnography that seeks to decenter dominantly positioned authoritative voices. Thus, I will read Hardy's narratives in respect to his use of privileged "traditionalizing" practices—"modes of creating textual authority" (Briggs and Bauman 1992:149)—as a means of authorizing his place, as a socio-cultural hybrid, "in the public realm of performance" (Kapchan 1993:311) while he simultaneously attempts to decenter privileged authority by invoking voices alternatively situated. To do this, I will focus on the seemingly disparate traditions of pastoral narrative and bawdy song, arguing that Hardy structures his narratives around the problematics of voice and visibility and that he uses sexual discourse as a means of disclosing the socio-cultural power-relations embedded in eroticized writerly-readerly negotiations of textualized bodies.

Preliminaries

Raised within the rural intermediate class but, as an adult, resituated by his position as a "'professional writer,' 'man of letters,' and London socialite" (Widdowson 1989:130), Thomas Hardy was part of and yet not part of traditionally configured spaces. His ambivalent response to his liminality is suggested by his desire for acceptance within a literary world controlled by the educated upper-class at the same time that he attempts to disclose the hidden relations of power (those of class, gender, and region) that control literary production and that structure everyday lived experience. Such relations of power were, for example, precisely those which constructed images of rurality in accordance with privileged needs and which sought to erase the contestability of Hardy's emergent hybrid voice through representations resituating him as a "peasant" writing about "peasants" (Williams 1973:199-200). In an age in which a privileged literary aesthetic called for what Hardy describes as "a precise transcript of ordinary life" (Florence Hardy 1975:150 in Widdowson 1989:161) and yet frequently used such transcripts, I would argue, as a means of constructing boundaries between self and others, Hardy's narratives both participate in and enable, while simultaneously contesting, such forms of representation and appropriation.

Commenting on his own literary method, Hardy writes:

> My art is to intensify the expression of things . . . so that the heart and inner meaning is made vividly visible (quoted in Widdowson 1989:161);

> I don't want to see landscapes, *i.e.*, scenic paintings of them, because I don't want to see the original realities—as optical effects, that is. I want to see the deeper reality underlying the scenic, the expression of what are sometimes called abstract imaginings. (quoted in Widdowson 1989:162)

"Original realities—as optical effects," I will suggest, should be read in relation to writerly-readerly negotiations of formal realism, salvage ethnography, and the impetus of edenic return embedded in pastoral narrative. However, "abstract imaginings" seems more closely related to the "realm of possibilities" Victor Turner associates with liminality (1969 and 1977), Mikhail Bakhtin defines in respect to the "grotesque" body, the carnivalesque, and the marketplace (1984), and Widdowson explains as Hardy's "embryonic conception of such modern critical notions as 'making strange' ('defamiliarization') and 'alienation'" (1989:160).

Although Hardy's narratives do construct the "scenic" (thereby participating in the underlying ideology of privileged pastoral) in order to court his readership (a type of "pimping" for his readership, as well as, at times, an indication of his own nostalgia), his narratives simultaneously disclose the socio-cultural power-relations that define the social order. In doing so, they provide a materialist critique of 19th-century rural capitalism and of metropolitan social and literary culture which is quite damning. But, perhaps more importantly, such disclosures enable an implicit critique of those closed ideological constructions of socio-cultural identity that attempt to marginalize and erase emergent socio-cultural bodies and those bodies' attempted constructions of their alternative identities. In doing so, Hardy's narratives attempt to break open a space in which to write the emergent hybrid body.

To address how Hardy writes the hybrid body, I will begin by envisioning Hardy functioning as an ethnographic tour-guide and ultimately, although not immediately, as his own ethnographic subject. In other words, Hardy plays appropriatively with identities, mixing and layering them in such a way that his narrative persona is both that of the "larger-than-local," frequently privileged, and predominantly urban participant-observer of rural and/or classed peoples (the "local" subject/object seemingly inscribed in many of his narratives) and, in a subordinated, muted way, that of the participant-observer of his own "localized" hybridity (an ethnographic subject who attempts self-inscription and who, in order to do so, at times appropriates the experiential subordination of rural and/or classed peoples for his own use, but a subject who should not be confused with those socio-cultural groups).

Thus, although I am positioning Hardy as a type of ethnographer, I want to stress that one cannot simply go to Hardy's narratives as a 19th- or early 20th-century metaphorical butterfly-collector hoping to net bits and pieces of vanished folklife (whether it be that of dominant or subordinate groups) any more than one should envision Hardy's narratives themselves as salvage projects although they do at times inscribe the politics of salvage ethnography.[3] While Hardy's "write-ups" might be discussed in terms of what Clifford Geertz has called "thick description," they are not products of scientific essentialism (if anything, they disclose the libidinal economy of scientific claims to objectivity); nor are they products of formal realism (see Widdowson 1989). Instead, they are interpreted and symbolically reconstructed ethnographic landscapes that frequently appropriate oppositionally situated socio-cultural bodies in order to map the border country that was literally and metaphorically Hardy's own body while negotiating that body's relationship as a hybrid to the larger culture, that within and that without its borders. In this way, Hardy writes fictionalized narratives which mediate between what George E. Marcus has called "closely observed cultural worlds" and the "impersonal systems" in which those worlds are embedded (1986:165-166), in folkloristic terms, between "local" and "larger than local" socio-cultural domains.

James Clifford has appropriately described hybrid locales or bodies as places of "struggle, policing and transgression" (1992:109). Similarly, Raymond Williams has emphasized their "conflicts of desire and possibility" (1993:198). Thus it seems appropriate that Hardy would draw on the situated socio-sexual politics of privileged pastoral and vernacular bawdry in attempting to reconfigure social spaces. The "low" aesthetic politics of bawdy song—a foregrounding of what Bakhtin (1984) has described as the transgressive grotesque body, in particular as such song traditions invoke images of copulative material and social bodies—provided Hardy with both a means of disclosing the situated "high" aesthetic politics of privileged pastoral and a means of espousing the alternatively situated and frequently marginalized border country's emergent creative potentialities.

Writing the Hybrid Body 47

Seeking Edenic Return: The Pastoral

> [a] fertile and sheltered tract of country, in which the fields are never brown and the springs [are] never dry. (Hardy, *Tess of the d'Urbervilles*, 1970:9)

In *Tess of the d'Urbervilles*, early in the first "Phase," entitled "The Maiden," the reader (who is gendered male by the text) is invited to observe pieces of rural life and to contemplate the pleasures of penetrating landscapes which are gendered female. Tess's village of Marlott is described as lying "amid the north-eastern undulations of the beautiful Vale of Blakemore or Blackmoor aforesaid, an engirdled and secluded region, for the most part untrodden as yet by tourist or landscape-painter, though within a four hours' journey from London" (1970:9). "Undulations," "engirdled," "secluded," "untrodden" rhetorically construct this landscape as female. The reader first views this pastoral landscape from above—a position of power fraught with the intermingled associations of 18th century colonialism, the Romantics' sense of the sublime, and 19th century imperialism. Thus, the reader's journey into Marlott and the people who live there is, by cultural inheritance, marked by feelings of personal and group power, self-assurance, superiority, and an implied promise of sublimity, each of which is constructed within the frame of erotic desire. The reader is asked to envision himself as a "tourist," a "landscape-painter," or an explorer who sees the country "extended like a map beneath him." And the narrator serves as the reader's guide while both "ramble" into the valley's "recesses," its inner life (1970:9). The narrator, thus, enables the reader to visualize, to contemplate, and vicariously to probe interiors: the Vale of Blakemore, Marlott, Tess's home, eventually Tess herself, and, I would argue, Hardy: the fictional inscription of those landscapes being the product (the textualized body) of Hardy's subjective construction of that which, as a socio-cultural hybrid, is within and without his own every-day lived experience.

The privileged narrative persona, through which Hardy courts his reader, is a blend of tour-guide, 19th-century folkloristic ethnographer, and storyteller. The narrator leads the reader through a picturesque landscape and, like a tour-guide, points out features of "historic" and "topographical interest" (1970:10), enlivening each with local legends, and drawing the reader's attention to discrepancies between the past—the environment and its inhabitants as they used to be and as the reader may have hoped or expected to see them—and the present (the environment and its inhabitants as they are): "The forests have departed, but some old customs of their shades remain. Many, however, linger only in a metamorphosed or disguised form" (1970:10). In pointing out such discrepancies, the narrator not only co-locates within the same frame of reference what he will later refer to as the "ideal" and the "real" (1970:11), but he shifts into an early version of a modern ethnographic mode that will celebrate in-depth, "objective," scientific observation over "casual" observation and "subjective" responses and constructions. As Mary Louise Pratt has noted, "In almost any ethnography dull-looking figures called 'mere travelers' or 'casual observers' show up from time to time, only to have their superficial perceptions either corrected or corroborated by the serious scientist" (1986:27). In this case, "The May-Day dance," the reader is told, is "to be discerned . . . in the guise of the club revel, or 'club-walking'" (1970:10), and the narrator as incipient ethnographer provides the reader with an intellectual context in which to understand the folk performance he is about to witness.

The reader is told that the performance's "real interest was not observed by the participants in the ceremony. Its singularity lay less in the retention of a custom of walking in procession and dancing on each anniversary than in the members being solely women," that few such clubs remained, and that those which did were "denuded . . . of this their glory and consummation," that "The club of Marlott alone lived to uphold the local Cerealia," and that it walked "as votive sisterhood of some sort." Finally, the event is introduced as "a gay survival from Old Style days, when cheerfulness and May-time were synonymous—days before the habit of taking long views had reduced emotions to a monotonous average" (1970:10-11).

What I find of interest here is not only the way in which an image of female bonding is disrupted by a male "will to know," but the way the narrator, first, initially localizes the folk event, hinting at an historicized context for the performance, then posits the possibility of the women speaking and thereby theorizing their own meanings of the folk event, and finally, rejects both possibilities, instead opting for a meaning which is the product of a privileged representation constructed from the point of view of that which is both external to the event and the female participants. The implicit subject-object positionings of this scenario are analogous to those described by Debra Kodish in her critique of male folklorists' tendencies to envision themselves as heroic figures who win entrance to "folk" abodes in order to awaken the women to their own "voicedness":

> Male collectors appear as powerful, magical outsiders, folktale heroes initiating action and reestablishing value. Female informants appear as passive vehicles, unwitting receptacles of knowledge, silent, unspeaking, to be wooed and won into speech. . . . These are sexualized concepts. (1987:574-575)

Kodish goes on to explore the differences between the ways in which the male ethnographers and the female ethnographic subjects make meaning out of the interview situation. In both Hardy's and Kodish's scenarios, privileged male discourse represents itself as objectively knowing and yet is clearly enmeshed in a representation of otherness constructed in accordance with the subjective needs of its own register, and, thus, might be understood in Foucauldian terms as a "'transfer point' of knowledge, power, and pleasure" (Linda Williams 1989:36).

In *Tess of the d'Urbervilles*, the event (the club-walking) is described as a "survival," a word which Edward Burnett Tylor—an ethnographer contemporary with Hardy—defines as "processes, customs, opinions, and so forth, which have been carried on by force of habit into a new state of society different from that in which they had their original home, and they thus remain as proofs and examples of an older condition of culture out of which a newer has been evolved" (1929 [1871]:16). While both the ethnographic narrator and Tylor hint at the possibilities engendered in emergent culture, the narrator's anthropological lecture ultimately frames and interprets the event the reader is about to witness within the discourse of what was to become known as "salvage ethnography," a discourse which Raymond Williams has identified with the Western pastoral desire for edenic return. As James Clifford has explained, "The other is lost, in a disintegrating time and space, but saved in the text" (1986:112). The pastoral "other"—the conduit of edenic return—is seemingly saved through rhetorical construction (here the privileged anthropological discourse inscribed in Hardy's fiction) while the "other" of everyday lived experience is, at least momentarily, eclipsed, present only as a disintegrating source who, constructed as lacking self-awareness, needs to be penetrated by an external intelligence (both writer and reader) in search of that which is no longer visible.

One might draw a parallel here between the ethnographic narrator's attempts to make the invisible visible and the modern hard-core porn film-director's attempts to do the same, particularly since the problems of both are constituted by bodies which are gendered female. Because the analogy seems so unusual, I am going to draw it out a bit so that the elements common to both can be more fully seen. Linda Williams suggests that the hard-core pornographer is beset by a particular dilemma. Drawing on Michel Foucault's (1985:91-92) differentiation between *ars erotica* (the passing of "general knowledge from the experienced to the initiate without specifying or classifying the details of this knowledge") and *scientia sexualis* ("a hermeneutics of desire aimed at ever more detailed explorations of the scientific truths of sexuality"), Williams analyzes the ways in which hard-core porn "obsessively seeks knowledge, through a voyeuristic record of confessional, involuntary paroxysm, the 'thing,' itself," the "thing" being sexual pleasure (1989:34-49). The problem for the director of hard-core porn is that,

> while it is possible, in a certain limited and reductive way, to "represent" the physical pleasure of the male by showing erection and ejaculation [referred to in the business as "the money shot"], this maximum visibility proves elusive in the parallel confession of female sexual pleasure. Anatomically, female orgasm takes place . . . in an "invisible place" that cannot be easily seen. . . . The history of hard-core film could thus be summarized in part as the history of the various strategies devised to overcome this problem of invisibility within a regime that is . . . an "erotic organization of visibility." (1989:49)

The problem surrounding the "money shot" is, I would argue, at the center of both salvage ethnography and pastoral constructions of edenic return. What is desired is visible proof—"the money shot"—of an invisible essentialism, both on the part of the ethnographer and on the part of the readers of ethnographic write-ups. But the members of the folk group, the bodies through which that proof is sought, are believed, when they do speak, either to lack self-awareness and therefore to be incapable of articulating that which is hidden within or to lie (whether that lie is constructed as the folk group members' theorizing of themselves in respect to their immediate local and historicized situation in a way that contradicts hegemonic representational practices or as their faking a representation of that which is sought to confirm hegemonic practices much as a woman might fake an orgasm). Thus, although the ethnographic narrator will continue throughout his narrative to probe the feminized folk group's interiors in search of the "involuntary paroxysm"—all the time directing his reader's gaze towards those interiors—, the "money shot" is ultimately a rhetorical construction: the product of the ethnographic narrator's reading and writing strategies and his audience's reading and rewriting strategies, both of which negotiate "truth" or "visibility" in accordance with the personal and cultural needs of the privileged register.

In respect to the folk event at hand, the narrator will describe individualizing differences among the women in terms of dress ("though the whole troop wore white garments, no two whites were alike among them"), age (there are middle-aged, elderly, and young women in the group), and appearance (the elderly women have "silvery-wiry hair and wrinkled faces, scourged by time and trouble" and the young girls have "heads of luxuriant hair [which] reflected in the sunshine every tone of gold, and black and brown," and some, the reader is told, "had beautiful eyes, others a beautiful nose, others a beautiful mouth and figure" although "few, if any, had all") (1970:11-12). And the narrator will suggest that "In a true view, perhaps, there was more to be gathered and told of each anxious and experienced one, to whom the years were drawing nigh" (1970:11) than he will describe. But while saying all this, the narrator is simultaneously redirecting the reader's attention towards a motifed image of erotic innocence—"white frock," "peeled willow wand," "a bunch of white flowers" (1970:11) and eventually "dancing on the green" (1970:13)—which is easily appropriated for his and his readers' own needs. Although age discrepancies are noted, the reader is directed to "let the elder be passed over here for those under whose bodices the life throbbed quick and warm" (1970:11). And although this subgroup is momentarily differentiated according to their individual beauties, they are immediately retroped as "genuine country girls," "each and all" of whom have a private spot within: "a private little sun for her soul to bask in; some dream, some affection, some hobby, at least some remote and distant hope, which starving to nothing, still live[s] on, as hopes will" (1970:12). It is, of course, this invisible, individually private but ultimately, in terms of privileged representational practices, cumulative domain to which the reader seeks voyeuristic access, a point brought home by the narrator's comment that the girls are "unaccustomed to many eyes" (1970:12).

The narrator's anthropological discourse provides Hardy with a means of gratifying his readers' needs by seemingly promising them the hard core "money shot" they want to see, but in fact what that discourse delivers is little more than a soft-core peep show in which those fleeting glimpses of Eden, that they may think they see, are fictions created through writerly-readerly negotiations. At the same time, by hinting at alternative ways for constructing meaning—ways which may not lead towards verification and fulfillment of privileged needs—, Hardy's novel inscribes the polysemic possibilities of a multivocal discourse that his contemporary readers were not always inclined to hear. It is in this domain of voices noted and hinted at but textually and extra-textually silenced that I want to locate Hardy as a cross-dressed body, for immediately after Hardy-as-narrator directs his reader's gaze towards the retroped "genuine country girls," he introduces Tess Durbeyfield as one of their members and locates her tentatively within the liminal domain of the hybrid: "The dialect was on her tongue to some extent, despite the village school" (1970:13). So that this point is not missed by the reader, it is repeated shortly thereafter when the reader is told that Tess, having "passed the Sixth Standard in the National School under a London-trained mistress," speaks "two languages: the dialect at home, more or less; ordinary English abroad and to persons of quality" (1970:21). Furthermore, the narrator differentiates her from the larger group of women by noting that "strangers" would sometimes "look long at her in casually passing by and grow momentarily fascinated by her freshness" (1970:14). But having noted her hybridity and differentiated her from the other women, the narrator then recuperates her as a trope of gendered rural otherness—"but to almost everybody she was a fine and picturesque country girl, and no more" (1970:14)—thus making her available for privileged appropriation. And any of this might be said of Hardy and Hardy's literary works' reception by the literary elite (Raymond Williams 1973:199).

Writing the Hybrid Body

As mentioned earlier, Hardy was himself a socio-cultural hybrid, and his fiction drew attention from a privileged readership who frequently attempted to control the threat of his difference by resituating him within the category of "peasant." Such appropriative and negotiated constructions of Hardy enhanced readings of Hardy's scenic sites/sights as being authentic (as in "he's one of them, so he should know"), while providing a means of marginalizing (as in "what else would one expect; he's one of them after all") the hinted at contestability of those sites: the possibility that what were made visible were not fleeting glimpses of Eden, but rather disclosures of post-edenic class, gender, and regionally based power-relations, as well as emergent possibilities that might threaten traditional socio-cultural givens. Writing himself as a metaphorically cross-dressed body, Hardy appropriates the female body for use as a semiotic object. His class-based frustrations with external forces that seek to construct and thereby control him he cross-codes in respect to the socio-cultural system of gender-dominance that constructs the female body as subordinate and voiceless, while the possibilities of self-construction (otherwise reserved for his male narrator and his privileged readers) he cross-codes in respect to female sexuality: its power to attract attention, capacity to produce pleasure (for itself as well as another), and its ability to procreate. Thus, as a semiotic object, the female body provides Hardy with a means of investigating and constructing himself as a contested site of cultural production (on contested categories, see Shuman 1993).

The May-day club-walking turns into a dance upon the green. The women initially dance with each other, but the narrator notes, "when the hour for the close of labour drew on, the masculine inhabitants of the village, together with other idlers and pedestrians, gathered round the spot, and appeared inclined to negotiate for a partner" (1970:14). The reader might here easily be included as one of the "idlers and pedestrians." Furthermore, the reader is informed that among "these on-lookers were three young men of a superior class" who are on a "walking tour through the Vale of Blackmour." The young men inquire "as to the meaning of the dance and the white-frocked maids," and Angel Clare (one of the three men) indicates his desire "to go and have a fling with" the women, an inclination his brothers respond to as being somehow unseemly: "Dancing in public with a troop of country hoydens—suppose we would be seen!" (1970:14-15). On the one hand, through Angel Clare the reader is provided a character with whom to identify and thereby a means of vicarious participation in the folk event. On the other hand, the reader's positioning as vicarious participant in the event and as readerly observer of the event are inscribed with the anxieties of the voyeur: "suppose we would be seen." What might be described as the reader's "will to knowledge" (Williams 1989:49) is thus momentarily deconstructed, disclosing the libidinal economy at the center of pastoral constructions: the pleasures (in respect to knowledge and power) and fears of the reader gone "slumming." It is at such moments as this—when Hardy's fictional lens frames both the viewed and the viewer—that Hardy seems most playfully and contestively asserting the deconstructive power of his hybrid positioning.

Although Angel's brothers move on, Angel fleetingly inserts himself into the landscape by inquiring of the women, "Where are your partners, my dears?" In reply, he is informed that "They've not left off work yet," and he chooses a partner somewhat indiscriminately from among the women and begins to dance (1970:15). Finally, the reader is told that "the village young men, who had not hastened to enter the gate while no intruder was in the way, now dropped in quickly" (1970:16), themselves negotiating for partners, suggesting that androcentric regional- and class-inflected power-relations are to be negotiated in terms of sexual access to and control of the female body. Interestingly, the "village young men" as potential sexual partners will disappear, for all practical purposes, from the novel at this point to be subsumed within the larger female gendered landscape, thus leaving that landscape open to unhindered privileged readerly appropriation. This act of appropriation is then simultaneously reinforced and contested by means of the referencing of a bawdy song in the scene that directly follows, when Tess, returning home from the May-Day Dance, overhears her mother's singing of "The Spotted Cow," a song which in the 19th-century circulated extensively both within oral tradition and by means of print (Preston 1992).

Of the song, what appears in the novel is the song's title and the lines, "I saw her lie do'—own in yon'—der green gro'—ove; / Come, love!' and I'll tell' you where!'" (1970:19), a textual variant of stanza 3, lines 3-4 of the following broadside text:

ONE morning in the month of May,
    As from my cot I stray'd.
Just at the dawning of the day.
    I met a charming maid.

Good morning, fair maid, whether, said I,
    So early, tell me now,
The maid replied, kind sir she cried,
    I've lost my spotted cow.

No more complain, no longer mourn,
    Your cow's not lost, my dear,
I saw your cow in yonder lawn,
    Come love and I'll sh[o]w you where.

I must confess that you are very kind—
    I thank you, sir, said she:
You will be sure her there to find;
    Come sweetheart go with me.

Then to the groves we did repair,
    And crossed the flowery dale;
We hugged and kissed each other,
    And love was all our tale.

And in the grove we spent the day,
    And thought it passed too soon,
At night we homeward bent our way,
    When bri[g]htly shone the moon.

If I should cross yon flowery dale,
    Or go to view the plough,
She runs and calls, ye generous swain,
    I've lost my spotted cow.

(19th-century broadside, Printed and sold by J. Pitts, Wholesale Toy and Marble Warehouse, 6, Great St. Andrew-street, Seven Dials.)

The sexual politics of gender, class, and region hinted at in Hardy's pastoral fantasy are blatantly revealed as being similar to those of pastoral's low other. The song invokes pastoral motifs ("charming maid," "generous [but more often 'gentle'] swain," "flowery dale," the freshness and innocence of spring and a new day) thereby suggesting the erotic sublimity of a mutually pleasurable encounter, only to conclude with a boast ("If I . . . [then] She . . ."), mapping the male narrator's assertion of dominance over the woman: the power-play implicit in his statement of her desire, his implied ability to use her desire for his pleasure, and his ability, having done so, to dismiss or ignore her at will. Furthermore, as I have explained elsewhere, class and regional conflict are suggested when the maid, who is a rural female laborer, specifically a milkmaid (Tess's position when she meets Angel for the second time), refers to the male as "Sir." By his own comment, he is someone who goes to "view the plow," not someone who labors behind the plow. Thus he might be a country squire, a 19th-century middle-to-upper-class gentleman (like Angel Clare in *Tess of the d'Urbervilles* who is out for a walk in the country), or, perhaps, some combination of the two, for example a man like Alec d'Urberville of the same novel whose money and values are identified with the city, but who, having acquired a country estate, presents himself as a country gentleman. He might also be a man like Fitspiers, a doctor in Hardy's *The Woodlanders*, who is of the city but for want of employment finds himself in the country. Or he might be the reader. If the narrator is understood as representing socio-economically privileged males, then through a transcoding of the woman's gender and socio-economic positioning, the song may be understood as mapping a privileged and perhaps urban hegemony over the rural laboring classes—female and male (Preston 1992:320-321).

Bawdry, although frequently associated by the privileged registers with the lower classes, has as a folk aesthetic tradition always crossed cultural registers. Furthermore, such crossings, because they encode meaning in accordance with localized and contextualized performance as well as recalling group-oriented histories of such performances, invoke individualizing group-identities as a means of constructing meaning. In *Tess of the d'Urbervilles*, the meaning derived from "The Spotted Cow" by a privileged singer or reader (male or female) may be negotiated somewhat differently than the meaning the song has for its performer, Tess's mother, Joan Durbeyfield (what the song might mean to Tess's mother will be discussed later) or, for that matter, for a rural male laborer who might resituate the song's politics based on his positioning and his needs. Here I want to emphasize the way in which the gendered socio-economic power-relations mapped by the sexual discourse of the bawdy song generally used by a privileged person to affirm privileged self-representation and validate privileged power ironically prostitute the very source through which the privileged registers otherwise seek edenic wholeness. In other words, whereas privileged pastoral constructs its female gendered landscape as virginal and innocent, privileged bawdry reveals privileged fears concerning previous contact and, in the process, reconfigures the maiden as "whore."

After the dance, Angel notices Tess standing "apart" from the group and "instinctively" feels that she was "hurt by his oversight," wishes that he had asked her to dance or had "inquired her name," "dismiss[es] the subject from his mind," and then moves on to join his brothers (1970:16-17). Angel will reappear later in the novel as a longer-term participant-observer of the landscape. This positioning will enable him to deconstruct privileged popular constructions of rural peoples as the stereotypical Hodge even though it will not keep him from constructing a reified reading of Tess that is dependent upon pastoral ideology.

> The conventional farm folk of his imagination—personified by the pitiable dummy known as Hodge—were obliterated after a few days' residence. At close quarters no Hodge was to be seen. At first, it is true, when Clare's intelligence was fresh from a contrasting society, these friends with whom he now hobnobbed seemed a little strange. Sitting down as a level member of the dairyman's household seemed at the outset an undignified proceeding. The ideas, the modes, the surroundings, appeared retrogressive and unmeaning. But with living on there, day after day, the acute sojourner became conscious of a new aspect in the spectacle. Without any objective change whatever, variety had taken the place of monotonousness. His host and his host's household, his men and his maids, as they became intimately known to Clare, began to differentiate themselves as in a chemical process. The thought of Pascal's was brought home to him: "A mesure qu'on a plus d'esprit, on trouve qu'il y a plus d'hommes originauz. Les gens du commun ne trouvent pas de différence entre les hommes." ["The sharper one's mind, the more one notices how many original men there are; the common run of people do not notice differences between men."4] The typical and unvarying Hodge ceased to exist. He had been disintegrated into a number of varied fellow-creatures—beings of many minds, beings infinite in difference: some happy, many serene, a few depressed, one here and there bright even to genius, some stupid, others wanton, others austere; some mutely Miltonic,

> some potentially Cromwellian; into men who had private views of each other, as he had of his friends; who could applaud or condemn each other, amuse or sadden themselves by the contemplation of each other's foibles or vices; men every one of whom walked in his own individual way the road to dusty death. (1970:151-152)

Equated in this passage are Angel's positioning as participant-observer of rural life and that of the scientist-philosopher. What is posited is that through close observation the object of his gaze reveals itself—its essentialistic components—as in a chemistry experiment. But simultaneously that chemical process is located within the observer, and revelation is shown to be the subjective construct of the reader (here the participant-observer of rural life) rather than the objective documentation of the ethnographic subject's self-revelation. Although one might be tempted to read—and through a negotiated belief indeed read—this as an ethnographic "money shot," the levels of narrative distancing embed within that "shot" its own means of deconstruction.

In this "shot" (as in the description of the May-Day dance), the ethnographic subject (Hodge) neither speaks nor acts but is spoken about, and even that is done not through the primary participant-observer's commentary but rather through the narrator's reconstruction of Angel's thoughts. The overdetermined nature of narrative distancing discloses the "money shot" as a textual fabrication which rhetorically 1) posits the possibility of the ethnographic subject as having spoken and acted only to appropriate the potential agency of that voice and those actions for another party, 2) claims authority for the participant-observer's interpretations (readings) of what he saw and experienced (he was there so he should know), but 3) does so by displacing the subjective quality of that experience with the "seeming" objectivity of the third-person omniscient narrator's writerly voice, a voice that thereby appropriates meaning to its domain. Where modern ethnography will rhetorically construct itself as objectively knowing by creating superficial disjunctures between subjective experience and "objective" inscriptions of that experience (for recent critiques of this practice, see Clifford 1986 and Pratt 1986), Hardy very early on exposes its subjective foundations. In the process, Hardy discloses the extent to which ethnography uses constructions of the "other" as a means of investigating and constructing the "self." By doing so, Hardy also contestively acknowledges his readers' powers (as participant-observers of his locale) to appropriate and rewrite his bodily text as a means of constructing and affirming their own.

If I linger on this textual moment, it is because I want to locate here Hardy's own frustrations with self-authorship, frustrations which stem from an acute awareness of the ways in which identity is always already constructed by forces external to the self which are internalized by the self, spoken, and then reappropriated by another. As participant-observer of his own hybrid bodily social chemistry, Hardy seeks knowledge of its essentialist elements, and as writerly-narrator of his fictions, Hardy seeks to author himself—all the while inscribing an acute awareness of the extent to which his voice has been and will be appropriated and thereby erased by readerly textual negotiations. The problem is one of agency. Just as Hardy appropriates the rural landscape and the female body for his purposes, so too his readers appropriate his textual fabrications of that/his domain for their purposes.

Angel will participate in and observe the local landscape and seem to learn from that experience a means of connecting with that landscape, but simultaneously he will continually relapse into traditional privileged constructions of self and otherness which reify and make a fetish of rural peoples. Angel's participation in pastoral ideology is revealed when, for example, he refers to Tess as a "fresh and virginal daughter of nature" (1970:155) and as the goddesses "Artemis" or "Demeter" (1970:167). Although Tess will attempt to reclaim herself by voicing her own reality, "Call me Tess" (1970:167), that voice will go unheard, just as her attempt at personal inscription (the letter she writes to Angel) will go unread. And when on her wedding day, she verbally confesses (speaks) her reality (a speech which one might note is mentioned by the narrator as having occurred although it is textually erased; it literally is not there), that attempted voicing of self-representation Angel will hear mixed with and thereby inflected by his own register's trope-laden constructions of rural and classed otherness. Where he had once envisioned her as "the most spotless creature that ever lived" (1970:227), only momentarily worrying that she played the "coquette" with him (1970:227), when he learns that he has married and thus linked himself with what might be termed "used goods," he retreats into a construction of self and otherness which frantically seeks to define difference and to establish distance between itself and that relegated to the category of "other." Referring to Tess as an "unapprehending peasant woman" of "different society and different manners" (1970:297) and as "too—childish—unformed—crude" (1970:305), Angel reverts to mapping Tess as low "other" and seeks solace in reaffirmation of his identity as a member of the privileged registers, the source of his folk identity. As Mark Workman has explained, "folk culture reasonably may be conceptualized as the site of ongoing tropic conservation and emergence, and, far more than any artifact or narrative, folk identity is its ultimate product" (1994:172). Having sought to "secure rustic innocence as surely as [he] should secure pink cheeks" through his union with Tess (1970:304), he—like his brothers before him—now, on some level, constructs Tess according to the trope-laden image of the country hoyden: "You were one person; now you are another" (1970:292). The statement seems an ironic inversion of his earlier comment on and attitude towards the "typical and unvarying Hodge" who, after close observation, "ceased to exist" being "disintegrated into a number of varied fellow-creatures" (1970:152).

Angel's prostitution of Tess to his own intellectual and emotional needs is mirrored in the text by Alec d'Urberville's prostitution of her to his physical needs. If, to Angel, Tess is initially an edenic landscape, an intellectual construct to love and cherish as a source of spiritual rejuvenation, to Alec she is, from beginning to end, a physical site to conquer, a material source of physical pleasure that is simultaneously fraught with privileged fears of rebellion and contamination. Thus, Tess is also represented as the proverbial country wench—an "artful hussy" (1970:66), a "mere chit" (1970:87)—and, as such, something either to prostitute to or already prostituted by one's own socio-economic register's needs and desires. Alec, having given Tess a "kiss of mastery"—which she wipes from her cheek—, exclaims, "You are mighty sensitive for a cottage girl!" (1970:65), suggesting that cottage girls are there for the mastering. And when Alec, meeting Tess after having seemingly reformed his ways, claims that it is Tess who subverts his higher nature, the reader is presented with the trope of the female laborer's potentially corrosive sexuality coupled with its "witch"-like power:

> You temptress, Tess; you dear damned witch of Babylon—I could not resist you as soon as I met you again! * * * * The religious

> channel is left dry forthwith; and it is you who have done it! . . . you find me a Christian enthusiast; you then work upon me, perhaps, to my complete perdition! . . . You have been the cause of my backsliding. (1970:411-422)

Insomuch as Angel and Alec mirror each other, constructions of idealized innocence come laden with fears of previous contact (and thereby contamination), guilts of appropriation, and worries of possible rebellion.

Tess, too, will alternate between constructing her identity in accordance with privileged constructions, particularly those which denigrate her, and persevering in accordance with a simple will to be alive. But although Tess will, at various times, attempt to speak her own reality in response to privileged tropic construction—"Did it never strike your mind that what every woman says some women may feel?" (1970:97); "Call me Tess!" (1970:167); "I am only a peasant by position, not by nature!" (1970:297)—, for the most part her voice will go unheard, bringing to mind both Gayatri Chakrovorty Spivak's question, "Can the subaltern speak?" (1988) and Margaret Mills's resituating of the question as "How, and under what circumstances, can or does the hegemonic hear?" (1993:174).

Unheard, Tess by the end of the novel will have resorted to physical violence as a means of espousing agency (she stabs and thereby murders Alec). But if the smooth, seemingly impermeable surface of dominant culture briefly shows itself to be penetrable, that surface quickly heals its wound by silencing the voice that would contest its hegemony (Tess is tried, convicted, and executed for the murder) and reasserts privileged representational power by displacing Tess (a contaminated source of edenic return) with her sister, Liza Lu, who is said by Tess to be "good, simple, and pure" (1970:503). That Tess, as fictional character, and Hardy, as author of that character, both participate in this displacement suggests the extent to which all voices, even those contestive of dominant social structures, are enmeshed within those structures. Having attempted to critique extant power-relations and representational practices, Hardy nonetheless provides his readership with a means of recuperating and thereby continuing those relations and practices.

Bodies in the Act of Becoming: Bawdy Song

> "Come Love, and I'll show you where."
> ("The Spotted Cow")

Traditional English male bawdy song uses sexual discourse to map cultural power-relations based on gender, class, and sometimes regional identity. Socio-economically privileged males assert their gender and class-based agency through acts of voyeurism (their ability to view coital couples of classes below their own, feminizing by means of their privileged gaze the coital bodies and the socio-economic register cross-coded onto those bodies) or through positing their abilities to have sexual intercourse with their "low others'" women (Preston 1992). In turn, those men marked as "low other" may assert gender and class-based agency by positing their ability sexually to satisfy women of their own socio-economic registers as well as women of the privileged socio-economic registers. Implicit in this discourse, as Claude Levi-Strauss has argued for other contexts (1969), is a representation of the female (or that gendered female through a male gaze) as a vehicle for male transactions. In other words, as Eve Sedgwick, quoting Gayle Rubin (1975), has noted, "Levi Strauss's nominative man uses a woman as a 'conduit of a relationship' in which the true *partner* is a man" (1985:26). Insomuch as Hardy's narrative performance is analogous to another man's singing of a bawdy song—masculine(ized) performer / feminized text / masculine(ized) audience—Hardy's performance maps, on the one hand, homosocial desire and, on the other hand, contestive sites within male homosociality.

Hardy's narrative is double-voiced. Whereas pastoral ideology provides Hardy with a means of seductively courting the privileged register, bawdy song provides Hardy with a means of both further courting that register and contesting his appropriation by that register, as well as a means of probing and attempting to construct a register of his own. The singing of bawdy songs was, as it still is, a tradition which foregrounded the disruptive possibilities of the material body: that which Mikhail Bahktin has called the grotesque body with its "protuberances" and "orifices and convexities" which in the process of penetrating and "swallowing up" constantly ignores and transgresses upon the "smooth" and "impenetrable surface that closes and limits" the bourgeois body, which, since the 17th century, has increasingly defined itself as a "separate and completed phenomenon" (1984:317-318). And this is what Hardy's intentional "coarseness" does for his narratives, whether, as George Wotton (1985) has suggested, it be Arabella's throwing of the pig's penis at Jude's head accompanied by her and the other girls' mocking and derisive laughter (*Jude the Obscure*) or, as I will argue, it is Farmer Cawtree's invoking of a bawdy song (*The Woodlanders*), Joan Durbeyfield's singing of that same bawdy song (*Tess of the d'Urbervilles*), or Hardy's performance of "The Tying of the Garter," a bawdy song he rewrites in his poem "The Dark-Eyed Stranger").

At the end of *The Woodlanders*, Farmer Cawtree—referring to Grace Melbury's impending reunion with her husband, Dr. Fitspiers (a community outsider who, having wooed Grace away from a local beau, is none-the-less unfaithful to Grace)—tells an anecdote about another husband and wife who had a tendency to fight like cats and dogs one hour and make up the next: "the next hour you'd hear 'em singing 'The Spotted Cow' together, as peaceable as two holy twins; yes—and very good voices they had, and would strike in like street ballet-singers to one another's support in the high notes" (1970:440). For Farmer Cawtree, "singing 'The Spotted Cow'" seems to be a euphemism for mutually playful and gratifying sex and functions as a bit of proverbial, if profane, wisdom. His commentary foregrounds the lower material body and its transgressive possibilities through the liminal locale created by collocating culturally inscribed low and high coital bodies: those of the street-singers and those of Grace Melbury and Fitspiers. This heteroglossic and transgressive moment, in Bakhtinian terms, is dialogized and thus fraught with the carnivalesque possibilities of the marketplace, as well as a laughter, at once, "gay [and] triumphant" and "mocking [and] deriding"—a laughter which "asserts and denies," "buries and revives" (1985:11-12). From one perspective, the slippage of street-singers into the realm of the pastoral is an act of contamination, a moment when that marked as low other invades one's pristine fabrications.[5] But from another perspective, such transgressions engender creative possibilities and sometimes contestively so. The result is the orgasmic transgressive humor suggested euphemistically by the street-singers' helping each other out on the "high notes" (1970:440).

In *Tess of the d'Urbervilles*, Tess, returning from a May-Day dance at which she catches the glimpse of a young man "of superior class" (1970:14), comes home to the familiar scene of her mother, Joan Durbeyfield, rocking a cradle and "singing, in a vigorous gallopade, the favourite ditty of 'The Spotted Cow'" (1970:19). The creative potentiality of co-mingling sexual bodies is symbolically evoked by the image of the child that Joan Durbeyfield rocks during her performance of the song as well as by the intensity of the rocking and singing. The scene, as initially described by the narrator, with its "thumpings," "violent rockings[s]," "vigorous gallopade[s]," "exclamation[s]," "high vocal pitch[es]," and "invocation[s]" is fraught with comic intensities both maternal and sexual (1970:18-19).

Reading *Tess of the d'Urbervilles*, the reader who does not know the song may initially gloss the performance with the traditionalizing motif of "mother singing a lullaby while rocking her infant child" and, through a negotiated reading (one requiring an erasure of the carnivalesque intensity of the performance), appropriate it to confirm an ideology that situates the mother-child relationship within the asexual sphere of 19th-century bourgeois domesticity, an ideology which is, perhaps, in some way further "naturalized" by the broad pastoral setting. But the reader who does know the song must read its situated performance as being somehow ironic in the sense that a bawdy song may not "seem" an appropriate choice for a lullaby, specifically because it draws attention to the mother's sexuality, thereby 1) broadly deconstructing bourgeois representations of the a-sexual mother's body (regardless of socio-cultural register) even as it simultaneously 2) recuperates the privileged female body by displacing and mapping the disruptive and dangerous potentialities of female sexuality onto the lower socio-economic, rural female body. If viewed as being ironic, the scene (as constructed in the second scenario) may be appropriated by the privileged reader and used to mark Joan's body (and by extension, Tess's body) as low other and thereby validate privileged use (economic and sexual) of it, or the scene (as in the first scenario) may be understood as a subversively coded performance during which, as Radner and Lanser have explained in respect to other performances, a member of a dominated socio-cultural group expresses covertly "ideas, beliefs, experiences, feelings, and attitudes" that the dominant socio-cultural register "would find disturbing or threatening if expressed in more overt forms" (1993:4).[6] In other words, whether one attributes the performance to Joan Durbeyfield or to Thomas Hardy, the scene is double-voiced, enabling privileged appropriation even as it contests such appropriation. And the performance may be attibuted to either or both performers: to the extent that it is Joan's performance, the scene functions as an inscription of an everyday artistic performance by a lower socio-economic women in rural 19th-century Dorset; to the extent that the scene is a literary representation, the inscribed performance of an "ethnographic/folkloric moment" has been decontextualized and recontextualized within Hardy's performance, another "ethnographic moment," but one whose referent is Hardy, not Joan Durbeyfield (on "decontextualization" and "recontextualization" in relation to the marketplace, see Bauman and Briggs 1990 and Kapchan 1993). In other words, Hardy appropriates the contestive properties of the female voice and body for his own subversively coded performance.

Through utopian fantasies, performances of bawdy song momentarily dismember the "impersonal systems" which seek to dominate all that has been transcoded culturally as the material body: everything that, since the 17th century, according to Peter Stallybrass and Allon White, has been mapped by bourgeois ideology "as low—as dirty, repulsive, noisy, contaminating" (1986:191), those "threats posed by bodies, by lower classes, by angry mobs[,]" as well as by emergent identities (Laura Kipnis 1992:337). Thus, the singing of bawdy song, here specifically "The Spotted Cow," like other forms of consciously transgressive folk humor (see Preston 1994), functions as a form of creative contestability. In this case the performances of the song (Cawtree's, Joan Durbeyfield's, and Hardy's) encode a typology of the larger plots in which people live their lives, as well as a challenge to the hegemony of those plots. Cawtree's anecdote is preceded by Grace's father's saying that "the woman walks and laughs somewhere at this very moment whose neck [Fitspiers will] be coling next year as he does hers to-night" (1970:439-440), and it is followed by the hollow-turner's comment, "She's got him quite tame. But how long 'twill last I can't say" (1970:442) as well as comments by other men foregrounding class and gender-conflict as mediating the nature of potentiality, but for just a moment the carnevalesque nature of the bawdy anecdote has opened a space for alternative imaginings. And although both the immediate setting for Joan Durbeyfield's performance—the interior of her home, of her social reality, which is described as a "one-candled spectacle," an "unspeakable dreariness," and a "yellow melancholy" (1970:19)—as well as Tess's less than satisfying alliances with Angel Clare and Alec d'Urberville, her eventual destitution, prostitution, and execution suggest a reading of the direction the song's events might go, given the song's lack of closure, particularly if sung by a woman, those "realities" are contested by the song's lack of closure. The song's open-endedness coupled with its bawdy nature breaks open a space in hegemonic social discourse for alternative imaginings.

Female bawdy song (either that involving female narrators and thus clearly meant to be sung by a woman or that appropriated from a male tradition and refocused by the gendered female voice in performance), like male bawdy song, functions as a gendered assertion of agency, in Joan's case, voicing a classed and regional identity as part of her gendered sexual desires and her ability to choose who may and may not, who can and cannot, satisfy her desires. Certainly gender-struggle is mapped in "The Spotted Cow" by the maid's assertion of female sexual desire and the potential power of that sexuality insomuch as the male is attracted to her even though the assertion seems to be countered by the male's implied ability to get her to disclose her desire, his implied ability to fulfill her desire, and then his implied ability to choose whether or not he will participate in a repeat performance. But whether female or male agency is mapped by the song may depend upon whether the performance is inflected with a female or male voice. Thus Joan Durbeyfield's performance asserting female agency through the power of female sexuality—the "trumpcard" that will get the gentleman to marry the milkmaid (1970:16) just as it got Joan's husband to marry her—invokes the descrepancy between what could be and what is and, thereby, both recognizes and is contestive of her own situation as well as that which eventually becomes Tess's.

Traditional bawdy song does not change reality, but it does challenge hegemonic authority by momentarily dismembering social structures and displacing them with utopian fantasies (on "utopian but not deterministic transformations," see Ashley 1990:xviii). Although the larger plots of Hardy's narratives define humanity as being caught in a maze of social determinism, the polyglossic textures of the narratives (those voices which speak and are recognized and thereby heard, those voices which speak but may go unheard, and those voices which are noted as existing but are textually erased) map a discourse of creative possibility, which is reinforced by Hardy's invocation of a bawdy song tradition that is itself dialogic: meaning and agency is asserted in accordance with textual negotiations which are responsive to the differing needs of individuals and groups situated differently in respect to social relations.

Tess of the d'Urbervilles is both an interpreted ethnographic inscription of such localized performances as those by Farmer Cawtree and Joan Durbeyfield and, figuratively speaking, Hardy's own performance of a bawdy song—a type of embodied auto-ethnographic inscription. Just as early ethnographers like the narrators of male bawdy song have frequently described their encounters with their "others" through the erotic language of penetration and conquest, so the narrator of *Tess*, as Penny Boumelha has argued, pricks, pierces, and penetrates Tess:

> The narrator's erotic fantasies of penetration and engulfment enact a pursuit, violation and persecution of Tess in parallel with those she suffers at the hands of her two lovers. . . . the phallic imagery of pricking, piercing, and penetration . . . serves . . . to satisfy the narrator's fascination with the interiority of her sexuality, and his desire to take possession of her. (1982:120)

Agency is thus situated with the male or masculinized ethnographer, singer of bawdy songs, and novelist. And the sharing of these texts by the writer-singer with the reader-audience provides a mechanism for, broadly speaking, privileged, more narrowly speaking, androcentric bonding: sharing one's ethnographic inscription (self-consciously fictional or otherwise) of another or one's bawdy song is analogous to sharing a female body. It is thus that Hardy, as male writer-singer, asserts a gendered agency and seeks a homosocial bond with his privileged reader. What is different about Hardy's voice is that it is a voice which recognizes its own fragility, an insecurity which is encoded through his cross-gendered identification with Tess as a representative socio-cultural "other." As that which "pricks, pierces, and penetrates" and as that which is "pricked, pierced and penetrated," Hardy maps his own liminal cultural status. But Hardy's writing of *Tess of the d'Urbervilles*, like another person's singing of a bawdy song, also flaunts the transgressive potentialities of his liminality.

Whether one inhabits a socio-cultural space traditionally defined as dominant or subordinate or one inhabits an emergent and hence liminal space, bawdry provides a means of reconfiguring cultural production as localized performances, but localized performances that are clearly touched by and thus responsive to larger-than-local power-relations. The bodies, material and socio-cultural, fleetingly produced (sung into existence) by such performances are images of Bakhtin's "bod[ies] in the act of becoming" (1984:317), a metaphor which Hardy literalizes in the last textual site I will read for this essay: "The Dark-Eyed Gentleman," from *Time's Laughingstocks*, 1909 (1976:243).

In "The Dark-Eyed Gentleman," Hardy invokes a bawdy song, "The Tying of the Garter," which he clearly associates with assertions of privileged male dominance, but whose contestive possibilities, if localized within the performance contexts of other registers, he seems equally aware of (for a discussion of the ways other registers' versions of this song map various assertions of agency, see Preston 1992). By referencing "The Tying of the Garter," Hardy once again draws upon the dialogic nature of the larger tradition of bawdy song, as well as bawdry's grotesque material body, in order to decenter and deconstruct mono-vocal assertions of authority. But in "The Dark-Eyed Gentleman," unlike many of his other narratives, the potential of contestive utopian fantasy, what Dominick LaCapra calls "experimental fantasy," is imaginatively realized, enabling a mapping of hybrid agency that rejects appropriation by hegemonic socio-economic others while participating in traditional gendered assertions of dominance. As LaCapra points out, carnivalesque phenomena test and contest "all aspects of society and culture through festive laughter; those that are questionable may be readied for change: those that are deemed legitimate may be reinforced" (1983:306).

Although there have been many versions of "The Tying of the Garter" (also know as "Tottingham Frolick"), I quote here the text from Thomas D'Urfey's *Wit and Mirth, Pills to Purge Melancholy* (1959), originally published in 1719-1720 and anonymously reprinted in 1876:

> AS I went from *Tottingham*
> Upon a market day,
> There I met with a bonny Lass

Writing the Hybrid Body

Cloathed all in Grey,
    Her Journey was to *London*,
        With Butter-milk and Whey.
To come Down adown,
To come Down, down a down a.

Sweet-heart quoth he,
        You're well overtook,
With that she cast her Head aside,
        And lent to him a Look;
Then presently these two
        Both Hands together shook:
To come, &c.

And as they rode together,
        A long side by side,
The Maiden it so chanced,
        Her Garter was unty'd;
For fear that she should lose it,
        Look here, Sweet-heart, he cry'd,
Your Garter is down a down, &c.

Good sir, quoth she,
        I pray you take the Pain,
To do so much for me,
        As to take it up again,
With a good will, quoth he,
        When I come to yonder Plain,
I will take you down, &c.

And when they came unto the Place,
        Upon the Grass so green,
The Maid she held her Legs so wide,
        The Young man slipt between,
Such tying of a Garter,
        You have but seldom seen,
To come down, &c.

Then she rose up again,
        And thank'd him for his pain:
He took her by the middle small,
        And Kiss'd her once again:
Her Journey was to *London*,
        And he from *Highgate* came,
To come down, &c.

> Thus *Tibb* of *Tottingham*,
>   She lost her Maiden-head,
> But yet it is no matter,
>   It stood her in small stead,
> For it did often trouble her,
>   As she lay in her Bed.
> *To come down, &c.*
>
> But when all her Butter-milk
>   And her Whey was sold,
> The loss of her Maiden-head,
>   It waxed very cold:
> But that which will away,
>   Is very hard to hold.
> *To come, &c.*
>
> You Maids, you Wives, and Widows,
>   That now do hear my Song,
> If any young man proffer Kindness,
>   Pray take it short, or long;
> For there is no such Comfort
>   As lying with a Man.
> *To come Down a down,*
> *To come Down, down a down a.*
>
> (1959 IV:179-181)

If performed by and among privileged males, this song might easily not only construct but confirm that register's extant view of appropriate social relations—in this instance, the sexual encoding the socio-economic. The young woman's willing participation in her loss of maidenhead and in the implied objectification and commodification of her own person—a possibility emphasized more fully in other versions of the song: "The maid to *London* came / To sell off her commodity / She thought it for no shame" (stanza 7, lines 4-6 in Ebsworth's *Choyce Drollery* [1656] 1876:45-47)—seems both to manifest dominant culture's view of her gender, class, and regional identity and to sanction that view, thereby marking her body like the products of her labor (buttermilk and whey) available for the satisfaction of privileged erotic and socio-economic needs. But one might note, as well, that there is the possibility latent in the song of a woman's voice—in other versions, "But that which will away, *quoth she*, / Is very hard to hold" and "*Quoth she* it is no matter, / It stood me in small stead, / But often times it troubled me / As I lay in my bed" (stanza 8, lines 5-6 and stanza 9, lines 3-6 in Ebsworth's *Choyce Drollery* [1656] 1876:45-47; my emphasis)—which might, contextualized by a woman's singing of the song, seek to reclaim her body for her own pleasures, both erotic and economic (see Preston 1993). Furthermore, just as a woman's voice might seek to reclaim the female body, so a non-privileged male's voice might appropriate the song for its own uses (see Preston 1992). It is as this web of differently situated identities that I want to locate Hardy's body and voice.

"The Tying of the Garter" is specifically invoked by Hardy in his short poem by way of the repeatedly occurring, refrain-like phrase, "he tied up my garter for me":

I

I PITCHED my day's leazings in Crimmercrock Lane,
To tie up my garter and jog on again,
When a dear dark-eyed gentleman passed there and said,
In a way that made all o' me colour rose-red,
    "What do I see—
    O pretty knee!"
And he came and he tied up my garter for me.
                    (stanza 1, 1976:243)

The initial difference between Hardy's narrative and the bawdy song lies in his choice of point of view. In Hardy's text, the narrator is a female rural laborer, not a privileged male. Thus within its fictional context, the narrative posits a woman's self-representation. Although by cross-dressing his voice, Hardy ultimately appropriates whatever potentialities lie in female sexuality for his own purposes, in the fictional context of the poem, the act of giving the woman a voice begins the process of rehumanizing and deobjectifying the otherness she normally represents. That the dark-eyed gentleman of the poem envisions and responds to her as objectified other is implicit in his comment, "What do I see— / O pretty knee," and his disappearance after he has gotten what he wants. She, like her bawdy song predecessors, is for him, as she has been for his predecessors, a pretty knee or body part, a loose garter or ephemeral object to be used and then discarded.

The maid's sexuality is represented as being active and responsive ("in a way that made all o' me colour rose-red") and yet innocent, bringing to mind Hardy's subtitle, *A Pure Woman*, to *Tess of the d'Urbervilles*. As Rosemarie Morgan has noted of Hardy's unconventional coding of female sexuality:

> Hardy's women experience their bodies in ways that drew shudders from his critics. . . . [But] whereas [the] critics reviled their [Hardy's women characters'] voluptuousness, Hardy kept firmly to his practice of celebrating the life of the senses and, most important, of presenting the voluptuous woman, the sexy woman, as neither dumb nor loose in morals. To bring seriousness and sexiness together in the single female form was not only to fly in the face of current convention, code and belief, it was also subversive. (1988:xi-xii)

The physicality of Hardy's female characters—their ability to labour, to weep, to sweat, etc.—suggests Bakhtin's image of the grotesque body which is also the body of bawdy song, that body which, as Kipnis argues (1992), through a cross-coding of bodily and socio-economic topography may be used by subordinated peoples to disrupt hegemonic power-relations. But while Hardy does use the laboring female body in this way, having done so, he also seeks to domesticate that body.

That the woman in "The Dark-Eyed Gentleman" is not a "whore" is highlighted throughout the poem by her emotional sensitivity which is implicitly contrasted with the baser representations of women in bawdy song texts:

II

'Twixt sunset and moonrise it was, I can mind:
Ah, 'tis easy to loose what we nevermore find!—
Of the dear stranger's home, of his name, I knew nought,
But I soon knew his nature and all that it brought,
       Then bitterly
       Sobbed I that he
Should ever have tied up my garter for me!
(stanza 2, 1976:243)

Her bitter sobbing—that follows her loss of virginity and the disappearance of the gentleman-stranger—differentiates her from the woman in "The Tying of the Garter" whose "heart [grew] cold" at the thought of her loss: a loss implied to be either something insubstantial and of little value to the woman in "The Tying of the Garter" or of such great value that it radically alters her perception of herself, of her socio-political reality, as well as potentially altering the nature of her behavior. But if, in "The Dark-Eyed Stranger," the narrator's comment, "But I soon knew his nature and all that it brought," hints at her pregnancy and her ensuing social condemnation, none of this actually appears in her narrative, nor is any mention made of her having opted for economic gain through a willing commodification of her body.

Instead, the woman's feelings of loss in "The Dark-Eyed Gentleman" are eventually displaced by her feelings of joy which emanate from her very human relationship with her son who is "comrade and friend":

III

Yet now I've beside me a fine lissom lad,
And my slip's nigh forgot, and my days are not sad;
My own dearest joy is he, comrade, and friend,
He it is who safe-guards me, on him I depend;
    No sorrow brings he,
    And thankful I be
That his daddy once tied up my garter for me!
(stanza 3, 1976:243)

That such fleeting sexual alliances as those presented in the bawdy song texts, in Hardy's poem, and in such novels as *Tess of the d'Urbervilles* do often end in the conception of a child is, in Hardy's poem, presented as neither comic nor pathetic, although it draws on both as stereotypical responses to a such an event. Instead, "Sorrow," the name of Tess's offspring, is transformed to "joy," a life-sustaining and potentially subversive creative force. In contrast to the shadowy figure of his father, the "fine lissom lad"—who is his mother's "dearest joy," her "comrade and friend," and the one "who safe-guards her"—suggests a solidarity between mother and child that one day might challenge privileged hegemonies. And yet, at the same time that a class-based solidarity is asserted, its cross-gendered nature is compromised by a mapping of active agency as male (the son), and the female body (the mother) once again becomes a conduit for a contestive male homosociality, this time envisioned as that between the father and son: socio-economic dominance is challenged, but gender dominance is ultimately kept in place.

Drawing on the work of Barbara Babcock (1980) as well as Bakhtin (1981), Debora Kapchan explains that "a hybrid form—like an ethnically or otherwise hybrid individual—can 'see' itself because it is more than itself; it is also other" (1993:305). To this one might add that what is seen or made visible is not some kind of essentialist truth or reality but rather a series of sometimes conflicting textual fabrications, appropriations of already appropriated locales. This inherent reflexivity is at the heart of Hardy's representation of his own bodily locale. Thus, as the dark-eyed gentleman, the female laborer, and the product of their socio-sexual intercourse—the "fine lissom lad"—, Hardy explores and seeks to construct the hidden text (that without and within the borders) of his own hybrid identity.

Conclusion

Clifford Geertz has suggested that "man is an animal suspended in webs of significance he himself has spun," that "culture" is those "webs," and that "the analysis of" culture is "not an experimental science in search of law but an interpretive one in search of meaning" (1973:10). He attributes to ethnography both the processes of writing and reading. It is a scientific writing up of "thick descriptions," but it is also interpretation. Geertz explains that "[d]oing ethnography is like trying to read (in the sense of 'constructing a reading of') a manuscript [the manuscript being the culture]—foreign, faded, full of ellipses, incoherencies, suspicious emendations, and tendentious commentaries, but not in conventionalized graphs of sound but in transient examples of shaped behavior" (1973:10). To this James Clifford has added the important observation that those doing the "readings" are themselves subject to "intersubjective dialogue, translation, and projection" (1986:109). Questioning the pretense of scientific objectivity, the comments of both Geertz and Clifford reposition ethnographic description as a literary genre, and Clifford and others have suggested the extent to which ethnographic inscriptions have, at times, embedded within themselves and merged with other literary genres, participating in literary tropes which have, for example, been borrowed from travel literature and personal memoirs and which may overlap with fictional and non-fiction accounts of "rites of passage," as well as heroic adventure tales of penetration and conquest (see, for example, Pratt 1986 and Kodish 1987).

It is the multivocality of mixed genres (Bakhtin 1981:262-263) that I have used as a transition between the ethnographer's reading (interpreting) and writing (as in creating or constructing) culture, the novelist's reading (interpreting) and writing (as in creating or constructing) culture, and situated folk performances (interpretive, creative, and hinting at alternative possibilities). In other words, I have attempted to read literary texts (specific pieces of Hardy's prose and verse narratives) as viable sites for historical ethnographic and folkloristic fieldwork, recognizing that they are "problematic outcomes of intersubjective dialogue, translation, and projection" (Clifford 1986:109) and that, while they construct readings of what Geertz has called "the web of culture," they are simultaneously enmeshed in that web.

Hardy's narratives participate in 19th-century constructions of what Amy Shuman and Charles Briggs describe as modernity's "quintessential 'other'" (1993:111), the folk: "traditional, peasant, working class, rural, poor, self-trained, and marginal" (1993:123). But those narratives also inscribe the trope-laden constructions used to define group-identity by that group's equally constructed opposites: privileged, urban, industrialized, "elite, mainstream, popular, academic, and modern" (1993:123). Hardy's narratives thus provide an incipient deconstruction of overly simplistic 19th- and 20th-century constructions of "folkness" while participating in them. In other words, in Hardy's narratives that which is frequently described as folklore's or folklife's "other" (the privileged register) is represented itself as a folk group whose "traditionalizing" practices (Briggs and Bauman 1992:149; Kapchan 1993:311) are documented and critiqued. The reflexivity of Hardy's hybrid socio-cultural positioning, in an essentialist way, situated him as a "natural" participant-observer (participating in and yet distanced from, part yet not part) of the folk groups inscribed in his narratives—narratives which, in turn, provided him with a means of encoding an auto-ethnographic inscription of the hybrid's frustrated attempts to investigate and voice in order to construct and make visible emergent identity(ies).

"Essentialist" and "natural" are, of course, currently awkward terms to use in reference to any individual or group unless one is critiquing the politics of such usage. I use them here, not because I fail to recognize the hybrid as a product of socio-cultural construction, but because I want a way to differentiate between Hardy's positioning as a hybrid within his "everyday lived experience" and his self-conscious writerly articulation and construction of that positioning, his literary ethnography. I want to foreground this split because of the way in which Hardy displaces the private, subjective, personal narrative "I" with the implied objectivity of a distanced, public (and sometimes, theorizing), third-person persona in his novels. The "I" gets mapped onto a character or characters in the novel who then become the object(s) inscribed by the third-person narrator, a voice which itself is, at times, participatory in the subject-object relations typical of salvage ethnography and of ethnographic participant-observation positionings incipient in the 19th century and formalized in the 20th century which I have been reading in relation to phalocentric and ethnocentric rhetorics of penetration and revelation.

Still, one might argue that by encoding the frequently muted, contestive voice of the ethnographic object-turned-potential-speaking-subject, however imaginary that voice might be, Hardy's narratives project his intense desire for that voice to exist and to be capable of speaking, in part, perhaps, because Hardy sees a need for subordinated peoples to have a voice, but also, in part, because their ability to speak validates his belief in his own ability to speak. Thus, when assuming a cross-dressed voice, Hardy might be seen as attempting a form of ethnographic inscription akin to current theories of a more feminized form of ethnography (one that foregrounds subject-subject relations and "experience-near" theorizing), but one which in Hardy's performances also demonstrates the potential dangers of feminized ethnographies: their ability, if not careful, to "swallow up," in an equally appropriative move, the ethnographic subject's voice (Mills 1990:11). What interests me here is the way in which Hardy's narratives (literary though they may be) argue that that which is constructed by the ethnographer (literary or otherwise) as the ethnographic other (whether object or subject) is sometimes an appropriated (consciously or unconsciously) positioning used to construct the voice of the ethnographer's own "imaginary," as in the following site from *Tess of the d'Urbervilles* in which Hardy speaks subjectively through Tess—a fictional construct of his own imagination—what he otherwise theorizes through the objective voice of the narrator.

Tess, asked by Angel to comment on "life in general" and "to tell [him] in confidence" of her hopes and fears, responds "shyly," thinking "that he meant what were the aspects of things to her":

> The trees have inquisitive eyes, haven't they?—that is, seem as if they had. And the river says,—"Why do ye trouble me with your looks?" And you seem to see numbers of to-morrows just all in a line, the first of them the biggest and clearest, the others getting smaller and smaller as they stand farther away; but they all seem very fierce and cruel and as if they said, "I'm coming! Beware of me! Beware of me!" (1970:159-160)

Tess is asked to speak, and when she (or is it Hardy?) does speak, s/he speaks the symbolic language of a reflexive surrealism that encodes her/his fears.

The terror s/he feels in the situation is then self-consciously and parodically appropriated by Angel and the narrator for hegemonic inscription as "the ache of modernism":

> She was expressing in her own native phrases—assisted a little by her Sixth Standard training—feelings which might almost have been called those of the age—the ache of modernism. The perception arrested him [Angel] less when he reflected that what are called advanced ideas are really in great part but the latest fashion in definition—a more accurate expression, by words in *logy* and *ism*, of sensations which men and women have vaguely grasped for centuries. (1970:160)

In this fictionalized ethnographic moment, we (as ethnographers, literary critics, or cultural theorists) might see ourselves asking our others to speak their meanings, meanings which we then appropriate and, like Angel or the narrator, inscribe within our "logies" and "isms"—a process which may, at times, benumb the contestive properties of our informant's own words. We might also see ourselves inscribing their words along with our own (a moment fraught with dialogic possibilities just as it is in Hardy's narratives) even though our books and articles, insomuch as they frequently carry only our names on the spines, materially argue that what we have done is appropriate the voiced performances of our others for the construction of our own. But although we might be tempted to fantasize the power of our voices—as "a more accurate expression . . . of sensations which men and women have vaguely grasped for centuries" (1970:160)—by imagining the ethnographic subject's validation of our work—"But *you*, sir, can raise up dreams with your music, and drive all such horrid fancies away" (Tess speaking to Angel; 1970:160)—, thereby relieving our guilts of appropriation, ultimately, we must recognize those "expressions" for the textual fabrications that they are.

Hardy's literary narratives (inscribing as they do that which is outside and inside his own socio-cultural bodily locale) disclose an identity politics hypothetically implicit in the acquired hybrid positioning of the "non-literary" ethnographer by suggesting that one's subjective and private positioning is inflected in one's public (writerly) performances and by hinting at the ways in which pieces of that identity may be cross-coded onto the ethnographic subject. This process at once appropriates and, at least partially, erases the ethnographic subject's identity while providing the ethnographer a means of exploring and articulating, through coded messages, meanings otherwise publicly and, in some cases perhaps, privately unarticulatable by the ethnographer. Seen from this perspective, the subaltern lies both without and within, a semiotic object caught between readerly and writerly textual negotiations.

Eroticising the subject-object relationships between and among performer-and-audience, ethnographer-and-ethnographic subject, and writer-text-and-reader in such a way that there is considerable slippage between categories, Hardy draws on the material body's disruptive potential, while reaching out to frame and mark all positional bodies within an "erotic organization of visibility" (Williams 1989:49). Thus the ethnographic "money shot" is, in Hardy's narratives, an heteroglossic image of variously situated material and socio-cultural bodies (including and perhaps most importantly Hardy's own) attempting to speak and act even as they are being spoken about and acted upon. One might read this in respect to Louis Althusser's argument that ideology (as a system of representations) positions people as "subjects" in a way that actually "subjects" (subordinates) them to hegemonic interests (1971:170-179), or one might foreground the creative and contestive nature of those bodies and, listening closely to their differently situated, mutually appropriative, negotiated voicings of meaning, hear the murmurings of emergent possibilities—those "bodies in the act of becoming" (Bakhtin 1984:317).

Notes

My earliest thinking towards this article occurred while writing my dissertation, "The Ballad and the Making of Meaning" (1976), under the direction of James R. Kincaid whom I would like to thank for his openness to and continued support of my work. I would also like to thank Michele Barale for her helpful commentaries on various versions of this essay and David Buchan, W. F. H. Nicolaisen, and Kenneth Goldstein for pats on the back when I needed them.

1. Kathleen Ashley, discussing Victor Turner's concept of "liminality," describes it as the "middle state" between "old and new statuses," as a state of "ambiguity, even paradox, outside or mediating between customary categories," as a "'realm of possibility' where new combinations of cultural givens could be playfully tested," and as the "'seedbeds of cultural creativity,' giving rise to new ideas and new paradigms" (1990:xviii). Mikhail Bakhtin defines hybridity as the mixing in one source of "two or more different linguistic consciousnesses, often widely separated in time and social space" (1981:429).

2. On liminality and reflexivity see Babcock 1980 and Babcock 1990.

3. As an example of such metaphorical "butterfly collecting," see Ruth A. Firor's *Folkways in Thomas Hardy* (1931).

4. The translation of the French is not in Hardy's text. I quote here David Skilton's translation which is provided in a note to the Penguin edition of the text (1978:527).

5. On 19th-century English metaphors of contamination, see Stallybrass and White 1986:125-148; on the 19th-century representation of the street-singer as a symbol of socio-cultural decay, see Preston (forthcoming).

6. One might note here that Joan Durbeyfield, even though a fictional character, is not the only woman to have sung a bawdy song as a lullaby. See, for example, Bess Lomax Hawes' (1974) discussion of "Slew-foot Sue."

References

Althusser, Louis. 1971. *Lenin and Philosophy and Other Essays*. New York: Monthly Review Press.

Anon. [19th-Century]. The Spotted Cow. Printed and sold by J. Pitts, Wholesale Toy and Marble Warehouse, 6, Great St. Andrew-street, Seven Dials, London. In the W. N. Harding collection of Broadsides, Box 11, item 1106.

Ashley, Kathleen M., ed. 1990. *Victor Turner and the Construction of Cultural Criticism*. Bloomington: Indiana University Press.

Babcock, Barbara A. 1980. Reflexivity: Definitions and Discriminations. *Semiotica* 30:1-14.

———. 1990. Mud, Mirrors, and Making Up: Liminality and Reflexivity in Between the Acts. In *Victor Turner and the Construction of Cultural Criticism: Between Literature and Anthropology*, ed. Kathleen M. Ashley, pp. 86-116. Bloomington: Indiana University Press.

Bakhtin, Mikhail. 1981. *The Dialogic Imagination*. Trans. Caryl Emerson and Michael Holquist. Austin: University of Texas Press.

———. 1984. *Rabelais and His World*. Trans. Helene Iswolsky. Bloomington: Indiana University Press.

Bauman, Richard, and Charles Briggs. 1990. Poetics and Performance as Critical Perspectives on Language and Social Life. *Annual Review of Anthropology* 19:59-88.

Boumelha, Penny. 1982. *Thomas Hardy and Women: Sexual Ideology and Narrative Form*. Madison: The University of Wisconsin Press.

Briggs, Charles L. and Richard Bauman. 1992. Genre, Intertextuality and Social Power. *Journal of Linguistic Anthropology* 2:131-172.

Clifford, James. 1986. On Ethnographic Allegory. In *Writing Culture: The Poetics and Politics of Ethnography*, ed. James Clifford and George E. Marcus, pp. 98-121. Berkeley: University of California Press.

———. 1992. "Traveling Cultures." In *Cultural Studies*, ed. Lawrence Grossberg et al., pp. 96-112. New York: Routledge.

D'Urfey, Thomas. 1959 [1719-1720; rpt. 1876]. *Wit and Mirth, Or Pills to Purge Melancholy*. Vols. I-IV. New York: Folklore Library Publishers.

Ebsworth, J. W., ed. 1876 [1656]. *Choyce Drollery: Songs & Sonnets*. Boston, Lincolnshire.

Firor, Ruth A. 1968 [1931]. *Folkways in Thomas Hardy*. New York: Russell & Russell.

Foucault, Michel. 1978. *The History of Sexuality, An Introduction*. Trans. Robert Hurley. New York: Pantheon Books.

Geertz, Clifford. 1973. *The Interpretation of Cultures*. New York: Basic Books.

Hardy, Thomas. 1970 [1887]. *The Woodlanders*. London: Heron Books.

———. 1970 [1891]. *Tess of the d'Urbervilles*. London: Heron Books.

———. 1976. *The Complete Poems of Thomas Hardy*, ed. James Gibson. London: Macmillan.

———. 1978 [1891]. *Tess of the d'Urbervilles*. New York: Viking Penguin Inc.

Hawes, Bess Lomax. 1974. Folksongs and Function: Some Thoughts on the American Lullaby. *Journal of American Folklore* 87:140-148.

Kapchan, Deborah A. 1993. Hybridization and the Marketplace: Emerging Paradigms in Folklorists. *Western Folklore* 52:303-326.

Kipnis, Laura. 1992. (Male) Desire and (Female) Disgust: Reading *Hustler*. In *Cultural Studies*, ed. Lawrence Grossberg et al., pp. 373-391. New York: Routledge.

Kodish, Debora. 1987. Absent Gender, Silent Encounter. *Journal of American Folklore* 100:573-578.

LaCapra, Dominick. 1983. Bakhtin, Marxism, and the Carnivalesque. In *Rethinking Intellectual History: Texts, Contexts, Language*. Ithaca: Cornell University Press.

Levi-Strauss, Claude. 1969. *The Elementary Structures of Kinship*. Boston: Beacon Press.
Marcus, George E. 1986. Contemporary Problems of Ethnography in the Modern World System. In *Writing Culture: The Poetics and Politics of Ethnography*, ed. James Clifford and George E. Marcus, pp. 165-193. Berkeley: University of California Press.
Mills, Margaret A. 1990. Critical Theory and the Folklorists: Performance, Interpretive Authority, and Gender. *Southern Folklore* 47:5-16.
_____. 1993. Feminist Theory and the Study of Folklore: A Twenty Year Trajectory. *Western Folklore* 52:173-192.
Morgan, Rosemarie. 1988. *Women and Sexuality in the Novels of Thomas Hardy*. New York: Routledge.
Pratt, Mary Louise. 1986. Fieldwork in Common Places. In *Writing Culture: The Poetics and Politics of Ethnography*, eds. James Clifford and George E. Marcus, pp. 27-50. Berkeley: University of California Press.
Preston, Cathy Lynn. 1992. "The Tying of the Garter": Representations of the Female Rural Laborer in 17th-, 18th-, and 19th-Century English Bawdy Songs. *Journal of American Folklore* 105:315-341.
_____. 1994. "Cinderella" as a Dirty Joke: Gender, Multivocality, and the Polysemic Text. *Western Folklore* 53:27-49.
_____. [Forthcoming]. "My Thing is My Own": Voice, Bodies, and Sexual Politics in Broadside, Drollery, and Oral Occupational Bawdy Song. In *The Other Print Tradition: Chapbooks, Broadsides, and Related Ephemera*, eds. Cathy Lynn Preston and Michael J. Preston. New York: Garland Publishing.
Radner, Joan Newlon, ed. 1993. *Feminist Messages: Coding in Women's Folk Culture*. Urbana: University of Illinois Press.
Rubin, Gayle. 1975. The Traffic in Women: Notes Toward a Political Economy of Sex. In *Toward an Anthropology of Women*, ed. Rayna Reiter, pp. 157-210. New York: Monthly Review Press.
Sedgwick, Eve Kosofsky. 1985. *Between Men: English Literature and Male Homosocial Desire*. New York: Columbia University Press.
Shuman, Amy. 1993. Dismantling Local Culture. *Western Folklore* 52:345-364.
_____ and Charles Briggs. 1993. Introduction to Theorizing Folklore: Toward New Perspectives on the Politics of Culture. *Western Folklore* Special Issue 52:109-134.
Spivak, Gayatri. 1988. Can the Subaltern Speak? In *Marxism and the Interpretation of Culture*, ed. Cary Nelson and Lawrence Grossberg, pp. 271-313. Urbana and Chicago: University of Illinois Press.
Stallybrass, Peter and Allon White. 1986. *The Politics and Poetics of Transgression*. Ithaca: Cornell University Press.
Tylor, Edward Burnett. 1929 [1871]. *Primitive Culture*. Vol I. London: John Murray.
Widdowson, Peter. 1989. *Hardy in History: A Study in Literary Sociology*. New York: Routledge.
Williams, Lynda. 1989. *Hard Core: Power, Pleasure, and the "Frenzy of the Visible."* Berkeley: University of California Press.
Williams, Raymond. 1973. *The Country and the City*. New York: Oxford University Press.

Workman, Mark E. 1993. Tropes, Hopes, and Dopes. *Journal of American Folklore* 106:171-183.

Wotton, George. 1985. *Thomas Hardy: Towards a Materialist Criticism*. Dublin: Gill & Macmillan.

5

"Writing" and "Voice": The Articulations of Gender in Folklore and Literature

Cristina Bacchilega

In her 1986 paper, "Taking Liberties, Writing from the Margins, and Doing it with a Difference," Barbara Babcock urged feminist folklorists to attend "not only to women's folklore and women folk but to examine and redefine disciplinary paradigms and discursive practices of folklore scholarship." Approached in such far-reaching and diversified ways, the ongoing project of feminist folkloristics is one of simultaneous cultural reconstruction and deconstruction, and has indeed counted "many and sometimes conflicting voices" (1986:391). Unfortunately, in the broad arena of American feminist theory today, the affirmation of women's experience and knowledge is often cast in outright opposition to, if not as separate from, French feminism which has learned much from deconstruction. I believe this binary opposition has further divided women and ignores the material and cultural conditions dynamically linking the two projects together. Thus, it is within the framework suggested by Babcock—and more recently by Beverly Stoeltje in her introduction to the special issue of the *Journal of Folklore Research*, "Feminist Revisions in Folklore Studies" (1988:141-153)—that I want to read a recent Italian novel in order to examine two paradigms—"writing" and "voice"—which have, consciously and unconsciously, been relevant to both patriarchal and feminist understandings of folklore and literature.

Dacia Maraini's *La Lunga Vita di Marianna Ucrìa* (1990; translated as *The Silent Duchess* 1992) provides a literary commentary on folklore which does not set one discourse in (hierarchical) opposition to the other; rather it foregrounds the "peopling" of the self in both. More specifically, like other contemporary women's novels (Toni Morrison's *Beloved*, Maxine Hong Kingston's *The Woman Warrior*, and Joy Kogawa's *Obasan*, to name a few), *La Lunga Vita di*

Marianna Ucrìa self-consciously addresses questions of gender precisely by articulating the paradox of "writing" and "voice" at work in folklore. My objective here is to show how, by informing our reading of such paradox in the novel, Hélène Cixous's—rather than Bakhtin's—rethinking of "voice" in contestation with Jacques Derrida's redefinition of "writing" can contribute to a dual feminist project of reconstruction and deconstruction in folklore and literary studies.

Theorizing Woman's "Voice"

In spite of folklore's reputed oral nature, its ties with writing have been strong in a variety of ways, including Thoms' introduction of the term "folklore" into the English language through his famous 1846 letter to the *Athenaeum*. At the heart of the discipline of folklore studies, then, lies a contradiction: to "preserve" and study folklore meant—especially in pre-cassette and pre-video recording days—to write, and thereby change the medium in which much folk communication and art actually took place. Furthermore, a great deal of folklore from premodern cultures comes to us mediated through written sources. How does contemporary critical theory affect our perceptions of this paradox and subsequently alter our understanding of the relationship between folklore and literature today?

The distinction between the illiterate and the learned is fortunately no longer the issue, but if most critics now would "admit that literary and oral artistry overlap" (Lindahl 1978:98), it is also true that little progress has been made in defining the terms of continuity between the two media and that speaking about unqualified "intertextuality" or "folklore as literature," for instance, is not sufficient. Derrida's redefinition of "writing" can help us 1) put into a broader cultural perspective the written/oral paradox at work in the conceptualization and pragmatics of folklore studies and 2) rethink the opposition between tradition-oriented and performance-oriented folkloristics.

Language writes us, claims Jacques Derrida, whose work calls into question the "metaphysics of presence" and the authority of the speaking subject. What matters here is his contention that Western thought has traditionally privileged the "speaking subject" and centered our scholarly and emotional interests upon him, while discounting writing both in its pervasively discursive and its specifically graphic meanings. Derrida points out that in speech the signifier's evanescence and the physical presence of the speaker contribute to the impression of the direct presence of a thought. But the spoken word is not unmediated. It has a material form which functions, like writing, as a system of differences. It can thus be misinterpreted, and it does not require the presence of the speaker, as both tape players and oral transmission in general abundantly prove. Rather than being in opposition to one another, writing and speaking share the important features of *mediated* meaning and *absence*, features traditionally used to put down writing as a poor substitute for the direct fullness of speech. "Writing" as language, then, has in practice shaped both our orthographic writing and our speech (Derrida 1976 and 1978).

Such poststructuralist rethinking of "writing" has had repercussions on literary studies, ethnology, and anthropology (see Clifford and Marcus 1986, Sahlins 1985, and Ashley 1990), and has opened up exciting possibilities for folkloristics. First, tape-recording, transcribing, and summarizing in written form are no longer merely or primarily conceived of as distortions of the immediate truth of speech. Yes, they increase the distance between the speaker and his words, but some distance was already there. Writing and speaking are of necessity implicated in one another. Second, the speaker—the tale-teller, the artist, the folk—need not be considered the immediate or unified origin of meaning. Modern folklorists have acknowledged in practice the limitations of such categories by invoking the concepts of audience, context, register, and tradition to address semantic transformations as well as to account for the at times contradictory positions taken by the individual speaker. But many folklorists still seem unwilling to connect the mediated and ambiguous nature of speech with the speaker's participation in the broader social process of language or, as Derrida would say, "writing." This resistance is understandable in part because Derrida's theory lends itself to the misunderstanding that writing is more important than the speaker—an elitist approach folklorists have struggled against—and also because Derrida's re-inscription of speech into writing inevitably calls into question other heavily-relied-on categories like "identity" and "authenticity." My point here is that, in spite of the apparent threats and the pointed questions it poses to the discipline of folklore studies, Derrida's theory of writing conceptualizes the continuity between the oral and the written without erasing their differences and presents their paradoxical relation as constitutive of language as a system. Third, the split between performance-oriented and tradition-oriented folklorists gains a different significance. Indeed folklorists have studied the unspoken premises of culture, what Dundes calls "folk ideas," all along; and folklorists have, often more than literary critics, been sensitive to what are now loosely called "discourses," the communal yet ideological, language-bound forces which shape our understanding and creative transformation of experience. In Derrida's terms, then, folklorists have studied "writing," even as they were working with oral materials; Derrida's theory would, thus, seem to a certain extent to valorize implicitly the past of folkloristics. But, as we well know, folklorists have studied "writing" by focusing on "speaking subjects," thereby participating even more than literary critics in the Western privileging of presence that Derrida criticizes. I am pushing the paradox to its extreme to point out that, within Derrida's redefinition of "writing," the dilemma between communal and individual focus is not discipline-specific, but philosophically "written" into Western thinking; what is discipline-specific is its visibility within folkloristics. To experience and to conceptualize this tension in different ways, folklorists must attend to it and exploit it rather than ignore it or univocally resolve it.

If, by redefining "writing," Derrida's philosophical investigations deconstruct the independent subject who speaks his own words and gives them meaning through his presence, Hélène Cixous exposes such a fiction as a specifically *patriarchal* one which has privileged speech not only over writing, but over "voice." Other feminists in Europe and the U.S. have fastened on the metaphor of "voice"—as the maternal, or as plural, historicized "voices," or as Bakhtin's double voicing—in order to articulate women's capacity to disrupt, contest, and subvert patriarchal language. In this essay I am focusing on Cixous's project because it participates explicitly in a double movement of deconstruction and reconstruction. Inscribing her position within Derrida's project, Cixous challenges the primacy of speech; however, she also challenges patriarchal deconstruction by

"Writing" and "Voice": The Articulations of Gender

affirming woman's "voice," a voice which claims a complex affinity with writing.

In agreement with other poststructuralist approaches to the "woman-question" (Derrida's woman-effect, Lacan's woman as lack, and Irigaray's mimicking woman) Cixous has shown women's position in relation to patriarchal language to be at best marginal, but always already implicated. By "accepting the challenge of the discourse controlled by the phallus" (1986:93), however, the "newly born woman" finds a way out of the victim position and turns her marginal feminine voice into privileged access to writing. Cixous affirms:

> Writing is the passageway, the entrance, the exit, the dwelling place of the other in me—the other that I am and am not, that I don't know how to be, but that I feel passing, that makes me live—that tears me apart, disturbs me, changes me, who?—a feminine one, a masculine one, some?—several, some unknown, which is indeed what gives me the desire to know and from which all life soars. This peopling gives neither rest nor security, always disturbs the relationship to 'reality,' produces an uncertainty that gets in the way of the subject's socialization. (1986:85-86)

Here Cixous celebrates the link between "writing" and feminine subjectivity: both are "the experience of not-me within me." Derrida's association of writing with ambiguity and absence is restated as *peopling*, and yet it does not rely on identity. "Writing," she says, "is woman's. That is not a provocation, it means that woman admits there is an other" (1986:85). She can do so because the illusion of self-presence and fullness of meaning has not historically been part of woman's experience with speech. "Listen to woman speak in a gathering (if she is not painfully out of breath): she doesn't 'speak,' she throws her trembling body into the air,... She exposes herself.... She *inscribes* what she is saying because she does not deny unconscious drives the unmanageable part they play in speech" (1986:92). To the "orator," Derrida's speaker, Cixous contrasts woman's "voice," which is "several," multiple, does not find its authority in presence, but refers to and materializes from the displaced body and song of the mother.

Cixous's staging of "voice" as a challenge to Derrida's "speaking subject" is not fully successful, and perhaps it cannot be. When she claims that woman "conveys meaning with her body" and that "her flesh speaks true" (1986:92), she seems to fall prey to a fiction quite similar to that of patriarchal thought. A woman's body is never present to itself, Cixous might argue, but then why is it associated with truth? My goal, however, is not to discuss the lack of coherence in Cixous's theory, but to suggest how useful her definition of "voice" is to the dual project of feminist folkloristics.

First, Cixous explicitly brings the question of gender to bear on the relationship between writing and orality. In so doing she furthers a deconstructive project, yet seeks to voice the perspective of women. By affirming the reciprocal implication of "writing" and "voice," she exposes speech as the patriarchal illusion of self-presence and self-sameness from which women should free themselves, especially since they/we have experienced this fiction only vicariously through men or in fragments—which makes it a contradiction in terms. A plurality of variously empowered and disempowered voices not only displaces (rather than opposes) the masculine speaker, but constitutes the practice of "writing." Second, this continuity between writing and voice is not, however, free of struggle. So many of the more powerful voices in "writing" reinforce patriarchal structures just as so much writing, literary or otherwise, models itself on the "selfsame" fiction of speech and does not want to "admit there is an other." Cixous offers a way into the struggle: by privileging "voice," she peoples language and makes Derrida's "writing" less overbearing and more diversified from the perspective of those who are marginalized by it, who are traditionally "other" in it. This helps in the specific analysis of a folk or literary narrative, say, where the object is not so much to explain how all narratives partake of writing as ambiguity and absence, but becomes one of articulating the struggles of meanings and voices at work in that narrative. Third, the displacement of speech through "voice" further legitimates the analysis of its strategies which, like those of writing, are *systematically* transgressive and, thus, may no longer be considered simply idiosyncratic or aberrant.[1] As examples of such research, I think of Gillian Bennett's study of women's storytelling (1989) and Jo Radner and Susan Lanser's strategies of coding (1987 and 1992).

This conceptualization of "voice," then, may help to address feminist and political concerns without relying on "identity." And this, I believe, is what Bakhtin's proposition that discourse is always at least

"Writing" and "Voice": The Articulations of Gender 89

double-voiced and we are always speaking the words of others—an argument more familiar to folklorists and to some respects analogous to that of Cixous's "voice" and Derrida's "writing"—cannot achieve.

What all three of these approaches have in common, I think, is the rejection of a simple application of Saussure's *langue/parole* polar opposition and the belief that, as Bakhtin states, "every concrete utterance of a speaking subject serves as a point where centrifugal as well as centripetal forces are brought to bear" (1981:272). But Bakhtin—or one of his paper-selves—also argues that while "words and forms are populated by intentions," another's, the speaker *appropriates* them by populating them with his own intentions and accent (1981:293). This process involves a raising of "socio-linguistic language consciousness" that could very well serve feminism as it did marxism; it would remind me of Cixous's theft of language, if it weren't that Bakhtin's appropriation or expropriation revolves around the *propre*, not as "proper" but as "own." In society as well as in artistic representations, the "speaking person" for Bakhtin is an "ideologue" (1981:333), who can achieve "independent thought" by assimilating another's words, an "internally persuasive discourse," with his own and into his own (1981:345)—yes, his speaker is always masculine. Dialogue as ideological struggle, then, involves the speaker and his listeners, not the voices *within* the speaker; in contrast, Cixous's "voice" does not stand for unified, representative position, since the words of co-option, collusion, disruption, giving, taking, etc. may and do speak through it. This "voice" is continuously implicated in "writing."

While the fragmentation or pluralization of the speaking person/voice is at issue in comparing Cixous and Bakhtin, it is the existential relationship between the speaker and language as "writing" or the discourse of others that sets Bakhtin's philosophy apart from Derrida's. For Bakhtin, an individual with an active "socio-ideological language consciousness" inevitably has to "choose" a language, and this choice in many cases accomplishes the mastery of another's words. Quotations can be made one's own through conscious choice, willful internalization; the individual, in other words, can rewrite the language that writes us. This antagonistically appropriative view of language rotates once again around the individual speaker whose reassuring self-presence controls the ubiquitous ambiguity of Derrida's "writing," where displacing is the rule of the game. Cixous's differential view of power in language, I suggested earlier, offers a feminist alternative to the chilling, immobilizing effects of Derrida's philosophy as well as to Bakhtin's pragmatics.

I do not wish to advocate dismissing Bakhtin—whose several paper-selves have much to offer to folklorists and whose theories I have undoubtedly simplified. Rather, my point is to clarify that his conceptualization of discourse does not problematize the speaking subject—patriarchal or otherwise. "I" am always doing the speaking and the listening; "I" can unmask, accept, in any case control the discourse of others; "I" can choose my voice. This approach to language, which seems to appeal to the "positive-thinking" folklorist, also invokes a particular narrative of identity and precludes our access to others (Workman 1989). Furthermore, from a feminist perspective, agency is far from unquestionable: women are increasingly aware of having limited access to it as well as having to sort out its implications of collusion.

What we can learn from Derrida and especially Cixous is not, I hope, to use more jargon but to approach the interweaving of "writing" and "voice," of tradition and performance, of patriarchal domination and women's subversion of it within a larger cultural project which seeks to promote the recognition, the admission—as different from the liberal acceptance or incorporation—of others within and without our selves. And what are the implications of this reconceptualization for the study of folklore and literature? Folklore, like literature, functions as both "writing" and "voice," in the specific meanings I have discussed. Furthermore, in both folklore and literature, the speaker—whether teller, character, or narrator—is to some extent called into question, and this has complex gender repercussions. To exemplify these dynamics more in detail, I will now focus on the doubly critical area of folklore *in* literature, where by definition the oral is always inscribed, and, more specifically, on a contemporary novel which self-consciously (re)writes folklore.

Dacia Maraini's *La lunga vita di Marianna Ucrìa*

La lunga vita di Marianna Ucrìa, Dacia Maraini's 1990 novel, is an extreme case in point. I will briefly recount its apparently straightforward plot since the book has only recently been translated into English as *The Silent Duchess* (1992). Marianna Ucrìa is a deaf-mute aristocratic woman in eighteenth-century Sicily, who reads voraciously and communicates with others through writing. Marianna's handicap and her consequent reliance on the written word shape her life, both negatively and positively. Forced at a young age to marry her stiff, conservative, and much older uncle, she gives birth to five children, has a villa built for her, and lives a fairly uneventful existence, increasingly seeking refuge in her library; yet following her husband's death, she becomes closer to the lower classes, experiences passionate love with a young servant boy, takes responsibility for his sister's violent behavior, and receives a marriage proposal from a sensitive and well-read senator.

Her mutilation, as the senator writes to her, makes her unique: "deprived of the privileges that you are nevertheless entitled to through your birthright, outside the stereotypes of your social position, in spite of it being part of your very flesh" (Maraini 1992:231) ("fuori dai privilegi nonostante ci stiate dentro per diritto di nascita fino al collo, fuori dagli stereotipi della vostra casta nonostante essi facciano parte della vostra stessa carne" 1990:261).[2] Underprivileged among the privileged, yet also free to be somewhat extravagant. But what is the cause of her silence? Her father almost has her convinced that she was born to it, while her mother seems to believe Marianna is somehow responsible for it: even when exposed to the "therapeutic" trauma of witnessing the hanging of a young boy, she did not speak, thereby demonstrating she lacked will.[3] Eventually, Marianna and the reader can answer this question, thanks to her openness to others' thoughts, a form of involuntary oneway telepathy. Marianna became deaf and mute as a result of her uncle raping her when she was five. The episode was then hushed, willfully forgotten by her family, and the uncle's later marriage proposal implicitly welcomed as a restitution of kinds.

Sustained by great intellectual and emotional strength, fortified by her readings of Hume and her brief discovery of bodily pleasure with the young Saro, Marianna is able in her forties to turn her victimization into a passport to economic and physical escape—even if this means emotional solitude.[4] She leaves her home, her young lover, her grown children, the book-loving senator, her known "chimeras," to travel on the mainland where, uprooted, she confronts the unfamiliar. The reader is not told what she finds, with the exception of muted questions.

The pervasiveness of folklore in a novel ostensibly about the violent silencing of women and the unexpected ways in which women talk back is what interests me here. Beliefs, formulas, rituals, proverbs, cautionary tales, sing-song rhymes, and family history constitute much of the outside world's communications with Marianna. She is exposed to them mostly through writing, so that in this novel folkloric forms are doubly inscribed as writing. For her knowledge of the world, in addition to this mediated assimilation of folklore, Marianna must rely on her reading of literature—another form of writing—, her highly socialized body, and haphazardly certain people's unuttered thoughts. Significantly the people whose thoughts she "overhears" are always emotionally or socially distant from her; their words are passed on in the absence of a conscious speaker and an intentional listener. Clearly, for Marianna communication can only occur through orthographic writing and absence; it is in both instances a form of "writing," in the Derridean sense.

To a certain extent folklore, the form of "writing" presently at issue, operates authoritatively in the novel; it reaches and writes Marianna in spite of her. When her husband-uncle Pietro first exercises his marital "rights" by raping her one morning in her sleep, the thirteen-year-old girl returns to her family home where mother and aunts assault her in turn with the many proverbs they write to her: "'Whoever marries and never repents, can buy Palermo for a hundred pence' and 'Marry for love and end up in pain' and 'Women and hens will go astray, if they ever lose their way' and 'A good wife makes a good husband" (Maraini 1992:31) ("'Chi si marita e non si pente, compra Palermo a sole cent'onze' e 'Cu si marita p'amuri sempri campa 'n duluri' e 'Femmina e gaddina si perde si troppu cammina' e 'La bona mugghieri fa bonu maritu,'" Maraini 1990:33).[5] Zeus's mythic couplings with Io and Leda—which Marianna recalls from time to time while her husband couples with her—also implicitly legitimate rape (1992:115; 1990:126).

If proverbs and myths prescribe sexual behavior, folk beliefs tell Marianna the sex of her children: when the belly is round rather than pointed expect a girl (1992:37;1990:39).[6] The striking account of her third child's birth exemplifies what this means. Even though she cannot hear the midwife's birthing formulas, Marianna knows them. She watches the midwife's lips and finds herself listening in on her thoughts.

> "Come out, come out, you little sod
> With help from our Almighty God."
>
> ... "What is the little *stinker* up to?... why don't you get born, eh?... ahhh but it's a little girl, ahi ahi...oh oh, oh my, oh my, nothing but girls come out of this ill-starred belly, what a misfortune. She doesn't have any luck, the poor dumb creature.... Get born, get born, *you stinking little girl*.... Suppose I promised you a little sugar lamb—no, you're determined not to come out...." (1992:35; emphasis is mine)
>
> ("Niesci niesci cosa fetenti
> ca lu cumanna Diu 'nniputenti."
>
> ... "Ca fa questo *fetente*?... perché non niesci?... ahhh ma questa è na picciridda! ahi ahi, tutte femmine ci escono da questo ventre sciagurato, che disgrazia! mutola com'è non ha fortuna... Niesci niesci *fetentissima* femmina... e se ti prometto un agnello di zucchero niesci? no, non vuole niescere..." 1990:37-38; emphasis is mine)

In the midst of customary injunctions and promises addressed to the baby,[7] the midwife pronounces the female's unworthiness: she is *fetentissima* (literally "you *biggest stinker* girl" and not simply "you stinking little girl" as in the printed translation) rather than simply *fetente* and if her family weren't noble and rich, she would be helped out of this world rather than into it (1992:36; 1990:38).[8] Folklore, then, seems to "write" Marianna into an inferior, subservient position, whether it be through stereotyping, compensation, collusion, or recuperation—for all of these ideological processes are at work here to reproduce gender ideology (Barrett 1980:108).

However, other "voices" people folkloric forms in this novel too, so that tradition cannot be indiscriminately interpreted as patriarchal "writing." The rituals performed on the newlyborn baby girl by that same midwife are not simply tied with Christian traditions: the cutting of her frenum to loosen up her tongue (*sgargiu*), then salt on the navel, sugar on her bloody belly, oil on her lips, and finally rose-water to rinse her little body (1992:36; 1990:38).[9] This is the same wisdom that guides women in the practice of abortion: the expert Pupara, "that's what they call her because she makes and unmakes the little ones" ("la chiamano così perché fa e disfa i picciriddi"), gives ladies and peasants alike parsley, roots and herbs which never fail (1992: 39 and 57; 1990:41 and 62).

Gossip, not surprisingly, does not spread in one direction either. It can destroy and, as we know, it is especially dangerous to a woman. Marianna's oldest and most conservative son Mariano, for instance, worries about the *malelingue* when she associates with her new friends. But gossip, as the senator reminds her, also "lies at the roots of literature" (1992:232) ("alla radice della letteratura" 1990:262): he cites none less than Montesquieu and Dante as examples. And Marianna's aunt Manina makes of gossip another artistic form for, following her death, her "witticisms continued to circulate, as salty and piquant as anchovies in brine" (1992:46) ("le sue battute continuano a circolare, salate e piccanti come alici in salamoia" 1990:49). Her lines become proverbial because they pinpoint excess: the Prince of Raù "despised money, but treasured coins like sisters" ("disprezzava i soldi ma trattava le monete come sorelle"); waiting for his wife to give birth, the very short Prince Des Puches had been "walking up and down nervously under the bed" ("camminando su e giù nervosamente sotto il letto"); and Hell was nothing worse than a Palermo without pastry shops— Manina did not care for sweets in any case (1992: 45-46; 1990:49). People laughed, feared her tongue, and kept repeating her lines.

In terms of gender what matters is not simply who is gossiping and at whose expense, but to what purpose.[10] While judgmental, Manina's gossip does not coerce; she points her finger at authoritative men mostly to entertain her audience. Gossip, then, can be a prescriptive form of "writing" as well as light and bubbly subversive "voices"; the senator's interpretation of Dante's *Commedia* as gossip best embodies this paradox.

Marianna's own joke about the Ucrìa being "nothing but turncoats" (1992:47) ("dei gran voltagabbana" 1990:51) brings humor to family history, a subject which in her husband-uncle's mind, deserves seriousness alone: "No making fun of the family's dead" ("Coi morti di famiglia non si può scherzare" 1990:51; translated as "It is not proper to joke about the family patriarchs" 1992:47). Unlike gossip, family history is a folkloric form over which men seek to retain control. Marianna's husband-uncle Pietro and her grandaunt Agata no longer speak to each other on account of their disagreement: for him the first Ucrìa ruled over Lidia in 600 B.C., while Agata swears it was Quinto Ucrìa Tuberone who became consul at the age of sixteen in 188 B.C. (1992:63; 1990:68). Two competing "speakers" in Derridean terms seek to assert their identities by establishing the official, true, family history; Pietro Ucrìa's authority, not surprisingly, triumphs in the family.

Yet these histories are equally questionable when one thinks of Pietro's distaste for books and Agata's reliance on saints' biographies. They are a form of "writing," and the external narrator leads us to reconceptualize them as such. Family history is more sacred to Pietro Ucrìa than the Bible. He treasures the painting representing the martyrdom of "Blessed Signoretto Ucrìa of Fontanasalsa and Campo Spagnolo, born in Pisa in 1269," never wondering how he got to Palermo or why the Turks killed him. Pietro has tried everything to recuperate the Blessed Signoretto's arm, a relic he claims some Dominicans possess; the Brothers say they gave it to some Carmelite nuns who gave it to the Poor Clares who say they never saw it (1992:47; 1990:51). This family history may be official, but it is also clearly legendary. The narrator does not attack it directly, the way Aunt Agata does, with a competing truth. Rather, through Marianna's eyes, we see the painting and notice the discrepancies between it and the written story of the Beato. With her we "hear" the various stories priests and nuns recount of the blessed man's precious arm. This proliferation of voices constitutes Pietro's family history and undermines it at the same time. It also opens the way for Marianna's grandmother's family stories.

Nonna Giuseppa learns to write in order to communicate with Marianna and teach her the history of Sicily (1992:101; 1990:111). She explains the origins of Bagherìa, the rich province where the Ucrìas have some property, as the "betrayal of an ambitious plot" (1992:107) ("il tradimento di un'ambizione" 1990:116), and she presents her own adventures as a child in a peasant insurrection in Palermo (1992:102-103; 1990:112-113).[11] While these oral histories tell of Giuseppa's family, its politics, and its status, this is not what motivates the telling. Giuseppa, even as she recounts her own experiences, laughs at the images of herself and her family; because of her grandmother's migraines, Marianna sees her as two, a split personality—and her stories tell us she is several. Giuseppa's seems to be a "voice" in Cixous's terms.

Other female voices, however, do not take on the challenge of patriarchy or of otherness. "To marry, to have children, to marry off the daughters, so that their daughters marry and have children, who in turn marry and have children..." (1992:193) ("Sposare, figliare, fare sposare le figlie, farle figliare e fare in modo che le figlie sposate facciano figliare le loro figlie che a loro volta si sposino e figlino...," 1990:218). This is the version of family history the "voices of family tradition" (1992:193), of familial reasoning ("voci dell'assennatezza familiare," 1990:218) proclaim. As the saying goes:

e pì e pì e pì	e pì e pì e pì
seven girls for one *tarì* [penny]	sette fimmini p'un tarì
e pì e pì e pì	e pì e pì e pì
one *tarì* is not a lot	un tarì è troppo poco
seven women for an apricot [tree]	sette fimmini p'un varcuocu...
(1992:17)	(1990:17)[12]

It would be wrong to say that these women have no or little value, but what they are is purely *exchange* value. The unity, strength, and power of the family comes from grafting, which is accomplished through "transplanting" the bodies of women. The narrator implicitly conveys a perspective on these sugary voices, yet tells us that even alienated and critical Marianna "has found herself drawn into an age-old family strategem: up to her neck in a scheme to unite the two branches of the family" (1992:194) ("si ritrova complice di un'antica strategia familiare, dentro fino al collo nel progetto di unificazione," 1990:218). Has she not by marrying her mother's brother and giving him children provided both branches of the family with descendents?

Marianna's implication and complicity with patriarchy as well as her womanly transgression and flight are not reconciled in the novel: she is and remains a "chimera" throughout, but the value of this metaphor changes. A man, the architect Intermassimi who defiantly shows his desire for Marianna while working on her villa, is the first to associate her with the mythic hybrid. His statues for the villa have beautiful leonine bodies, bird-like claws, long coiled tails, and Marianna's head; some of them bear a goat's head on their backs, and all have a surprised look—mirrored by Marianna's when she sees the architect's drawings (1992:33; 1990:35).[13] These statues remind Marianna of her mother's cautionary tales, where chimera-like dogs with long forked tongues would chase the little deaf-mute if she dared to do anything at all (1992:10; 1990:8).[14] The cautionary message has been internalized, those deceitful tongues have taken over hers. But when she is older and stronger, she feels small wings growing on the side of her ankles (1992:233; 1990:264). She has not become whole. She is a monstrous assemblage of patriarchal beliefs, victimization, complicity, critical awareness, womanly desire, but she has acquired wings and brings change, flight, to her stone image.

Marianna, then, is the mythic creature that patriarchal "writing" has constructed for us, but also the transformation, the paradoxical voicing of this myth from a woman's perspective. Fragmentation and hybridization are written into her body, yet she exploits her lack of identity in transgressive, creative ways which re-shape her. This movement is not restorative, however: even as she cracks the mold by flying away, she remains muted and carries with her the long tails, the forked tongues, the pointed claws.

Maraini's narrative also seeks to maintain the inner tension of "voice" even as it challenges patriarchal tradition; it carefully presents Marianna "writing" rather than "speaking," on the three levels of fabula, story, and text (Bal 1985). Literally, Marianna is mute and must communicate through writing, reading, and involuntarily hearing others' unintentional thoughts. "Can she then retain something of her own that does not originate in other minds, other constellations of thoughts, other wills, other interests? A repetition in her memory of images [simulacra] that appear real because they dart like lizards, squirming beneath the sun of everyday experience?" (1992:99) ("Di suo poi cosa ha che non sia la suggestione di altre menti, altre costellazioni di pensieri, altre volontà, altri interessi? un ripetersi nella memoria di simulacri che appaiono veri perché si muovono come lucertole sbilenche sotto il sole dell'esperienza quotidiana?" 1990:108).[15] This is her condition, the condition of "writing," and it is both victimizing and empowering. This muteness works in the fabula—she never speaks—and in the text—she never narrates explicitly, though there is much free indirect discourse. On the story level, she is the focalizor, the eyes through which the external narrator sometimes sees; at other times, she is the object of the others' gaze. Marianna Ucrìa does not find her "own" voice, does not appropriate others' thoughts to construct her "identity," does not become a "speaker." Rather she is "written" by others (including Maraini) at the same time that she transforms that "writing" through the inscription of her several "voices," whether muted or not, in and against that "writing."

Dacia Maraini's deliberate narrative strategies engage her readers in the contradictory and multiple play of "voice," staged both as "writing" and as challenge to the forked tongue of the patriarchal speaker. To this purpose, folklore serves her well.

Notes

1. Pamela Banting's essay "The body as pictogram: rethinking Hélène Cixous's *écriture féminine*" proposes an understanding of the relationship between the body and verbal language along the lines of translation rather than representation (1992). I find my interpretation of Cixous's "voice" to be akin to Banting's much more developed argument.

It should be noted that when I wrote this essay, Maraini's *Bagheria* (1993) had not been published. This fascinating memoir accounts for Maraini's childhood discovery of Sicily, following two very hard years in a Japanese concentration camp. In it we get yet another perspective on Marianna Ucrìa, whose portrait in the villa Valguarnera intrigues the young girl: *Bagheria* re-inscribes Marianna and other characters like Felicita into Maraini's "self-constructed" image—a paradoxical mix of rigor, intellectual curiosity, and voluptuousness; she writes, Marianna "holds a piece of paper on which an unknown and lost part of my Bagheria past is written" (tiene fra le dita un foglietto in cui è scritta una parte sconosciuta e persa del mio passato bagariota," 1993:168).

2. All quotations are from the 1992 translation; at times I have added my modifications in brackets; passages in the original are also provided. In most cases, the folkloric materials in the original are in a Sicilian dialect rather than standard Italian; unfortunately this contrast is not apparent in the English translation. My thanks to

Professor Gaetano Cipolla, from St. John's University, New York, who helped me with the translation of some of the Sicilian words. I am also grateful for Lee Haring's comments on an earlier draft of this essay.

Dacia Maraini was born in 1936 and has been an influential and prolific feminist writer in Italy. Among her works are novels such as *L'età del malessere* 1962 (The Age of Discontent), *Donna in guerra* 1975 (translated as *Woman at War*, 1989); plays like *I sogni di Clitennestra e altre commedie* 1981 (Clytemnestra's Dreams and Other Plays), *Lezioni d'amore* 1982 (Love lessons) and *Veronica, meretrice e scrittora* 1992 (Veronica, prostitute and writer); collections of poems such as *Crudeltà all'aria aperta* 1968 (Cruelty Out in the Open) and *Mangiami pure* 1979 (Devour me too); an interview with Alberto Moravia in 1986, *Il bambino Alberto* (The Child Alberto) and a life history in collaboration with Piera degli Esposti, *Storia di Piera*, 1980.

3. It should be noted that Maraini's novel is historical. Her account of the procedures leading up to a young boy's execution finds confirmation in Giuseppe Pitrè's volume XXVIII of the *Biblioteca delle tradizioni popolari siciliane, La vita in Palermo cento e più anni fa* (*Life in Palermo One Hundred and More Years Ago*, 1940-1949). Particularly striking are the description of the executioner's traditionally red and yellow attire (Maraini 1992:18-19; 1990:18 and Pitrè:289) and the reference to the *Scarichi di coscienza*, a book in which the culprit's confessions were recorded (Maraini 1992:17; 1990:17 and Pitrè:298). Similarly accurate in relation to this unofficial history of Sicilian customs are her descriptions of entertainment, travelling conditions, religious orders, the fad of French fans, and Bagherìa as a vacation resort (see Pitrè, volumes XXVII and XXVIII). Pitrè's large collection of Sicilian lore covers the second half of the eighteenth century.

4. The analysis of *La lunga vita di Marianna Ucrìa's* literary intertexts would require another essay. Suffice it to say here that if Hume is a major influence in Marianna's transformation (which is not surprising given her historical context), quotations from Michelangelo Buonarroti's sonnets, Gaspara Stampa's and Boiardo's poetry, *Song of Songs, The Book of Job, The Odyssey*, and the poetry of the Sicilian Paolo Maura, as well as references to her knowledge of St. Augustine, Socrates, Saint-Simon, and Pascal give us a sampling of the range of her reading.

5. In Pitrè's IX volume of *Biblioteca*, we find "Cui si marita e nun si penti,/ A Palermu si ò pigghia cient'unzi cuntanti" (Maraini's version of the dialect is more accessible), "Cui si marita pr'amuri/ Sempri campa 'n duluri," and "La bona mugghieri fa lu bon maritu" (1940-1949, vol. IX:73, 74, and 85).

6. In Volume XV of *Biblioteca*, Pitrè cites several beliefs in connection with the baby's sex; one of them: "Panza pizzutedda, figghiu masculu" confirms Marianna's which is, in any case, a still broadly-held belief among women today (1940-1949, vol. XV:122).

7. In the same volume of *Biblioteca*, Pitrè quotes a midwife from Ragusa reciting the following formula during a difficult delivery: "Niesci, niesci, cosa fitenti,/ Ca' lu cumanna Diu 'nniputenti" (1940-1949, vol. XV:142).

8. In *Customs and Habits of the Sicilian Peasants*, Salvatore Salomone-Marino notes that Sicilian mothers administered "the juice of the cane rootstalk, a teaspoon the first day, two the second, three the third" to sick babies: "this juice, believed to be a

very potent poison, either cures quickly or quickly kills" (1981:210). The midwife in Maraini's novel thinks this is how a poor family would get rid of the little girl.

9. In volume XV of *Biblioteca*, Pitrè also describes the midwife cutting the cord with scissors, burning its end with a candle, cutting the baby's frenum loose with her long fingernail, giving the baby some honey to console it, bathing it in aromatic water, applying a cloth dipped in oil and egg-white (*conzu*) to the mother's genitals, and stretching the placenta out in the light to show it is not torn (1940-1949, vol. XV:140-153). Dacia Maraini employs all of these details in her telling of the baby girl's birth (Maraini 1992:34-37; 1990:37-40).

10. Martha Weigle has discussed "gossip" as a form of lore in *Spiders & Spinsters: Women and Mythology* (1982).

11. In volume XXVII of *Biblioteca*, Pitrè quotes the Spanish lines on the frontispiece of Prince Branciforti's villa in Bagherìa ("Ya la speranza es perdida/ Y un sol bien me consuela,/ etc.," 1940-1949, vol. XXVII:383); Giuseppa quotes the same lines and explains to Marianna why the Prince retired there.

12. I have so far been unable to locate this rhyme in Pitrè.

13. In volume XXVII of the *Biblioteca*, Pitrè describes the monstrous and famous statues surrounding the Palagonia villa in Bagherìa and they bear an uncanny resemblance to the ones in Maraini's novel (1940-1949, vol. XXVII:386).

14. Maraini also refers to the popular werewolf stories Marianna's daughters enjoy listening to and dread remembering at night (1992:39; 1990:42).

15. Other images of Marianna reinforce the split within her: she is "half-fox and half-siren" (1992:226) ("mezza volpe e mezza sirena" 1990:256); she is a grandmother of forty, a sleeping rose waking to ask for her share of honey (1992:169; 1990:190); she is like a character from *A Thousand and One Nights* who cannot escape his destiny by escaping, but doesn't know it (1992:226; 1990:256). None of these images has negative connotations even though it is fragmented. (Cixous's Medusa laughs in the background.)

References

Ashley, Kathleen M., ed. 1990. *Victor Turner and the Construction of Cultural Criticism.* Bloomington: Indiana University Press.

Babcock, Barbara A. 1987. Taking Liberties, Writing from the Margins, and Doing It with a Difference. *Journal of American Folklore* 100:390-411.

Bakhtin, M. M. 1981. Discourse in the Novel. In *The Dialogic Imagination*, ed. Michael Holquist. Translated by Caryl Emerson and Michael Holquist. Austin: University of Texas Press. (Original: *Voprosy literatury i estetiki*, Moscow, 1975).

Banting, Pamela. 1992. The body as pictogram: rethinking Hélène Cixous's *écriture féminine*. *Textual Practice* 6 (Summer):225-246.

Barrett, Michele. 1980. *Women's Oppression Today*. London: Verso.

Bennett, Gillian. 1989. "And I Turned Round to Her and Said..." A Preliminary Analysis of Shape and Structure in Women's Storytelling. *Folklore* 100, ii:167-183.

Cixous, Hélène. 1986. Sorties. In *The Newly Born Woman*, ed. Hélèn Cixous, Hélène and Catherine Clément, pp. 63-132. Translated by Betsy Wing. Minneapolis: University of Minnesota Press. (Original: *La jeune née*, Paris, 1975).

Derrida, Jacques. 1976. *Of Grammatology*. Translated by Gayatri Chakravorty Spivak. Baltimore: Johns Hopkins University Press. (Original: *De la Grammatologie*, Paris, 1967).

_____. 1978. *Writing and Difference*. Translated by Alan Bass. Chicago: University of Chicago Press. (Original: *L'écriture et la différance*, Paris, 1967).

Lindahl, Carl. 1978. On the Borders of Oral and Written Art. *Folklore Forum* 11:94-123.

Maraini, Dacia. 1992. *The Silent Duchess*. Translated by Dick Kitto and Elspeth Spottiwood. London: Owen. (Original: *La lunga vita di Marianna Ucrìa* [Marianna Ucrìa's Long Life]. Milano: Rizzoli, 1990.)

_____. 1993. *Bagheria*. Milano: Rizzoli.

Pitrè, Giuseppe. 1940-1949. *Biblioteca delle tradizioni popolari siciliane. Opere Complete di Giuseppe Pitrè*, L volumes. Firenze: Barbèra.

Radner, Joan N. 1992. *Feminist Messages: Coding in Women's Folk Culture*. Champaign: University of Illinois Press.

Radner, Joan N. and Susan S. Lanser. 1987. The Feminist Voice: Strategies of Coding in Folklore and Literature. *Journal of American Folklore* 100:412-425.

Sahlins, Marshall. 1985. *Islands of History*. Chicago: University of Chicago Press.

Salomone-Marino, Salvatore. 1981. *Customs and Habits of the Sicilian Peasants*. Translated by Rosalie Norris. London: Associated University Presses.

Stoeltje, Beverly J. 1988. Introduction: Feminist Revisions. *Journal of Folklore Research* 25:141-154.

Weigle, Martha. 1982. *Spiders & Spinsters: Women and Mythology*. Albuquerque: University of New Mexico Press.

Workman, Mark. 1989. Narratable and Unnarratable Lives. Paper presented at the American Folklore Society Meeting. Philadelphia. Published in *Western Folklore* 1992 51:97-107.

6

Social Protest, Folklore, and Feminist Ideology in Chicana Prose and Poetry

María Herrera-Sobek

> It is essential to destroy the widespread prejudice that philosophy is a strange and difficult thing just because it is the specific intellectual activity of a particular category of specialists or of professional and systematic philosophers. It must first be shown that all men are "philosophers", by defining the limits and characteristics of the "spontaneous philosophy" which is proper to everybody. This philosophy is contained in 1. language itself...[,] 2. "common sense" and "good sense," 3. popular religion and, therefore, also in the entire system of beliefs, superstitions, opinions, ways of seeing things and of acting, which are collectively bundled together under the name of "folklore".
>
> —Gramsci 1978:323

Although the Italian, Marxist, theoretician Antonio Gramsci's statement quoted above at first glance would tend to privilege folklore as an area of important cultural thought production, he in fact views it in an overall negative light; his ultimate goal is its total destruction. This is indeed unfortunate but is in keeping with the general contempt a substantial number of intellectual elites view folklore.

There are, however, enlightened intellectuals, and indeed, even opportunistic members of the hegemonic class who appreciate the significance of the political and artistic forces contained within folk genres and folk philosophy.

In this study, I examine the literary oeuvres of Chicana intellectuals and their role as mediators between folk and literary genres and suggest that their insertion of folk genres within their artistic creations serve both political and aesthetic purposes. As such, Chicana writers also become mediators or "hinge intellectuals" between the ruling class elites and the pueblo or Chicano working class since through their artistic renditions Mexican-American women literary authors articulate the social injustices visited upon their ethnic community as posited by Gramsci.[1] I further contend that the interconnections between social protest, folklore, and feminist ideology as rendered in their artistic works, be they visual or written, can be traced to the politically charged historical context in which Chicana/o intellectuals arose.[2] From its very inception in the 1960s, the Chicano Movement was characterized by the artistic production of politically committed artists. Indeed, the Chicano Movement privileged those works that were committed to La Causa (The Cause—i.e., the Movement's search for justice). Such is the case with the birth of contemporary Chicano theater led by Luis Valdez and the Teatro Campesino. The Teatro Campesino was the product of the farm workers struggle to gain justice in America's agricultural fields.[3] Other renown novelists and poets such as Tomás Rivera, Alurista, José Montoya and numerous others filled their stanzas with politically charged lyrics and their prose with politically charged commentaries.

The cadre of artists producing works in all areas of artistic endeavor were engaged in the nationalistic mythmaking project they were politically committed to construct. They were engaged in the Aztlán nation building-effort and in what I call ethnic construction. In this sense Chicano intellectuals were fulfilling the function delineated by Gramsci:

> A human mass does not "distinguish" itself, does not become independent in its own right without, in the widest sense, organizing itself; and there is no organization without intellectuals, that is without the theoretical aspect of the theory-practice nexus being distinguished concretely by the existence of a group of people "specialized" in conceptual and philosophical elaboration of ideas. (1978:334)

And Gramsci is particularly insightful when he acknowledges that "The process of development is tied to a dialectic between the intellectuals and the masses" (1978:334).

This might lead to the erroneous conclusion that Gramsci privileges intellectuals which, in fact, he does not, for his conceptualization of intellectuals is extremely broad. His cautionary statements against reifying intellectuals and his statement that "all men are philosophers" as quoted in my epigraph, provide a firm basis from which Gramsci can defend himself against accusations of privileging intellectuals.

Having pointed out how all men are philosophers because "even in the slightest manifestation of any intellectual activity whatever, in 'language,' there is contained a specific conception of the world," Gramsci suggests a second state or level "which is that of awareness and criticism" (1978:323).

Chicanas are engaged in critically revisioning the world and not "passively and supinely" (Gramsci's phrase) accepting other's conceptualization of the universe. I submit that Chicanas are actively reordering, rewriting and recreating. Through their artistic creations, they are offering audiences a new vision and a new definition of reality. This can be clearly perceived in their reworking of the Virgin of Guadalupe, La Malinche and La Llorona myths, for example.[4] The Virgin of Guadalupe, venerated icon of Mexico and the Americas since the 1530s, commonly has been represented as the ideal woman, the exemplary paragon of virtue and motherhood. The catalogue published recently in conjunction with the critically acclaimed touring exhibition of Chicano art, titled "Chicano Art: Resistance and Affirmation" (CARA), posits the following statement vis-a-vis Chicana artists:

> Chicana visual artists, in particular, provided a perspective that helped to revitalize Chicano art in this later, postnationalist period. These artists produced artworks of self-affirmation and empowerment by creating new imagery and reinterpreting established cultural and religious icons such as the image of the Virgin of Guadalupe and the legend of La Llorona. They expressed their resistance to the male dominated structures of Chicano nationalism and to the larger social and class structures that affect women and children even more than men. Their visual and conceptual transformtions of the female image from victim to role model and heroine was an important step in the stage of Chicano liberation. (Del Castillo 1991:322)

In other genres Chicanas also are rewriting master narratives. In poetry, for example, Pat Mora redefines her relationship with the Virgin Mary in the poem, "To Big Mary from an Ex-catholic":

> Will you kick me in the teeth?
> Will your foot spike so fast
> from under your blue robe
> no one will see

> but I will bleed?
>
> My fault. I stopped the bribes
> hoarded soft petals
> didn't lay them at your feet
> didn't speak to you at all.
>
> If some day in a dark church
> I wait for a nod, smile, wink,
> will you just smash your foot
> into my mouth?
> (1986:77)

In the above poem Pat Mora has reconceptualized the relationship between devotee and sacred female deity and most importantly shows the transformation in the personality of both of the female protagonists. The poetic voice is no longer the dutiful, devoted Hija de María [Mary's daughter] bringing flowers to Mary in the month of May as is the custom but has indeed left the church and competed with the sacred icon by hoarding for herself those rose petals intended for the Virgin Mary. She has not rendered unto God what is God's. Mary's personality has likewise evolved from the loving, devoted, passively smiling, and forgiving Mother to a potential big, kicking, aggressive avenging, and violent Mary.

A second major icon that has been reconceptualized by Chicana poets is the much maligned Malinche, Doña Marina, the mistress of Hernán Cortez, conquerer of the Aztec Empire. Mexican history has condemned this Aztec woman as the second Eve who lost the Mexican paradise. Both Chicana creative writers and scholars have reconceptualized her in a different mode: She was a dreamer and a mystic, one who saw the inevitability of the fall of the Aztec Empire and sought to save it as much as she could. The Texas Mexican poet Carmen Tafolla presents La Malinche's story in a new vein:

> Yo soy la Malinche
> My people called me Malintzin Tepenal
> The Spaniards called me Doña María
>
> I came to be known as Malinche
>   and Malinche came to mean traitor

> They called me —chingada
> ¡Chingada!
> (1985:17-18)

and she revises this view of Malinche's role in the poem's closing lines:

> But Chingada I was not.
> Not tricked, not screwed, not traitor
> For I was not traitor to myself
> I saw a dream
> and I reached it.
> Another world
> la raza
> la raaaaaa—zaaaaaaaa
> (1985:17-18)

In other words Malinche is the founder of a new people, the Latin American/Mexican/Chicano people. And this is a creative act, not a destructive deed as Octavio Paz (1959) and Carlos Fuentes (1971) would have us believe.

An even more recent example is Sandra Cisneros's nationally acclaimed work, *Woman Hollering Creek and Other Stories*, published in 1991. In the short story by the same name Cisneros rewrites the folk legend of La Llorona and impregnates it with strong doses of feminist ideology.

Two strands exist and intermingle in La Llorona legend: one Mexican and one Aztec (aside from its interconnections with the European Weeping Woman legends).[5] On the one hand, according to the former version, La Llorona was originally a beautiful young mestizo woman madly in love with a wealthy Spanish *caballero*. The fruit of this love are various children (one to nine, the number varies) born out of wedlock, the Spaniard having promised to eventually marry her. It came to pass that one night the young, mestizo mother was informed of her *caballero's* impending wedding. On the night of her lover's wedding, after peeking through the window of her lover's house and witnessing the wedding scene, she returns to her own home intensely distraught. There, in a fit of rage and/or insanity, she kills all her children. Having realized her deed, she madly rushes out of her house screaming "¡Ayyyy, mis hijos!" As punishment for this barbaric deed, she roams the waterways, any dark street or road screeching, "¡Ayyyyy, mis hijos!"—forever in search of her lost children (see Arizpe 1963:7-12). On the other hand, according to the Aztec version, La Llorona was a woman who, before the conquest, predicted the fall of the Aztec empire and was seen in the streets of the Aztec capital in a white dress, long hair in disarray, and screaming in anguish, "¡Ayyyy, mis hijos!"—in anticipated pain of the loss to come (Sahagún 1950-1968:25).

Texas anthropologist/folklorist José Limón has undertaken a perceptive analysis of the La Llorona legend, proposing that

> La Llorona is the third major female symbol of Greater Mexican socio-culural life. If articulated with this history and not merely with local contexts, she may be understood at two levels: first, as a positive, contestative symbol for the women of Greater Mexico and second as a critical symbolic reproduction for a socially unfulfilled utopian longing within the Mexican folk masses.... (1986:60)

Limón views La Llorona as addressing the "social and psychological needs of both Greater Mexican sectors, needs left unmet by the hegemonic, hierarchical, masculinized and increasingly capitalistic social order imposed on the Mexican folk masses since their beginning" (1986:60).

La Llorona is sometimes viewed as a figure who has been eternally condemned to roam the waterways of the world for having murdered her children. For some critics she is symbolic of the punishment a woman receives for not fulfilling her mother's role in the expected fashion. For other scholars, such as Clarissa Pinkola Estés, she is the "tale about the river of life that became [the] river of death. The *protagonista* is a haunting river woman who is fertile and generous, creating out of her own body. She is poor, breathtakingly beautiful, but rich in soul and spirit" (1992:301). In her best-selling book, *Women Who Run with the Wolves: Myths and Stories of the Wild Woman Archetype*, Pinkola Estés amplifies:

> "La Llorona" is an odd tale, for it continues to evolve throughout time as though it has a big inner life of its own. Like a great marching sand dune that pushes across the land, taking up what is before it, building with and upon it till the land becomes part of its own body, this story builds on the psychic issues of each

> generation. Sometimes the *La Llorona* tale is told as a story about *Ce. Malinalli* or *Malinche*, the native woman said to have been translator and lover to the Spanish conqueror Hernán Cortés.
> But the first version of "*La Llorona*" I ever heard described her as the female protagonist in a union-busting war up in the north woods, where I was raised. The next time I heard the tale, *La Llorona* was dealing with an antagonist involved in the forced repatriation of Mexicans from the United States in the 1950s. I heard the story in numerous versions in the Southwest, one being from the old Spanish Land Grant farmers, who said she was involved in the land grant wars in New Mexico; a rich developer took advantage of a poor but beautiful Spanish daughter. (1992:301)

The most recent version reported by Pinkola Estés is truly startling. The author reports an informant narrated a La Llorona tale where the twin boy babies of the Weeping Woman are born deformed—"blind with webbed fingers, for the *hidalgo* had poisoned the river with the waste from his factories" (1992:303). La Llorona threw the malformed twin boys in the river and dies of grief. She is condemned to roam the waterways looking for her children (1992:303).

La Llorona has been perceived both as victim and as an active incipient feminist who was a lover, unwed mother, and child killer. As Limón points out the legend has not mystified or obscured her sexual being. She is the "counter-hegemonic denial of the first pole in the madonna/whore" symbolic, ideological configuration of women" (1986:75).

In Sandra Cisneros's short story "Woman Hollering Creek" the subtext underlying the work is the legend of La Llorona. This Weeping Woman structures the feminist ideological components of the story line. She is "La Gritona" the one who yells out, speaks out, is not voiceless, silent. As such, she eventually becomes a role model for Cleófilas the dreamy, innocent and ingenious Mexican bride brought to the United States. In the short story Cleófilas had experienced a rude awakening in her new country when her husband began to abuse her physically by beating her mercilessly. Cleófilas eventually finds the courage to leave her husband and return to Mexico with her children.

The nexus between La Llorona and a feminist conceptualization of life is explicitly made when Felice, the woman who is driving Cleófilas to the bus station, drives up to the arroyo or creek and "the driver opened her mouth and let out a yell as loud as any mariachi"

(Cisneros 1991:55). Eventually Cleófilas is able to laugh exactly as the liberated Felice: "Then Felice began laughing again, but it wasn't Felice laughing. It was gurgling out of her own throat, a long ribbon of laughter, like water." (1991:56)

As is evident, a folk legend serves as the substratum underlying the feminist ideology and social protest explicit in Cisneros's short story. The story is not merely retelling the La Llorona legend but is creatively transforming it into a feminist narrative of liberation and self empowerment. Read in this light the story approximates Limón's theoretical postulations vis-à-vis La Llorona and patriarchal society: "...It is here that the legend poses a more fundamental oppositional threat to men because by La Llorona's act she symbolically destroys the familial basis for patriarchy" (1986:76). There are, however, as Limón notes, two stages to her story: "The symbolic destruction of the nuclear family at one stage, and the later possible restoration of her maternal bonds from the waters of rebirth as a second stage. One must conclude that waters will also heal her patriarchally induced insanity" (1986:76). Limón additionally points out that in the restored world of love, men, as La Llorona experienced them, are basically absent. The figure of La Llorona is indeed a powerful and subversive figure which Cisneros has incorporated within her narrative. The Chicana author has artistically rewritten the legend and, at the same time, has retained its underlying feminist ideology.

Cisneros has transformed in a similar manner the *retablo* tradition in her collection "Little Miracles, Kept Promises" (in *Woman Hollering Creek*, 1991). *Retablos* may be translated as "ex-votos" and are related to the Mexican *manda* or "promise" made to a saint in time of need. When the special request or favor made to the saint is granted, the devotee is obligated to keep the promise made. For example if an individual has been seriously injured in an accident he/she may promise to visit the Virgin of Guadalupe in Mexico City upon successfully recovering. After recovering fully he/she is obligated to undertake the trip. When the person makes the visit to the Virgin, he/she may also want to commission a folk painter, a painting called a *retablo* depicting the details of the accident and of the recovery. A short narrative encapsulating the events accompanies the painting. The *retablo* bears witness to the efficacy of a particular saint or virgin in producing the "miracle" and to the gratefulness of the individual who receives the favor.

The *retablo* narrative structure informs Cisneros' own narratives in the section titled "Little Miracles, Kept Promises." Her *retablos*, however, are impregnated with sardonic humor, mordant criticism at the injustices visited upon Chicanos/Mexicanos and a definite feminist perspective. They are, in addition, in the epistolary form. The following examples explicitly delineate the above concerns:

> Dear San Martín de Porres,
>   Please send us clothes, furniture, shoes, dishes. We need anything that don't eat. Since the fire we have to start all over again and Lalo's disability check ain't much and don't go far. Zulema would like to finish school but I says she can just forget about it now. She's our oldest and her place is at home helping us out I told her. Please make her see some sense. She's all we got.
>
>   Thanking you,
>   Adelfa Vásquez
>   Escobas, Texas
>   (1991:117)

> Dear San Antonio de Padua,
>   Can you please help me find a man who isn't a pain in the nalgas. There aren't any in Texas, I swear. Especially not in San Antonio.
>   Can you do something about all the educated Chicanos who have to go to California to find a job. I guess what my sister Irma says is true: "If you didn't get a husband when you were in college, you don't get one."
>   I would appreciate it very much if you sent me a man who speaks Spanish, who at least can pronounce his name the way its supposed to be pronounced. Someone please who never calls himself "Hispanic" unless he's applying for a grant from Washington, D.C.
>   Can you send me a man man. I mean someone who's not ashamed to be seen cooking or cleaning or looking after himself. In other words, a man who acts like an adult. Not one who's never lived alone, never bought his own underwear, never ironed his own shirts, never even heated his own tortillas. In other words, don't send me someone like my brother who my mother ruined with too much chichi, or I'll throw him back.
>   I'll turn your statue upside down until you send him to me. I've put up with too much too long, and now I'm just too intelligent,

too powerful, too beautiful, too sure of who I am finally to deserve anything less.

Ms. Barbara Ybáñez
San Antonio, TX
(1991:117-118)

Saint Jude, patron saint of lost causes,
     Help me pass my English 320, British Restoration Literature class and everything to turn out ok.

Eliberto González
Dallas
(1991:124)

As is evident from the above examples, Chicanas are fulfilling the function of organic intellectuals who, according to Gramsci, work "out and make coherent the principles and the problems raised by the masses in their practical activity, thus constituting a cultural and social bloc" (1978:330). The intellectuals' roles include those of organizers and leaders. They reconceptualize and elaborate ideas, never forgetting their connection to the masses. Chicana writers follow this paradigm in that their works are permeated with folk genres and with oral literature. In the eloquent words of Lorna Dee Cervantes, they are "scribes" who transcribe for their people that which is deeply felt (1987:11). They effectively mediate between an outside written word and an inside oral tradition.

In spite of Gramsci's correct postulations vis-à-vis the dialectic between intellectuals and the masses, he incorrectly conceptualized the relationship between folkloric and official cultures. Furthermore, he was never able to perceive folklore's relationship to intellectual creativity nor to the uses and abuses of folklore by hegemonic powers. His erroneous conceptualization of folklore as remnants of the ruling elites' cultural productions did not allow him to detect how the cultural elites appropriate folklore for their own ideological purposes. A case in point was the utilization of the folktale for nationalistic purposes during Germany's Third Reich. Christa Kamenetsky in her article, "Folktale and Ideology in the Third Reich," posits how

> In German folklore the Nationalist Socialist Party recognized an excellent means to educate young and old in the spirit of the new *Weltanschauung*. In a systematic effort, Party ideologist Alfred Rosenberg had developed as early as 1933 a highly specialized

mechanism of controls in order to carry out more efficiently the cultural politics of the Third Reich. (1977:168)

As Kamenetsky notes further, Hitler's Party leaders wanted a

> revival of national folklore including the folk heritage of Nordic Germanic origin. This involved a cultivation of the German folktale and of Norse mythology and Icelandic sagas, as well as of Nordic Germanic symbols, customs, laws, and rituals. Folklorists were obliged after 1935 to consult carefully also the related disciplines of Nordic Germanic history and race theory which were thought to belong together with folklore in the general research concerning "folkdom" (*Volksforschung*)." (1977:168-169)

Scholars who did not focus on cultivating folklore for the purpose of Third Reich ideology and propaganda suffered by not being published and by being denied funding for research. Deformed versions of German folklore were extensively promoted by the Third Reich through inexpensive editions of collections of folktales in bookstores, libraries, public schools, and so forth.

In Hitler's Nationalist Socialist Party, the indoctrination program incorporated the use of the German folktale and was employed as "an ideological weapon" meant to serve the building of the Thousand Year Reich. Thus, Party official Alfred Eyd announced in 1935, "The German folktale shall become a most valuable means for us in the racial and political education of the young" (1977:170). Unfortunately, as Kamenetsky perceptively points out, the German version of the folktale used by the Third Reich was "no longer a true reflection of the common peasant folk, but only a medium for the Nazi ideology, and a mouthpiece of racial propaganda" (1977:178).

Although Alberto María Cirese avers that Gramsci "is able both to criticize the limitations of popular ideology and to maintain a solidarity with those classes which are at the moment subaltern because he takes the ideology of the mass of the population as the starting point for a transformation of things as they are" (1982:212), if read correctly, Gramsci's ultimate goal was the extermination of folklore. Anne Shawstack Sasson rightly states that "there was no romantic quality about Gramsci's interest in folklore" (1982:212). Gramsci intuited that "folklore and ideology in a wider sense had to be analyzed seriously and critically because it was a factor influencing people's daily lives" (1982:212) and not because of the intrinsic worth of folklore.

Cirese does point out that Gramsci's view of folklore is not monolithic but has a bipartite structure and can be viewed through two separate lenses:

> On the one hand, [Gramsci] considers folklore as an object of study and as such he validates it in full. But on the other, he looks at it as a force or factor in real life and its process of development, and from this point of view he characterizes it with a long, and so far systematic and unbroken, series of negative, low-value, qualities.
>
> While Gramsci grants importance to folklore since it is a particular conception of the world and thus worthy of scientific research, he deprivileges it by placing it low in a hierarchy of values. He denies to it all the formal qualities of coherence, unity, consciousness, etc., which are typical of the hegemonic classes and their 'official' conceptions." (1982:223-224)

Gramsci's binary system in which folklore is obviously in the negative side of the equation includes: Folklore is to official culture as the subaltern is to the hegemonic class, the simple to the cultured, the unorganic to the organic, the fragmentary to the unitary, the implicit to explicit, the debased to the original, the mechanical to the intentional, and the passive to the active (Cirese 1982:220). And, although Gramsci correctly views much of folklore to be in conflict and in contestatory opposition to official culture, he nevertheless characterizes this opposition in negative terms.

Gramsci's perception of folklore denies much of what is creative in subaltern culture and, in fact, rewrites literary history, for much of cultured writing is derivative or inspired by folk motifs and genres. Some of the greatest stories ever written are derived from folk legends: *Don Juan, Romeo and Juliet, Hamlet,* and *Faust*—all find their origins in folk material. Folklore has been a source of literary inspiration to writers in Western Europe and America from the medieval period, the renaissance, the romantic movement, to our present postmodernist age. Such writers as El Conde Lucanor, Chaucer, Shakespeare, Lope de Vega, Cervantes, García Márquez, Juan Rulfo, and García Lorca have incorporated folk motifs and folk genres within their works. Chicana intellectuals too have incorporated within their literary works folk genres through which they have masterfully weaved not only the words of the people but their grievances and their struggle against social injustice.

Notes

1. In a discussion with Hernán Vidal, a highly respected Latin American Marxist theoretician, he elucidated on the concept of intellectuals as "mediators" and indicated the term "hinge intellectuals" was a more popularly accepted term within Latin American intellectuals.
2. Angie Chabram-Dernersesian traces early feminist challenges to the male oriented, "macho" ideology that permeated the Chicano Movement in its early stages in her article, "I Throw Punches for My Race, but I Don't Want to be a Man: Writing Us—Chica-nos (Girl, Us)/Chicanas—into the Movement Script" (1992).
3. Luis Valdez states the goals of the Teatro Campesino and particularly the *Actos* thusly: "Actos: Inspire the audience to social action. Illuminate specific points about social problems. Satirize the opposition. Show or hint at a solution. Express what people are feeling" in *Actos: El Teatro Campesino* (1979:6).
4. For a discussion on the Virgen de Guadalupe myth, see Lafaye (1976). For a discussion on the La Malinche myth, see Cypess (1991). For a discussion on the La Llorona myth, see Limón (1986).
5. For a partial bibliography, Limón (1986); see also Botton-Burlá (1992), Barakat (1965), Aragón (1980), Horcasitas and Butterworth (1963), Kearney (1968), Kirtley (1960), Kraul and Beatty (1988), Leddy (1948), and Palacios (1991).

References

Arizpe, Artemio de Valle. 1963. La Llorona. In *Leyendas y sucedidos del México colonial*, pp. 7-12. México, D.F.: El Libro Español.
Barakat, Robert A. 1965. Aztec Motifs in La Llorona. *Southern Folklore Quarterly* 29:288-296.
Botton-Burlá, Flora. 1992. Las coplas de 'La Llorona.' In *Estudios de folklore y literatura dedicados a Mercedes Díaz Roig*, ed. Beatriz Garza Cuarón e Yvette Jiménez de Báez, pp. 551-572. México, D.F.: El Colegio de México.
Cammett, John M. 1967. *Antonio Gramsci and the Origins of Italian Communism*. Stanford: Stanford University Press.
Chabram-Dernersesian, Angie. 1992. I Throw Punches for My Race, but I Don't Want to be a Man: Writing Us—Chica-nos (Girl, Us)/Chicanas—into the Movement Script. In *Cultural Studies*, eds. Lawrence Grossberg, et al., pp. 81-95. New York: Routledge.
Cirese, Alberto María. 1982. Gramsci's Observations on Folklore. In *Approaches to Gramsci*, ed, Anne Showstack Sassoon, pp. 212-247. London: Writers and Readers Publishing Cooperative Society.

Cisneros, Sandra. 1991. *Woman Hollering Creek and Other Stories*. New York: Random House.
Cypess, Sandra Messinger. 1991. *La Malinche in Mexican Literature: From History to Myth*. Austin: University of Texas Press.
De Aragón, Ray John. 1980. *The Legend of La Llorona*. Las Vegas, New Mexico: The Pan American Publishing Company.
Del Castillo, Adelaida R. 1977. Malintzin Tenépal: A Preliminary Look into a New Perspective. In *Essays on la Mujer*, ed. Rosaura Sánchez, pp. 124-149. Los Angeles: Chicano Studies Center Publications, University of California at Los Angeles.
Del Castillo, Richard Griswold. 1991. *Chicano Art: Resistance and Affirmation, 1965-1985*. Los Angeles: Wight Art Gallery, University of California at Los Angeles.
Estés, Clarissa Pinkola. 1992. *Women Who Run with the Wolves: Myths and Stories of the Wild Woman Archetype*. New York: Ballantine Books.
Fuentes, Carlos. 1971. *Tiempo mexicano*. México, D.F.: Joaquín Mortiz.
Gramsci, Antonio. 1970. *Antología*. La Habana, Cuba: Instituto Cubano del Libro, Editorial de Ciencias Sociales.
_____. 1978. *Prison Notebooks*. New York: International Publishers.
Hoare, Quintin, ed. 1977. *Antonio Gramsci: Selection from Political Writings (1910-1920)*. London, England: Lawrence and Wishart.
Horcasitas, Fernando and Douglas Butterworth. 1963. La Llorona. *Tlalocan: Revista de fuentes para el conocimiento de las culturas indígenas de México* 4:204-224.
Kamenetsky, Christa. 1977. Folktale and Ideology in the Third Reich. *Journal of American Folklore* 90:168-178.
Kearney, Michael. 1968. La Llorona as a Social Symbol. *Western Folklore* 27:199-206.
Kirtley, Bacil F. 1960. La Llorona and Related Themes. *Western Folklore* 19:155-168.
Kraul, Edward García and Judith Beatty. 1988. *The Weeping Woman: Encounters with la Llorona*. Santa Fe, New Mexico: The Word Process.
Lafaye, Jaques. 1976. *Quetzalcoatl and Guadalupe: The Formation of Mexican National Consciousness, 1531-1813*. Chicago: University of Chicago Press.
Leddy, Betty. 1948. La Llorona in Southern Arizona. *Western Folklore* 7:272-277.
Limón, José. 1986. *La Llorona*: The Third Legend of Greater Mexico: Cultural Symbols, Women and the Political Unconscious. In *Renato Rosaldo Lecture Series Monograph*, Vol 2, Series 1984-85 (Spring, 1986):59-93.
Marzani, Carl, trans. 1957. *The Open Marxism of Antonio Gramsci*. New York: Cameron Associates.
Mora, Pat. 1986. *Borders*. Houston: Arte Público Press.
Nemeth, Thomas. 1980. *Gramsci's Philosophy: A Critical Study*. New Jersey: Humanities Press.
Palacios, Mónica. 1991. La Llorona Loca: The Other Side. In *Chicana Lesbians: The Girls Our Mothers Warned Us About*, ed. Carla Trujillo, pp. 49-51. Berkeley: Third Woman Press.
Paz, Octavio. 1959. *El laberinto de la soledad*. México, D.F.: Fondo de Cultura Económica.
Sahagún, Fray Bernardino de. n.d. *Historia general de las cosas de Nueva España*, vol. 3. Mexico City: Nueva España.

Sassoon, Anne Showstack. 1982. *Approaches to Gramsci*. London: Writers and Readers.
Tafolla, Carmen. 1985. *To Split a Human: Mitos, Machos y la Mujer Chicana*. San Antonio: Mexican American Cultural Center.
Valdez, Luis. 1979. *Actos: El Teatro Campesino*. San Juan Bautista, California: Menyah Productions.

Part II: The Traditional, Vernacular, and Local

7

"Sidebar Excursions to Nowhere": The Vernacular Storytelling of Errol Morris and Spalding Gray

John D. Dorst

Super Mario Five

It took me some time to realize recently that my eight year old son's casual references to playing a game he called Super Mario Five were not reflections of second grade afternoons squandered in dim basements, where "play" consists of endlessly repeated electronic scenarios enacted through the frantic tapping of controller buttons. There is, in fact, no such thing as Super Mario Five, at least not in the form of the programmed cartridges that are the object of weekly pilgrimages to the Nintendo section of the local video store. Rather, Super Mario Five is the name of a playground game devised by a regular play group of eight or nine second graders. They play it during daily recess at their public school.

The details of the game are not important here, but it is significant that there *are* a great many details and nuances in what turns out to be a remarkably complex and flexible form of fantasy play. The basic game consists of nothing more than the players imagining themselves inside the video apparatus and moving around the playground as if it were the three dimensional realization of video space. The play involves confronting obstacles, defeating imagined enemies (all the players are "good guys"), receiving messages, gathering special powers, discovering "warp zones", in short, all the things that go on at one remove in the video game universe. The difference, of course, is that in the schoolyard game imagination is given its head. Though based on the conventions of the video game, Super Mario Five is an opportunity to *create* fantasy worlds rather than merely to traverse the same preprogrammed video landscapes over and over again. The participants cooperate and lend aid to one another, in contrast to the individualization of play that video games require.[1] Where the programmed scenarios of the electronic device control the shape of action in Nintendo, on the playground no one has complete control over events. Any of the participants can "discover" a message in, for example, a broken open chunk of snow and thereby change the direction of play, or come upon the piece of playground flotsam that he identifies as the magic flute which, when played, blows everyone to some entirely new world of his imagining, with new sets of obstacles and adversaries.

This game is of course an example of a type of cultural activity that clearly falls into a realm—children's play—that folklorists have long assumed to be within their scholarly purview. But at the same time it has peculiarly emergent properties which the field of folklore is not very well equipped to address. The performance paradigm, for example, can help us organize our thinking about the physical enactments of such play, but it becomes a blunt instrument if we try to use it to understand the wider system of cultural production for which this game might be taken as a symptom.

Consider, for instance, the fact that if in the course of play one of the participants needs to go to the bathroom, he doesn't call "time out;" instead he puts himself "on pause." That is, he imagines pushing the button on the video controller that freezes the action and frees the player to do other things. This seemingly trivial detail suggests the complexity of the imaginative space in which the game operates. The participants are actually some nebulous blending of physical actors, external manipulators of action ("controllers"), and the very apparatus itself. This third component is discernable in such things as the invention of theme tunes for the various worlds the players construct. Someone will propose that they are in "jungle world" and make up on the spot the repeating tune that becomes the signature of this realm. As far as I can make out from their comments, it seems that the players move around the playground with the new tune running in their heads, at least at the beginning of play. They also on occasion will sit down and actually map out in advance the world they are about to negotiate, incorporating into their play the role of video game programmer.

The complexities suggested by such features make performance oriented studies of such things as the "It" role in children's play, or the ethnographic discovery of manipulative strategies children use to enhance their standing in a play group, seem decidedly limited in explanatory power. At least this is so if we accept that such things as Super Mario Five may herald to folklorists whole new orders of cultural production.

The sort of folk culture/mass culture studies we are most accustomed to also seem inadequate to emergent conditions. These tend, I think, to operate from a paradigm in which the processes of framing and reframing are central. That is, one either looks at how folk culture is appropriated in professionalized, bureacratized, commodified contexts—for example, public sector discussions about the presentation of folklife in professionally managed festivals—or, more commonly, one examines how folk culture appropriates mass culture productions and retools them in vernacular, face-to-face situations.

The point I want to make here is that it is limiting to see the playground game as an invasion of children's imaginative space by the commodified apparatus, thereby simply demonizing the machine, or to see it as another example of childhood's infinite capacity to liberate through imagination even the most degraded and passive of spectacles, thereby glorifying the folk process. Either of these readings restricts our ability to recognize the cultural novelty, the emergent qualities of the play space charted in Super Mario Five.

I am tempted to suggest that there is some connection between what is happening on this second grade playground and what happens in the so-called hyperspaces that theorists of postmodernism are so concerned with. As I have suggested, for example, there is a certain undecideability of the "subject of play" in Super Mario Five that seems analogous to the undecideability of location characterisic of postmodern spatial experience.[2] I make this connection here not because I want to announce the appearance of some sort of postmodern folk play, but rather to suggest that the fully developed consumer culture we now inhabit requires a more thoroughgoing reconsideration of the concept of folklore than folklorists have so far entertained. If the word postmodernism is to be of any use at all, it must be taken as the name for a general cultural condition, one that requires us to reshuffle our deck of terms and concepts. Folk, popular, elite, mass, vernacular, industrial, official, unofficial, etc.: while such terms certainly have had and continue to have useful referents, much of the cultural production that has come to characterize our world can only be fit to them at the expense of much being lost to view.

Just as most of our field's analytical paradigms seem less than adequate for capturing important qualities of advanced consumer culture, so too is it inadequate merely to look for instances of a new species called "postmodern folklore" which we can locate in some stable zone of cultural production alongside all the kinds of folklore we're already familiar with. "Postmodern" is not a genre designation.

This, it seems to me, is the sort of mistake Gerald E. Warshaver makes in what is nevertheless his valuable essay, "On Postmodern Folklore" (1991). In distinguishing a three-fold scheme of "levels" of folklore, he takes for granted (and thereby mystifies) "the lore produced by a given folk" as the "first instance" in his scheme (1991:220), to be distinguished from its second level reframing as an object of academic knowledge, where the lore continues to be connected to its context of production, but now through the medium of scholarly representation. And this in turn is marked off from the third, truly postmodern level in which first level folklore is recontextualized in such a way as to detach it from its original cultural referents and make it available to a much wider range of reception and, most importantly, consumption. Examples of this last category are the increasingly professionalized therapeutic applications of ritual practices (human potential movement, New Age sciences), the "folklorized" festivals managed by folkloristically sophisticated consultants, and the professionalized storytelling movement that has become such a common feature of contemporary public discourse (1991:225-227). Certainly the proliferating atavisms of the "Men's Movement" are another apt example.

There is no question that Warshaver is recognizing a very real and truly emergent phenomenon, especially in his acknowledgement that the forms of cultural production he identifies as postmodern are bound up with "new social classes, new methods of consumption and new politics" (1991:225). However, his scheme helps us hardly at all in trying to locate such complex and evanescent phenomena as Super Mario Five. An advanced consumer culture (or postmodernism), I would argue, is every bit as much a basic condition of possibility for this game as it is for the commodified third level productions Warshaver equates with postmodern folklore. But the playground game is at the same time the product of social relationships that most folklorists would be likely to ascribe to Warshaver's category of first level folklore. My point is that contemporary consumer culture is a structurally pervasive historical moment which requires us to rethink entirely our analytical apparatus for making sense of cultural production. Merely adding new categories to expand the typologies we now have in place will not accomplish the tasks of cultural analysis and critique that seem most urgent.

To make this point from another direction, using forms of cultural production drastically different from children's play, I would suggest that folklorists might look to certain contemporary artists as guides, albeit unwitting ones, to new territories which can fairly be called postmodern, and where both the folklorist and the folklorist's object of study must be constructed differently. Two people I have in mind for my purposes here are Spalding Gray, who is usually associated with that movement vaguely referred to as "performance art," and the idiosyncratic documentary filmmaker Errol Morris. Each in his way has been concerned with the nature of what I will loosely call vernacular storytelling, that fact alone making them of some interest to folklorists. But true to their postmodern context, both are also interested in how story gathering and storytelling are interwoven. In this they can be said to make problems for folklorists, who generally depend on keeping these sphere's separate. Gray and Morris, then, I will position here as examples of postmodern cultural producers who very directly question the applicability of folklore studies as currently practiced to the conditions of advanced consumer cultural life.

Spalding Gray and Errol Morris

Gray and Morris occupy similar positions in the larger structure of the contemporary arts. Both have emerged from the obscurity of afficiando interest into a middling celebrity. Morris has been the subject of a *New Yorker* profile (Singer 1989), and both he and Gray have been featured in the *New York Times* magazine section (Gourevitch 1992; Gray 1992). Gray's recently published novel, *Impossible Vacation* (1992), has received national attention, and Morris's films have received critical acclaim and international awards.

His fourth and most recent documentary (1992), an adaptation of Stephen Hawking's widely read *A Brief History of Time* (1988), reflects Morris's movement closer to the center of film industry power. Nevertheless, I think it is fair to say that both he and Gray continue to speak to fairly specialized audiences, in part because the media they work in are marginal to the national entertainment market.

Gray is probably best know for his widely admired stage monologue *Swimming to Cambodia*. Typical of the postmodernism he has been said to exemplify (Gitlin 1989), it is difficult to categorize his performance. Ostensibly an account of his involvement in the film *The Killing Fields* (1984), Gray sits on stage with a couple of maps, a pointer and a notebook, and proceeds to deliver a rehearsed (but not formally scripted), highly digressive monologue that is part history and geography lesson, part self-analysis, and part narrative of encounters and experiences. Although there is almost no stage machinery and no physical action, save for hand gestures and facial expressions, the performance is highly "acted." Gray imitates accents, recreates emotional and mental states, and shifts tone and tempo constantly, from rather extreme histrionics to subdued irony, all contributing to an atmosphere of uncertainty about how one is to interpret what is being said. This feeling of imbalance is also a quality typical of postmodern style.

If Gray's monologues are, at least in their overt features, about himself, some might even say self-indulgent, Morris's documentaries are notable for the filmmaker's absence. A first time viewer of his work is likely to be most struck by their air of contrivance. The signature of his style is the static interview, often referred to (misleadingly, I think) as "talking heads." He places his subjects in fixed positions, sets a camera in front of them and simply records their conversation, without direct questions from him, or camera movements, or even much in the way of editing. In many cases one seems to be getting extended segments of raw footage. One of the oddest effects he achieves is the impression that the subjects are simply "turned on" and allowed to run, just like the camera itself. He has even invented a device, which he calls the Interrotron, that projects his own video image over the lens of the camera his interviewee speaks into. In this way he literally removes his physical presence from the interview situation and gets the film subject to speak more directly to the recording device than is possible (or, presumbly, desirable) in more conventional documentaries. His goal is to achieve what he thinks of as true "first person" film (Gourevitch 1992:18).

Their differences in medium and approach notwithstanding, Gray and Morris come together, it seems to me, in precisely the area that makes them of some moment for folklorists, that is, in the centrality to their work of vernacular storytelling. Each in his way seems preoccupied with the unglamorous, out-of-the-way, and frequently bizarre stories that are being told around us all the time. In this they come as close to the interests of professional folklorists as anyone working in the contemporary arts.

This is perhaps most obviously true of Morris's work. Two of his films and a number of his ideas for unrealized film projects have arisen from his interest in marginal communities or striking events that have generated local folk traditions. His second film, *Vernon, Florida* (1981), though it consists of little more than a series of interviews with residents of this Florida panhandle town, presents vignettes of a quirky regional folklife (e.g. worm farming, turkey hunting) that puts one in mind of some studies done by good professional folklorists—of, say, fox hunters in the Pinelands of New Jersey or buckaroos in Paradise Valley, Nevada (see Hufford 1992 and Marshall 1981).

For another of his projects, Morris spent a year in Plainfield, Wisconsin, drawn there by the grotesque story of Ed Gein, a local farmer and amateur taxidermist who in the 1950s killed several women and exumed corpses from the local graveyard. Gein served as partial inspiration for both Alfred Hitchcock's 1960 film *Psycho* and Tobe Hooper's more recent *Texas Chainsaw Massacre* (1974). Morris even obtained a interview with Gein shortly before the latter's death at the regional mental hospital. Gein is the subject of a well-developed body of legendry and joke-lore that flourished in Wisconsin in the 1960s and persists today. Like professional folklorists, Morris is interested in the complexities of vernacular experience and expression, but he differs from them in his emphasis on the strangeness, even the impenetrable weirdness that is so often part of local cultures. Folklorists are more likely to downplay these qualities in the interest of dignifying, and frequently romanticizing, the folk. This is a point to which I will return.

Though less concerned with exploring local cultures of the sort folklorists might undertake to study, Gray shares with Morris an interest in "the irrelevant, the tangential, the sidebar excursion to nowhere that suddenly becomes revelatory" (Singer 1989:39). "Stories," Gray says, "seem to fly to me and stick":

> They are always out there, coming in. We exist in a fabric of personal stories. All culture, all civilization is an artful web, a human puzzle, a colorful quilt patched together to lay over raw indifferent nature. So I never wonder whether, if a tree falls in the forest, will anyone hear it. Rather, who will tell about it. (1987:7)

In *Swimming to Cambodia* he describes a stragegy of hanging around where the stories are told, a strategy familiar to many folklorists:

> Whenever I travel, if I have the time, I go by train. Because I like to hang out in the lounge car. I hear such great stories there—fantastic! Perhaps it's because they think they'll never see me again. It's like a big, rolling confessional (1987:31).

Gray has made a career of telling his personal stories, which frequently entail retelling the tales others have recounted to him. Having been schooled in the underground theater of Artaud and Grotowski (Gray 1987:8), in which narrative expression was decidedly secondary, he has become one of the premier performance artist to return to stories—but not the sort of stories familiar to classical theater. Rather this new movement takes, like Morris's films, the personal, the local, the vernacular—I am tempted to say "folk"—as its primary dramatic resource. Not surprisingly, Gray spent five years, beginning in 1970, with Richard Schechner's Performance Group (Gray 1987:8). Schechner is of course an important figure in a performance tradition that has drawn upon anthropological sources for theatrical inspiration.

It is not my goal here either to bring Morris and Gray into the fold as quasi-folklorists or to locate them among the professional storytellers who appear with growing frequency in summer park amphitheaters, artists in the schools programs, and storytelling conferences (one of Warshaver's instances of postmodern folklore). Rather, I'm suggesting that in their work we see a relocation—perhaps "dislocation" is the better word—of storytelling that is the self-conscious analogue in the elite arts to the minor and unself-conscious relocation of play in Super Mario Five.

It has become virtually an article of faith with the theorists of postmodernism, at least those who use the word to name a general shift in the nature of cultural production, that our age is marked by a loss of faith in the master narratives of western civilization. The "big stories" that heretofore seemed to account for whole domains of cultural experience fail to capture the fragmentation and localization of advanced consumer culture.[3] In place of these *grand recits*, the modest and mundane narratives of local relevance—precisely the sort of stories that are the foundation of Gray's and Morris's work—take on a new importance. That this is also the general arena in which many folklorists operate makes our field potentially a critical one under the current conditions of cultural production.

But along with the simple fact that local stories become in postmodernism the definitive type of story, and not merely, as traditional folkloristics would have it, the marginal bypaths woven through some "Great Tradition," they are relocated in a second and, I think, more interesting way. The postmodern relocation of narrative foregrounds what, for want of a better word, I will call the mystery of vernacular story. It seems to me the merest truism that folklorists are in the business of making sense of local stories, and the history of folk narrative study is a history of strategies for sense-making, from the spatio-temporal sense of historic-geographic studies to the micro-social sense of communicative subtleties in narrative performance. In contrast, what postmodernism brings into view and makes central to its project is the indeterminacy of stories and storytelling.

The postmodern fascination with this quality of vernacular narrative should not be mistaken, as it often is by postmodernism's critics, as a turn toward vulgar obscurantism. The best of the postmodern artists are intent on revealing what we might call complex indeterminacy, expressed in their work by a constant and often playful movement back and forth across the boundary of coherence, another word that is not quite adequate to the circumstances but that will have to do. Both Gray's and Morris's work display this quality abundantly.

Mark Singer, author of the *New Yorker* (1989) profile of Morris, identifies a particulary good instance of the quality I'm talking about. It occurs in Morris's second film, *Gates of Heaven* (1978). In my view this work, which takes as its unlikely subject two California pet cemetaries, is the fullest realization of Morris's cinematic technique and of the sensibility that makes him most relevant to the present discussion. The film is built up largely of a series of static interviews, though "monologues" would perhaps describe their quality better. Morris is never present, either visually or on the soundtrack. We never hear the questions or promptings that the speakers might be responding to, nor do we usually know the names of those who appear. There is neither voiceover narration nor superimposed text to tell us how these people relate to the film's theme. What we mostly have, in other words, is people talking—talking about their own lives, their pets, their aspirations, there views of the world or opinions of others. Just as in the overall arrangement of the film it is not always clear what the significance of this or that element might be, so in any given monologue it is not always easy to discern complete coherence in what is being said. This is most strikingly true in the long discourse of an elderly woman whom Singer identifies as one Florence Rasmussen. Sitting tightly framed in what is presumably her own front doorway (typically, this is never made clear), she delivers a remarkable continuous monologue in which she alternates between absolute assertions and elaborate qualifications of those assertions that border on being, and sometimes actually are, complete contradictions (she bought her son a car/she didn't really buy it but she gave him four hundred dollars; this son, who is really a grandson, never got married and never will/he was married once but is now divorced).

Singer says this scene is emblematic of Morris's work: "a seamless monologue from someone who has been allowed to talk until the truth naturally sorts itself out" (1989:39). This seems to me not quite accurate. He is right about the method, but the result is hardly sorted truth. What we see, rather, is someone in the process of working out an account of something, though that "something" is never entirely clear. It is the activity of vernacular story making that is his subject, and this includes all the uncertainties, false starts, qualifications, self-fictionalizations, and incoherencies endemic to that process.

Not all the monologues are as fey as Florence Rasmussen's, but in all of them we see common people struggling to get a grip on their local realities through their vernacular storytelling. The well ordered tale, the unequivocal opinion, and most important, the unqualified truth, are undercut at every turn. We are left in the end with no easily calculated meaning or message, no definitive sense of how we are to feel about all we have just seen. There are some moments that pass into low comedy, while others tend toward genuine pathos; some scenes of ludicrous pomposity and others of dignified modesty. The perhaps surprising result is that one does not come away feeling cheated by this indeterminacy. Our discovery of its very complexity recuperates it for us. What we get is the revelation that the most trivial, even sordid seeming subject turns out to be both rich and strange.

One possible criticism that folklorists might be likely to level against Morris is that he is disdainful of his subjects, depicting them in such a way that invites his sophisticated audience to condescend. This would be to mistake him, I think. Certainly there are moments in his films where we see people behaving less than admirably, or more commonly, moments where people appear just plain silly. But overall Morris's films come off as being sympathetic to, and certainly fascinated by the everyday and the vernacular. The complexity of his vision, his unwillingness to reduce vernacular experience to a single reading, either admiring or disdainful, is his way of dignifying it. He lets it have its mystery and indeterminacy.

In this perhaps folklorists have something to learn. Along with our professional need to identify the coherence of vernacular expression, we generally feel compelled to suppress whatever might seem negative in our depictions of those we study. Usually this means we focus our research on materials, groups and individuals we can admire and present in a positive light. Unfortunately, this also often means we downplay the frequent intractability, the undecideability, and simply the weirdness of much vernacular experience and expression. We tend, I think, to push these qualities either in the direction of picturesqueness or in the direction of profound meaningfulness, rather than to leave them with their utter strangeness in tact.[4] One salutary feature of postmodernism, and of Morris as its exemplar, is the willingness, even the necessity, to take seriously the everyday weirdness of advanced consumer culture.

Most of what I have been saying about Errol Morris's films applies also to Spalding Gray's performances. I have already pointed out how Gray's monologues keep us off balance in our attempts to identify a message or find a stable position from which to evaluate what we are hearing. One might see him as the self-conscious dramatizer of precisely the processes and qualities of vernacular telling, what he calls personal stories, that Morris is after in his films. It is tempting to think of Morris as recording directly what Gray collects and then reshapes for theatrical presentation. But this would miss the important point that under the conditions of advanced consumer culture those sorts of distinctions are becoming less and less tenable.

For one thing, Morris is hardly a recorder of "natural" discourse, in the sense that folklorists use that term. In fact, he purposely underlines the unnaturalness or constructedness of so-called natural settings. His subjects are generally recorded in "real" environments, like Florence Rasmussen in her doorway, but he uses tight framing, the unrelievedly static camera, and obviously manipulated lighting to produce the effect of artificiality. These are the appropriate physical correlatives of the fictiveness and artificiality of the "real life" monologues he gets from the people who speak into his camera.

Nor are Gray's stories any less "natural" than those of Morris's raconteurs. He identifies his first attempt at personal storytelling as the time when, as a college student working on at a night job, he would tell the "story of his day" while running the dishwasher or working the garbage truck (Gray 1987:7). When he later began to approach such storytelling as a dramatic resource, his method was to tell his tales on stage and let them grow from one night to the next as more details came to him and new memories emerged. This focus on the emergent properties of everyday stories is, as we have seen, a quality that appears in Morris's films. One of the strengths of Gray's monologues is that he is able to preserve the feel of this "natural" feature of stories. He allows it to invest his performances with the digressiveness and sense of indeterminacy that I have been arguing is a hallmark of postmodern vernacular experience.

One might say of Morris, and of Gray as well, that they take the idea of vernacular expression as performance to a more radical conclusion than folklorists who subscribe to the academic performance paradigm. A consumer culture in which performance spectacles are the very substance of experience makes any easy distinction between the natural and the artificial more misleading than illuminating. That is one of the conventions of folkloric practice that Morris and Gray's brand of postmodernism calls into question.

Another is the line between the figure of the folklorist and the folk, as well as between the folklorist and the artist who draws on folk expression as raw material or inspiration. As we have just seen, Gray uses his own personal stories *as* his theatrical performance. But as we have also seen, he collects the stories told to him and makes them part of his own story. The sort of blending of roles and narrative positions we see in his work seems to me quite like the blending of the roles and positions I pointed out in the playground game.

This sort of boundary crossing is even carried a step further in one of Gray's more recent monologues, *Monster in a Box* (1991). Gray's initial narrative impulse here is to tell about his inability to complete the novel a publisher has solicited from him. The novel is about a man who is unable to take a vacation, and Gray carries the boxed manuscript—the monster—on stage with him as his only prop (the novel has now been published as *The Impossible Vacation*, 1992).

In his monologue, Gray tells us that among the distractions keeping him from completing the novel are the acting roles and theater projects that have come his way. Among these is an invitation from the Mark Taper Forum Theater in Los Angeles to be in residence there for a year and travel around the city looking for interesting people to invite in and be interviewed on stage in front of an audience. HBO also approached him for a similar project in which he was to travel around the country looking for people who have been taken onto UFOs, with the intention of having him interview them on stage. Here the very activity of interviewing and collecting stories becomes the performance itself. It is not much of a stretch to see in this the folklorist's own role being brought on stage, and thereby inserted into the play of shifting positions that so typifies the postmodern cultural experience.

The Complex Undecideability of Vernacular Storytelling

In his classic essay on storytelling, Walter Benjamin displays his characteristic prescience in seeing the displacement of meaning in stories by what he called "information" (1969). True storytelling, as he constructs it, is news that comes from afar, either in time or space; it is the giving of counsel and the offering of meanings that are not exhausted in the act of telling, but that ramify over time and become amplified by the experiences of the listeners. Information, on the other hand, "lays claim to prompt verifiability. The prime requirement is that it appear 'understandable in itself'" (Benjamin 1969:89). True storytelling is at its purest in the orally mediated tale from vernacular experience. The paradigm of information is the hard news newspaper article.

From a current perspective it seems obvious that the resources of information have exploded beyond what even Benjamin might have imagined. The impoverishment of experience he was beginning to observe is now an inescapable condition of existence. Storytelling, though, is a more complicated issue. Benjamin's pessimism seems based on a principle of limited good that may not apply as clearly to communicative resources as he suggests. If information simply displaced storytelling, then one would expect the latter to have disappeared altogether by now. That is far from the case. It has been my contention here that rather than disappearing, storytelling is being relocated under the regime of advanced consumer culture. As postmodern theorists tell us, the grand narratives, which presumably would include the mythic/epic narratives of oral tradition that Benjamin looked to, are no longer available to us as broad explanatory resources. What perhaps takes their place are the local, vernacular, personal stories that operate in a close orbit, but make up for their limited scope of application with their profusion.

In any case these are the sort of stories that artists like Morris and Gray direct us to. Although they may not offer grand patterns of coherence on which to anchor a stable moral order, still they are far from Benjamin's information, which exhausts itself in the moment of its reporting. In fact their very mystery and strangeness can be a cultural resource of great importance in our attempts to resist the profound reductiveness of information. What I have focused on here, and what I find central in both Gray and Morris, is the complex undecideability of such storytelling as it operates under current cultural conditions. This may not be a very satisfying quality to those who desire narrative stabilities, but it is a fact of vernacular stories in our age and so worthy of folklorists' attention. And linked to it is the breaking down of the old stabilities of teller/tale/told to. The idea of natural storytelling situation, of the collector/ethnographer versus the folk performer, of folk artist versus folklorist versus fine arts user of folk material are all disrupted to such a degree that professional folklorists must begin to amend their practice accordingly. It requires first of all that we acknowledge the relocations that are occurring all around us, and to us as folklorists. And in this we might look to things like Errol Morris's films and Spalding Gray's performance pieces—and maybe to second grade playgrounds—for assistance.

Notes

1. For a thorough discussion of the properties and effects of Nintendo type video games, see Eugene F. Provenzo, Jr. (1991).

2. For the seminal formulation of the idea of postmodern hyperspace, Frederic Jameson (1984); for an effective application of the idea, see Giuliana Bruno (1987).

3. The *locus classicus* for this point is Jean-Francois Lyotard (1984[1979]).

4. One begins to find in the work of cultural anthropologists some attempts to convey the impenetrable otherness of ethnographic subjects. See for example Dan Rose (1987).

References

Benjamin, Walter. 1969 [1955]. The Storyteller. In *Illuminations*, ed. Hannah Arendt, pp. 83-109. New York: Schocken Books.

Bruno, Giuliana. 1987. Ramble City: Postmodernism and *Blade Runner*. October 41:61-74.

Gitlin, Todd. 1989. Postmodernism Defined, At Last *Utne Reader*. July-August:53.

Gourevitch, Philip. 1992. Interviewing the Universe, *The New York Times Magazine* Aug. 9:18-19, 44-48, 53.

Gray, Spalding. 1987. *Swimming to Cambodia: The Collected Works of Spalding Gray*. London: Picador.

_____. 1991. *Monster in a Box*. London: Pan Books.

_____. 1992. Gray's Anatomy: A Preview. *The New York Times Magazine* May 17::42-48.

_____. 1992. *Impossible Vacation*. New York: Alfred A. Knopf, Inc.

Hawking, Stephen W. 1988. *A Brief History of Time: from the Big Bang to Black Holes*. New York: Bantam Books.

Hufford, Mary. 1992. *Chaseworld*. Philadelphia: University of Pennsylvania Press.

Jameson, Frederic. 1984. The Cultural Logic of Late Capitalism. *New Left Review* 144:53-92.

Lyotard, Jean-Francois. 1984 [1979]. *The Postmodern Condition: A Report on Knowledge*, trans. by Geoff Bennington and Brian Massumi. Minneapolis: University of Minnesota Press.

Marshall, Howard W. 1981. *Buckaroos in Paradise: Cowboy Life in Northern Nevada*. Lincoln: University of Nebraska Press.

Morris, Errol. 1978. *Gates of Heaven*.

_____. 1981. *Vernon, Florida*.

_____. 1992. *A Brief History of Time*.

Provenso, Eugene F. 1991. *Video Kids: Making Sense of Nintendo*. Cambridge: Harvard University Press.

Rose, Dan. 1987. *Black American Street Life: South Philadephia, 1969-1971*. Philadelphia: University of Pennsylvania Press.

Singer, Mark. 1989. Predilections. *The New Yorker* 64(Feb.6):38-72.

Warshaver, Gerald E. 1991. On Postmodern Folklore. *Western Folklore* 50:219-229.

8

Shakespeare's Step-Sisters: Romance Novels and the Community of Women

Clover Williams and *Jean R. Freedman*

Introduction

> Re-vision—the act of looking back, of seeing with fresh eyes, of entering an old text from a new critical direction—is for us more than a chapter in cultural history: it is an act of survival.... A radical critique of literature, feminist in its impulse, would take the work first of all as a clue to how we live ... and how we can begin to see—and therefore live—afresh.
> —Adrienne Rich ("When We Dead Awaken: Writing as Re-vision")

> Shakespeare had a sister; but do not look for her in Sir Sidney Lee's life of the poet. She died young—alas, she never wrote a word. ... Now my belief is that this poet who never wrote a word and is buried at the crossroads still lives. She lives in you and me, and in many other women who are not here tonight, for they are washing up the dishes and putting the children to bed. But she lives; for great poets do not die; they are continuing presences; they need only the opportunity to walk among us in the flesh. This opportunity, as I think, it is now coming within your power to give her.
> —Virginia Woolf (*A Room of One's Own*)

Most scholars of women's romance novels have described the genre in terms of contradiction or paradox. Though the nature of this theoretical dichotomy varies, what remains fairly constant is the fact that this paradox is interpreted as a tension between positive and negative aspects of the romance. Even many who explicitly consider the genre's duality a reflection of the female psyche want to transcend the paradoxes implicit in both, to unify them, usually by doing away with the "bad" parts. Yet if this ambiguity within the romance is what makes it resonant to so many women, then this very heterogeneity—of ideology, of perspective, of reader identification and response—is itself positive. The romance invites identification with both the text and its place in society and gives the reader a framework to reflect upon these, while simultaneously focussing her consideration upon her own life and values. Reader reflections often create a literal community through discussion with other readers (and authors); they also create the impression of what Thomas Roberts (1990) calls a "virtual" fellowship with other fans. Either way, because the romance paradox echoes paradoxes in women's own situations, it acts as a positive force in that it stimulates the re-vision that Adrienne Rich describes above, and with it, community among women.

In the first part of this essay we will compare ambiguities posited by various scholars for the romance with those current in feminist theories of woman's difference. Where positive aspects of women's culture may be linked—directly or indirectly—to the paradoxes in women's lives, women's literature (which reflects these paradoxes) may be given a positive (re)interpretation. For example, if object-status has divided the female self, leaving her to spy at her own keyhole, this self-reflection is as true a model of human identity as the more individuated monad attributed to the male psyche. Likewise, a genre of literature which repeats woman's incorporation and reinterpretation of both types of identity is valuable because the combination and juxtaposition are valuable, as is the act of negotiation itself. According to many fans, the romance provides a framework for this type of negotiation by thematically asserting and reasserting for women a right to both affiliative identity and monadic recognition and by refusing to see them in opposition.

Given the variety of interpretations the romance has inspired, an attention to how enthusiasts themselves understand the romance becomes especially important. Louise Rosenblatt, pioneer of reader-response theory, wrote that "a literary experience gains its significance and force from the way in which the stimuli present in the literary work interact with the mind and emotions of a particular reader" (1938:35).[1] Moreover, since this effect is cumulative, regular readers of a genre will probably respond differently than newcomers:

> What the reader has elicited from the text up to any point generates a receptivity to certain kinds of ideas, overtones, or attitudes. . . . As the reading proceeds, attention will be fixed on the reverberations or

implications that result from fulfillment or frustration of those expectations. (Rosenblatt 1978:54)

It is thus probably not enough for the scholar to read romance or any other relatively formulaic genre as an outsider, and then to project from her own impressions what effect the books might have on the enthusiast. (Though Stanley Fish asserts that all textual interpretations are valid insofar as readers describe their own responses, this validity is individual rather than determinate, and does not grant license to second-guess the responses of others. See Fish 1980:338.)

Nor is reader-response always solitary: it creates, and in a sense is created by, community. Rosenblatt points out, and Radway has suggested in her study of the Smithton women, that literary interpretive tastes and techniques occur "in a social matrix," with relationships between readers also influencing interpretation (Radway 1991:55; also Rosenblatt 1978:28). Discussion of the romance plot consolidates these social matrices, or "interpretive communities," of many readers, who negotiate and share values (Fish 1980:14). Other readers may have little desire or occasion to discuss their reading habits, but may participate in what Thomas Roberts calls "a virtual fellowship of characters, readers, and writers" (1990:218). Widespread scorn for the genre and those involved in it causes many readers and authors to feel a pronounced solidarity with unseen others in the romance community. This very marginalization has stimulated many women to identify and assert themselves in collective terms, as readers and women. (See also Radway 1991:101.) The second half of this paper presents several overlapping romance groups, made up of readers, booksellers, authors, and others.

But who are the women who make up these communities of interpretation? By all informed accounts they are both normal and numerous.[2] Jean Radford writes that half of all women reading at any time will probably be reading a romance novel (1986:15). The romance's sales have "leveled out" from a high of about fifty percent of all North American paperback book sales, to a steady twenty-five percent, yet because of ever more organized venues for sharing and buying used books, actual readership has probably remained much higher than even these statistics would indicate (Burack 1983:ix; Falk 1990:xx). Thus any theory of the romance which concludes with contempt for the reader, however sympathetically couched, is denigrating a significant proportion of women. Though critiques are not necessarily untrue on that account, we cannot afford to accept generalizations about readers without close attention to both unspoken assumptions and alternate interpretations of the same material.

Indeed, romance readers are diverse enough to defy most generalizations. Janice Radway cites Harlequin's findings that the average reader "matches the profile of the 'North American English-speaking female population' in age, family, income, employment status, and geographical location" (1991:55). Though Harlequin press is hardly a disinterested party, these statistics coincide with those of Peter Mann (1974, 1981), whose study of British readers led him to call the Mills and Boon reader "Everywoman."[3] Studies cited by Carol Thurston have found that the educational level of romance readers in the United States matched that of the female population almost exactly, and that romance readers tend to be slightly more liberal and egalitarian than other women, and significantly more likely to vote (1987:118-19, 121, 123).[4] Readers are also well-adjusted in other ways. Psychologists Claire Coles and M. Johanna Shamp found only two significant differences in the romance reader's profile: Readers of the erotic historical romance reported engaging in twice as much sexual intercourse and using sexual fantasy far more frequently than did "nonreaders" (cited in Thurston 1987:10-11).

Beyond the most general guidelines, romance books themselves are difficult to characterize. Traditional Harlequin (or Mills and Boon) novels are around 190 pages, with a naive heroine, an often cold (even brutal) hero, a strict code of decency, and sometimes other features dictated by publisher's guidelines. Even these strict guidelines allow for endless variation and creativity to those familiar enough with the genre to recognize the interplay of innovation within tradition. Nor was this model necessarily repressive: in a 1965 Mills and Boon novel by Violet Winspear, the heroine reflects that it is better never to marry than to do so for the sake of tradition or without total freedom of communication, and that women's work (whether in or out of the home) should be a meaningful career, rather than a mere job or substitute for love (Winspear 1965). Though this author was somewhat exceptional, her popularity shows that readers recognized the difference and preferred her to many others.

Since Ms. Winspear's initial popularity, these early rules have been expanded and subgenres intermixed so much that many feel the only constant features remaining are the romance itself and the temporary problem—usually one of gendered miscommunication between the two main characters—that thwarts it. The thematic problem of communication between the sexes is variously interpreted: Many theorists see the romance novel's portrayal of gendered miscommunication as an exaltation of gender hierarchy, while readers and authors usually refer to the romance as a model of liberation and a vehicle of solidarity, and aver that the romance is itself the victim of gender hierarchy. Since there is no single intrinsic meaning to be drawn from these texts and because theories and techniques of folklore fieldwork complement the aims of reader-response theory so aptly, we asked readers and authors of the romance to talk with us about their reactions to the genre.

Our fieldwork was conducted primarily in southern Indiana during the first half of 1992. During this time, Clover visited several used bookstores that specialized in romance novels and discussed romance with readers both at these stores and on the campus of Indiana University, where several readers approached her to discuss the genre. On the weekend of May 2, 1992, we both attended romance conferences. Jean's event was held in Indianapolis by the Indiana branch of the Romance Writers of America and was attended by writers, readers, one agent, and one editor, many from Indiana or nearby states. Clover went to Savannah, Georgia for the Booklover's awards convention sponsored by *Romantic Times* magazine. This was a larger, more mixed event, dominated by published and "unpublished" authors, but also well attended by readers, booksellers, agents, reviewers, cover models and artists, and all other imaginable members of the romance community. Thus Jean had the opportunity to focus on writers and readers in a locally-oriented, grass-roots group, while Clover divided attention among individual writers, booksellers, readers, and others, as well as on the interactions between these groups. The ideas put forth here have been culled from our combined interviews, observations, and discussions.

And we read. Thomas Roberts (1990) has demonstrated throughout his study of genre fiction that in order to understand any popular genre, one needs to be familiar enough with what is part of an unspoken tradition to know when and how that tradition is being revised, reinterpreted, or changed. To that end we both read romance novels that we enjoyed, romance novels that we hated, romance novels with more variety and novelty than scoffers would ever expect, and romance novels until they came out of our ears. We agreed about the merits, flaws, and possible effects of some, and disagreed about others.

The Integrity of Ambiguity: Romance and Theories of Difference

> What the liberated woman will look like cannot be imagined with any certainty or detail at the moment, let alone how she will be experienced. In order to live through this transitional space between the *no longer* and the *not yet* without going mad, it is necessary for woman to learn to look in two diverging directions simultaneously.
> —Sigrid Weigel ("Double Focus: On the History of Women's Writing")

> Do I contradict myself?
> Very well then I contradict myself,
> (I am large, I contain multitudes.)
> —Walt Whitman ("Song of Myself")

It has long been a commonplace of feminist theory that assumptions of universality and subjectivity are patterned after a male model and in contradistinction to the female Other, and that these assumptions leave the female subject divided between an internalized Otherness and a male-identified subjectivity. This divided selfhood, combined with a social structure which defines women in relation to others, theoretically makes women more self-monitoring, more apt to identify themselves with others and to define themselves relationally instead of following a masculine model of oppositional identity. Feminist psychologists like Nancy Chodorow (1994) and Jean Baker Miller (1976) have added that the process of female individuation involves a less radical differentiation from the mother than does male individuation, and that women's identities are thus more fluid, less oppositional. According to feminist literary scholar Judith Kegan Gardiner, this creates a processual rather than a fixed model of identity in much of women's fictional and autobiographical writing, with the result that women writers and readers tend to approach a text "with the hypothesis that its female author is engaged in a process of testing and defining various aspects of identity" (1982:187) by shifting identification throughout the text, alternating between immersion and separation, "ego violation and mutual identification" (1982:188).[5] These theories of female Otherness and reflexivity are interrelated, but separable: one need not embrace the whole theoretical complex to make use of the parts. The following suggested feminist revisions of theories about romance novels alternate between several interrelated theories of female identity to address scholarly objections to the genre and its fans.

From Simone de Beauvoir's first formulation of Otherness as intrinsic to women's experience, many theorists have regarded female ambiguity as something to be overcome or transcended (1989[1949]:680). Similarly, Tania Modleski disparages the romance novel, which she tells us "both reflects and contributes to. . . . a kind of 'double conscience,'" later described as common to the "normal female personality" (1990:32, 58). The romance, she tells us, both promises and thwarts the "self-forgetfulness" necessary to transcend female self-reflection (1990:47-48, 53). Modleski's argument is too multifaceted to be reproduced here, but is based on the supposition that the reader's foreknowledge of the romance formula inhibits straightforward identification with the heroine's distress. Reader familiarity with the romance formula thus heightens both intellectual distance from and emotional identification with the heroine, and emphasizes a self divided into observed and observer, object and subject. That part of the reader which identifies with the heroine "turns against her own better self, the part of her which feels anger at men," while the distanced reader "turns against her own 'worse' self, the part which has not yet been liberated from shameful fantasies" (1990[1982]:14). Modleski suggests that as long as women use the romance and other popular culture media to solve their problems vicariously, they will continuously reproduce the structures of sexism, and thus never come to "real" solutions.[6]

Carol Thurston points out that some of what has been considered objectionable in romance fiction follows a pattern common to other types of literature for hundreds of years. This, she says, is "characterized by a schizoid portrayal of the female persona . . . the chaste, self-sacrificing, domestic, tractable heroine, and the sexy, selfish, aggressive Other Woman" (1987:36). The naive heroine of early romance novels was often contrasted with a female "foil," a sophisticated, sexual Other Woman who competed for the hero's affections. In this area, romance novels have made good progress: most readers now demand heroines whom they consider sexually aware, self-motivated, and very assertive, and this is the type of heroine most modern authors create. Though several commentators have described the romance heroine as weak or childish, readers' descriptions of favorite romance novels describe strong women who fight for love and identity on their own terms (Radway 1991:77). With the qualities of the "Other Woman" now being embraced and integrated rather than denied, female "foils" and one-dimensional heroines are becoming rare in today's romance. (And the portrayal of positive relationships among women is increasing.) Real women are, to use Modleski's example, both independent and empathic, both angry at and sexually attracted to men.[7] To suppress this ambiguity in women's literature or psyche is to modernize the good woman/bad woman structure which dehumanizes all women, the "good" as well as the "bad."

Thurston applauds modern romance novels for portraying characters who possess both stereotypically female and stereotypically male qualities. Spokespersons from both men's and women's movements have discussed the benefits, to members of both sexes, of a range of potential feelings and expression which contain elements traditional to both. Carol Thurston discusses several studies showing that men and women who report high levels of both traditionally masculine and traditionally feminine personality traits also have "higher levels of self-esteem and are exceptionally well-adjusted" (1987:80-81). When the female foil is still found, she is usually more, not less, traditional than the heroine and is often explicitly portrayed as insecure or unbalanced.

While feminist scholars usually agree that the construction of Otherness as measured by deviance from a male norm is harmful, many have also seen the interrelated ambiguities of female immanence, reflexivity, and fluid ego-boundary as potentially positive configurations. Feminists in general, and French feminists in particular, have allied themselves with a recognition of physical and ethical immanence, the latter characterized by a privileging of contingence and circumstance over abstract or rigid moral principles. Though there is a variety of opinions about whether a distinctly female writing exists, whether it is realizable, and how it might be manifested, many suggest that it would express the immediacy and simultaneity of the immanence associated with women. As such, an *écriture feminine* would, Kristeva writes, "name what has thus far never been an object of circulation in the community: the enigmas of the body, the dreams, secret joys, shames, hatreds of the second sex" (1982:50). Others have added that it would "privilege not the look [which is associated with masculine detachment] but the tactile, the simultaneous, the fluid," and would reflect the "split between the two sexes, but also the constitution of the subject and the organization of male/female sexuality" (Jacobus 1986:64; Rodenas 1989:42). The proponents of an *écriture feminine* would probably not think of romance novels as an example of "writing the body"—Julia Kristeva warns against "market-place romanticism which would otherwise have been rejected as anachronistic," and other feminist scholars have equated the romance novel with political regression (Kristeva 1982:50; also Fowler 1991; Douglas 1980). But perhaps they would reconsider if they knew how the romance is read and interpreted from within its own circles. Whether one agrees that the qualities associated with *écriture feminine* are distinctly female properties or not, many members of the romance community seem to share and applaud a very similar understanding of women's writing, for manifestly similar reasons.

How-to books for budding romance writers routinely contain advice like the following, written by Vivian Stephens, former editor for Harlequin's American Romance series, who says that romance writers "must be either born or trained sensualists." She writes:

> Writers have to really get in touch with life . . . . Their five senses must be aroused. They should eat food they really like; listen to music that can be so poignant it makes them cry . . . . Anything that is tactile or will stimulate the senses can then be translated into words . . . . It's important to realize that the sensuality you're sharing will be between you and the reader. You are making her vulnerable by letting her share those feelings . . . . This whole exercise is to provoke thoughts that have been generated by the emotions, that have been set off by the sensuality of (1) *touch*, (2) *scent*, (3) *seeing*, (4) *hearing*, and (5) *taste*. (1983:55-56; see also Burack 1983:15; Barnhart 1983:77-79)

This and other books prescribe exercises to stimulate the would-be author's sense awareness on and off the page. Exercises include uses of silks and other materials, bubble baths, flowers, and perfumes to evoke mood; a comparison of the sensations of eating a lemon and eating a persimmon; and various sense-memory exercises (e.g., Stephens 1983:56; Barnhart 1983:44). Rosemary Guiley writes that sensual description "is not limited to sexual description, but involves the senses in all things. Women notice details, such as colors, textures and smells, but it's a subtle awareness" (1983:237). One book even gives the explicit advice to cultivate synesthesia, especially in the experience and description of sight (Lowery 1983:66-67). Though Ms. Lowery never describes this method explicitly, she seems to suggest that, by creating synesthetic linguistic metaphors ("light creaks"), women can evoke corresponding physical sensations.

For many women in the romance community, as for many feminist theorists, the privileging of vision over the other senses is a predominantly male way of distancing one's self from experience. Men who want to write romance are warned that both detachment and overvisualization are seemingly interrelated flaws common to male attempts at the genre. In a discussion of male romance authors, Kathryn Falk tells us that romance editors claim to know when a novel has been written by a man because they feel that men tend to use language which depersonalizes women (impersonal descriptions like "flank" or "mound," and instrumental verbs like "push" and "pull"), to focus on men's feelings, and to lack intimacy with their surroundings and with others. She quotes Mills and Boon editor Heather Jeeves as saying, "They write too voyeuristically, as though they're watching through a window, not experiencing it directly" (1990:321). Other editors she spoke with described most male-authored romance as unemotional, or "graphic and mechanical" (1990:321). Carolyn Nichols, senior editor for Bantam's "Loveswept" line, says, "I believe this is part of nurture, not nature. Culture teaches such things differently to men and to women. A woman has generally been taught to be more aware of her surroundings" (Guiley 1983:237). Thus, Guiley explains, even male writers who notice and try for this difference in awareness have trouble "grasping the subtlety of it. They tend to describe things too pointedly and in excess" (1983:238). This view of male writing is shared by the "Smithton" readers who told

Janice Radway that "very few men are 'perceptive' or 'sensitive'" enough to create within this women's genre (1991:83).

Bantam editor Carolyn Nichols also asserts that "in many of the stories either edited or written by men, rape is seen as nothing wrong," and that "it's never portrayed that way in any book written by a woman" (Guiley 1983:237). While it is certainly true that women-authored romances have occasionally glorified rape, a female author who regularly does so was said by a Smithton reader to write "man's type book[s]," and suspected of having a male editor, and perhaps a male readership (Radway 1991:83). Though the—usually implicit—threat of violence is still a fairly common feature of the romance, this automatically creates an adversarial relationship between the hero and heroine. The fans and authors we spoke with confirmed Radway's report that romance readers believe the genre opposes brutality against women (Radway 1991:124; Snitow 1979; Modleski 1990). The heroine must neutralize the threat of violence (and bring the hero to penance, if his threat was intentional), before she allows herself to become emotionally intimate with the hero. In a sense these are "quests" or morality plays: the struggle between Everywoman and the threat of male violence should not be confused with a glorification of dominance, nor should it be assumed that readers care little who "wins" the struggle.

Leslie Rabine's study of the romantic quest from Tristan and Isolde to the Harlequin novel points out that the genre has always been concerned with a definition of selfhood as the romance hero struggles to define himself (1985:2). Harlequin's twentieth-century feminization of the romance hero, author, and readership, then, necessarily reflects a very different quest and model of selfhood than that of the "quintessentially phallocentric subject" and accompanying suppressed female voice found in male romance quests (Rabine 1985:10). These modern women's romances show a quest for selfhood that struggles "against an order that represses an autonomous female voice," and which threatens to subsume her simultaneity into a compartmentalized linearity:

> Instead of a desire to return to an original unity of self and other, feminine historicity . . . reveals itself as the desire to heal the devision [sic] of society into the separate spheres of the feminine domestic and the masculine sociopolitical, which according to many

> feminists grounds the social and sexual oppression of women. Rather than a *synthesis*, these feminine voices seek to rediscover the already existing but invisible *interconnections* between domestic and sociopolitical, public and private, sexual and historical spheres. Rather than a unified totality, the feminine voices seek a network of difference. The wholeness they seek does not transcend history and is not a resolution of contradictions, but an entry into history which women have been denied. (Rabine 1985:13)

Romance heroines thus embody, as Thurston has pointed out, a complex wholeness: Their competences in male domains "often become the selling point that distinguishes one romance from another," and may even help to validate the fact that "for them sexual sensation, feelings of love, and rational thought are all intimately connected" (Rabine 1985:167, 176-177). Because the romance heroine's quest for identity entails the struggle to vindicate and maintain this simultaneity and interconnectedness, she is alternately threatened by both a "dissolution of her self into the male self" and a self-control which closes her off and denies her needs (Rabine 1985:175). The resolution lies in bringing the hero to "recognize and adopt the relational, feminine form of self" (Rabine 1985:175). (This change in the hero, however, may sometimes be indicated by what we considered a token gesture on his part, or only after great sacrifice on the part of the heroine.)

The concept of a definitively female standard of writing is as problematic as that of a distinctly female form of self. To many, both concepts re-enforce stereotypes which have caricatured and limited women. If there is a women's writing, it is no more standardized than woman's selfhood: both are a process of revision and experimentation. Self-definition lies in flux, in the process of women creating a sphere in which to define themselves and their writing. This sphere and process of definition, whether enacted in academic debate or popular fiction, may define women's writing more productively than any theoretical model that might be abstracted from them.

Reading Women

> If this fluidity carries with it a unique capacity for bonding—for merging, for empathy, for the joy and terror of "being girls

together"—we must pause to consider seriously what we have entered into in the act of reading these texts.
—Marilee Lindemann ("'This Woman Can Cross Any Line': Power and Authority in Contemporary Women's Fiction," 1989)

A note in Janice Radway's study of romance readers tells us that she has learned of at least five other groups in the United States similar to the one she studied, and that "if these groups are widely relied upon to mediate the mass-production publishing process by individual selection, then a good deal of speculation about the meaning of mass-produced literature based on the 'mass-man' hypothesis will have to be reviewed and possibly rewritten" (1991:249). Re-vision of the romance as mass culture and of the romance reader as "mass-man" is long overdue, since there are countless groups of women engaged in constructing the romance text. Over two-thirds of Harlequin readers in Margaret Ann Jensen's study had been introduced to the genre by established readers, and many maintained friendships in which exchanging, discussing, or shopping for romance novels played an instrumental role (1984:144-145). Jensen found that the novels "furnish people with a common experience that forms a bond" (1984:144-145) often transcending social or cultural differences, or strengthening intergenerational bonds between female family members. (See also Christian-Smith 1990:103.)

These informal readers' groups are found wherever women are: Jensen (1984) found women sharing books and opinions in homes and neighborhoods, Linda Christian-Smith (1990) studied schools, Kristin Ramsdell (1987:16) praises romance reader groups in libraries, and Radway (1991:249) mentions that co-workers create informal romance networks. The most visible type of reader group, though, is centered around new or used bookstores specializing in romance novels. Informal romance reader groups have probably been common for at least as long as the romance has been popular: since the romance has always suffered public derision, it is unlikely that so many women from so many different backgrounds would have begun or continued reading romances if their interests had not been awakened and nurtured by female friends and family. The industry boom that gained force in the 1970s has made these groups known to one another and given them the sense of belonging to a larger community. As with more explicitly feminist groups, the sense of a sisterhood that reached beyond their immediate circles helped many romance readers to define and assert themselves as women and readers, and to form and draw strength from local groups. A formal national network, mirroring and enhancing the support women's circles shared spontaneously, is relatively recent. Romance Writers of America and *Romantic Times* magazine, founded in 1980 and 1981 respectively, represented the first organized efforts to promote a sense of broad community, both actual and virtual, among romance authors and readers. Overwhelming response to both efforts demonstrates that many women felt, as described in a recent letter to *Romantic Times*, that they had found their family.

Romantic Times, the first publication to review romance novels, began as a bimonthly newsletter quartered in a walk-in closet. Within a year, creator Kathryn Falk had 12,000 subscribers, was selling 50,000 copies of each issue printed, and had received "stacks of letters from women who wanted to join the staff" (Falk 1989:10; Jensen 1984:68). The publication now offers a number of services for fans and authors, including manuscript evaluation, celebratory and educational events, a bed-and-breakfast inn, and an informal hotline, all of which facilitate identification and blend categorical divisions between groups. Published authors regularly write features in the form of chatty letters telling how they started, giving writing tips, or describing the evolution of a recently written book in terms which invite the reader to identify with and perhaps to join this fellowship of creative professional women, most of whom began as romance fans. Readers are almost invariably invited to write to authors, and while many writers have stopped giving their home addresses, those who do not answer their mail are labelled "prima donnas" (Falk 1989:301). In the magazine, homey, amateurish group-photos published on newsprint provide a striking and, one suspects, intentionally witty contrast to vividly stylized high-gloss "centerfolds" of romance book covers. This playful contrast of glamour and homeyness is common to women in the romance community: Radway (1991) found that readers usually discussed both the act of reading and the romance plot in the context of their own lives. Even the word "escape," so often used by readers to describe romance reading, indicates that an overlapping awareness of text and reading context are an essential part of the romance reading experience. As a further example of play and contrast, the 1990 Booklovers conference offered women a choice between attending a costume ball and a slumber party, though participants played with these boundaries as well, staging raids on one another's events. Letters to *Romantic Times* portray in-store slumber parties, breakfast clubs, and other groups, usually formed under the auspices of a member of "Bookstores That Care," a network of independent stores.

The "Bookstores That Care" (BTC) motto recalls the romance community's weariness of the condescension they receive from the general public, and echoes what they find positive in their own community: "Booklovers are equal. No author is better than her readers or booksellers. No reader is better than her authors or booksellers. No bookseller is better than her readers or authors. We fight for what's write." This ideal was taken seriously by the bookstore owners Clover spoke with, who are proud of having achieved success on their own terms. Surrounded by the books they love, they described the responsibility they felt for knowing both a very prolific genre and a wide variety of readers, and spoke of providing a supportive environment for women's interests. Perhaps because BTC owners had chosen to make personal interactions central to their lives, they were extremely articulate about the role of romance novels in women's friendships.

Owners of a bookstore in South Carolina that regularly encourages book swaps, parties, and discussions said that romance plots are often used by readers as a framework to discuss issues that might otherwise seem too controversial or too personal. Not surprisingly, these issues often—though not always—were directly related to expectations and negotiations of gender. They talked about the soul-searching that had been inspired by a romance plot in which a woman who had always been the responsible member of her family had unexpectedly rebelled, plots about women healing themselves after abuse, and plots depicting unconventional relationships. They also described heartfelt discussions which had been brought to life under the mantle of fiction. Even negative scenarios were used in positive ways by these romance fans, who sometimes used fictional examples to discuss self-destructive patterns of thought or behavior with fellow readers who might otherwise resent the intrusion. And while some women dislike reading about objectionable heroes, other readers relish the adversarial relationship they invoke. One woman said that she dislikes books which she feels degrade women but that, "I kind of like it, though, when the guy starts out cold or a jerk, because I think, 'yeah, you'll get yours, buddy.' And then I can't wait to read it." One of Radway's informants, who said that when a book upset her, she could not put it down but instead had to "read [her] way out," may have been referring to a similar desire for resolution (1991:71). Tolerance of this adversarial relation varies from reader to reader just as tastes do. But by responding to the novels, they are responding to their own lives and convictions; and in discussing them, these women share a unique and special form of intimacy.

Finally, the Romance Writers' of America (RWA) and other romance writers' organizations, though more guild-like than less formal groups, provide another component in the construction of community among romance fans. From the beginning, RWA has rallied members to the defense of their genre as a valid form of women's literature, and has concerned itself with improving author's rights in contract negotiations (Rabine 1985:183). Several authors told Margaret Ann Jensen that they had come to identify themselves as feminists through the experience of writing and publishing romances, and that one of the first things many successful writers do with their money is to build a room of their own to work in and retreat to (1984:72). Even the many members of RWA who have not yet published learn to claim time for themselves, to use criticism constructively, and to persist in the face of rejection. Jensen has called romance writers a rare "Horatio Alger" figure for women—a goal which does not depend on "marrying up the social ladder," and which "features 'ordinary women' . . . and 'just housewives' who work their way to the top by their own imagination, market savvy and self discipline" (1984:71). The romance author's image also reinforces cooperation among women, not a common model of success in most other fields.

Just as Radway suggested that reader groups challenge theories which consider mass-media an impersonal influence, Leslie Rabine calls the RWA a "crack" in what she considers an otherwise dehumanizing "mass-marketing machine" (Radway 1991; Rabine 1985:185). Because of the fluid division between readers and authors, and between face-to-face and media interactions, the romance community also creates a convergence of the interpretive community described by Stanley Fish (1980) and the virtual fellowship of Thomas

Roberts (1990). Women at the Booklovers conference attributed the differences between interpretive models and the reality of the romance community to gender: Most models, whether of reading, mass market relationships, or group behavior, are patterned after male ideals and responses, they pointed out, and men tend to build hierarchies of influence. Several women compared their event with other types of conferences or literary events from other genres, pointing out differences in interaction and ideological patterns, and attributing these to gender differences. Others noted that for them, a shared feeling of "safety in numbers," and of release from marginalization contributed to a heightened sense of community. Asked about the reasons for that marginalization, authors and other readers talked about sexism and a good deal more.

Writing Women: The Romance Writers of America 1992 Spring Conference

> Fie, fie upon her!
> There's language in her eye, her cheek, her lip,
> Nay, her foot speaks; her wanton spirits look out
> At every joint and motive of her body.
> —William Shakespeare (*Troilus and Cressida*)

> The good ended happily and the bad unhappily. That is what Fiction means.
> —Oscar Wilde (*The Importance of Being Earnest*)

The Indiana Chapter of the Romance Writers of America held its spring conference on May 2, 1992 at the Ramada Inn South in Indianapolis. The event was relatively small, particularly in comparison with the conference sponsored by the national affiliate, with probably no more than several hundred women (and a few men) in attendance. Featured speakers were predominantly published romance writers, but also included one editor and one literary agent. Chapter members included writers as well as enthusiastic readers, many of whom planned to write or were in the process of writing a romance novel of their own. The purpose of the conference, as stated in its promotional brochure, was "to supply the aspiring writer with information that will help sell that first manuscript, and to support and promote our published authors."

Because of the relatively low cost and easy access of Indianapolis to most parts of the state, many women were able to attend this conference who would have been unable to afford the time or money required for the national event. The participants included professional women and urban housewives, factory workers and farm dwellers. Thus Jean was able to interview a very eclectic group of people who had gotten together for the express purpose of discussing romance novels. She conducted both formal interviews set up by the conference organizers and more informal discussions in the hotel lounge. The formal interviews were one-on-one discussions with women who were professionals in the field of romance fiction. The informal interviews, with both individuals and groups, included enthusiastic readers and aspiring authors as well as published writers. Each interview situation had its advantages; individual interviews allowed Jean to explore one person's views in some depth, while group interviews enabled her to hear many different viewpoints on the same topic.

Despite the diverse and eclectic backgrounds of these informants, they had certain things in common—including a fondness for romance fiction and a desire to defend this genre against constant slights and denigration. Early questions about why the women enjoyed romance novels were not perceived as neutral, although they were intended as such. Very quickly, the negative image of the romance novel, and by implication, the romance writer and reader, emerged as a common concern.

Like the women we interviewed, we were familiar with the enormous amount of disapproval that the genre excites. When we told friends and colleagues about our research on romance novels, they responded with the kind of raised eyebrows and derisive chuckles that might accompany disclosure of some sub rosa activity. Scholars of romance fiction spend a good deal of time defending their choice of topic or distancing themselves from the genre by treating it with one of the three attitudes identified by Tania Modleski: "dismissiveness; hostility—tending unfortunately to be aimed at the consumers of the narratives; or most frequently, a flippant kind of mockery" (1990:14). The women we interviewed encountered similar denigration as a part of their daily lives. These women—both professional writers of romance novels and fans—were eager to defend either their chosen profession or their preferred genre of fiction. They were also eager to discuss the reasons they felt stood behind these criticisms and the reasons they did not accept the criticisms as valid.

Because of this continual need to defend one's profession or hobby, romance readers are a highly reflexive group and are unusually articulate about their activities. As every fieldworker knows, most people do not spend a great deal of time meditating upon their actions; romance readers, however, are forced to do so. In his study of the nude in art, John Berger remarked, "Men look at women. Women watch themselves being looked at" (1973:47). Similarly, romance readers are forced not only to examine and defend their daily actions, but to view themselves through the eyes of others. Because of the scorn and disapproval that this genre evokes, romance readers must develop sophisticated rationales for their literary choices and simultaneously must fight against the negative perception of the romance reader that exists both in the academy and in the general public. In defending romance novels, they end up defending—and to some degree, defining—themselves.

All the women to whom we spoke had encountered people who denigrated the genre. The objections they encountered seemed to come from two opposing and seemingly contradictory sources—romance detractors trivialize the novels, yet simultaneously view them as far more serious than do the romance readers themselves. These two points of view are also common in the scholarly community, as is shown in the following comments by Tania Modleski and Tom Henighan. In 1982, Modleski noted that: "Although Harlequin romances, gothic novels, and soap operas provide mass(ive) entertainment for countless numbers of women of varying ages, classes, and even educational backgrounds, very few critics have taken them seriously enough to study them in any detail" (1990:11). Yet Henighan, an English professor at Carleton University, said in a radio interview in 1984: "[I]f I became dictator, God forbid, maybe the first thing I would do would be to ban Harlequin romances and burn down the factory that makes them, and society would be much better thereby, because women would have to go out and face reality instead of reading those fantasies" (quoted in Thurston 1987:114). Romance novels are too unimportant to be studied by critics of popular culture, yet powerful enough to divorce women from reality and cause an English-professor-turned-demagogue to make their destruction the primary act of his reign.

Romance devotees, on the other hand, claim a more moderate course for the novels. Virtually all of the women who were interviewed cited entertainment, escape, or relaxation as the primary function of the romance novel. This is consistent with the findings of Radway (1991 [1984]) and Thurston (1987). One woman Jean interviewed, a romance writer with degrees in English and psychology, was interested in women's political issues and was used to reading "literary-type work" and nonfiction. When she had children, however, she "just wanted to pick up something to relax at the end of the day . . . They're books by women, for women, and that's what appealed to me." She explained that romances appeal to many women because "They're escape books, because they're light reads, they're fast reads, they get through them, they leave the reader with an upbeat feeling." She did not abandon her interest in women's issues, but placed them in her books: "I . . . take on causes or issues relevant to women. Problems of our time, so to speak." In other words, relaxation and escape need not constitute a denial of everyday life.

On the other hand, many women value romances because they do offer a break from quotidian activities. Another woman, an avid reader who plans to write romances in the future, said: "It's my escape, my fantasy, my way to relax. I can be somebody else, somewhere else, doing something more interesting than what I'm currently doing." Not surprisingly, she prefers the intrigue and suspense romances, with their hint of the extraordinary. She has published articles and would like to write an intrigue of her own, but with five children, a full-time factory job, and a farm that she and her husband run, she knows that this goal must wait a few years. In the meantime, she reads novels, discusses them with her mother and eldest daughter, and learns as much as she can at events such as the Indianapolis meeting of RWA.

It soon became apparent that romance readers are neither helpless dupes who hide from life behind a screen of romance novels nor benighted fools who confuse fantasy with reality. To the contrary, they are busy women with full lives who use romances for specific purposes and, in the process, support a huge industry dominated by women.[9] If particular romances do not please a reader, she will not recommend them to her friends—and personal evaluations are extremely important to romance readers (see also Radway 1991). One woman said that if she didn't like the way a romance ended, she would rewrite it to suit herself. An avid reader for many years, she had won third place in a romance writing contest and then sent a query letter to Harlequin. The query letter elicited a request for a manuscript, and, despite the demands of a full-time job in a large urban hospital, graduate courses in journalism, two children, and a husband, she managed to turn out a manuscript in six weeks. Though the manuscript was rejected, rejection is common for a writer's first book, and the writer is currently planning revisions. But she admits that her husband, while helpful and supportive, does not take her romance writing very seriously. She is very aware of the double vision that a romance writer or reader must apply—that of seeing oneself through one's own eyes and through the eyes of a mocking public. She says:

> Even though I love to read romance, I find myself, you know, kind of like hiding the cover when you're out in the doctor's office so they don't see that you're reading a romance. . . . [I]t's kind of double-edged . . . I can see both sides of it . . . there's that lower-down perception of romance.

When asked why she thought people had this negative perception, she answered without hesitation, "Well, I think our society values men more. And so the books that women write and the books that women read are valued less."

In 1949, Margaret Mead wrote:

> In every known society, the male's need for achievement can be recognized. Men may cook, or weave, or dress dolls or hunt hummingbirds, but if such activities are appropriate occupations of men, then the whole society, men and women alike, vote them as important. When the same occupations are performed by women, they are regarded as less important. (quoted in Rosaldo and Lamphere 1974:xiii)

While romance readers would agree that their society celebrates the activities of men and denigrates the activities of women, they would not agree that "the whole society, men and women alike" share in this valuation. To the contrary, they fight for equal respect for women's activities and consider the valuation of men's work at the expense of women's to be an unfair and inaccurate double standard. Another romance writer—a tall, strikingly articulate woman who holds a Master's degree in library science—explored this point in some detail by comparing romance novels with other forms of popular fiction. In her remarks, we see how romance fiction has been both belittled and considered slightly dangerous:

> There is no difference between the romance genre and the mystery genre and the science fiction genre. There is good in it, there is bad in it, but there is good science fiction and there is crappy science fiction, and we all know this. It's been said that romance is stigmatized because it really is women's fiction and the fact that it's women's fiction causes people to sneer at it. . . . You know, frequently a hostile reaction is born out of a sense that you're threatened.

Why should people feel threatened by a genre they consider trivial, frivolous, and even stupid? She suggested, somewhat hesitantly, that perhaps men feel that they cannot measure up to the standards set by heroes in romance fiction. Though romance readers do not expect their husbands or lovers to behave like romance heroes and in fact make clear that part of the genre's appeal is its ability to provide an escape from reality, we can see why a genre that celebrates female pleasure and depicts sexuality from the female point of view could be construed as threatening. Carol Thurston points out that modern erotic romance novels constitute "the first large and autonomous body of sexual writing by women addressed to the feminine experience" (1987:10). Several of the women studied by Thurston report that romance novels encouraged them to behave in a more assertive manner and to seek a more imaginative, active sexual role (1987:133-134). Similarly, Radway (1991) and Christian-Smith (1990) reported that women and girls seek independence and equality in many areas after reading about the spunky, intelligent heroines of romance novels. Though romance novels certainly suggest that a woman's place is with a man, they also suggest that this place should become one of sharing, trust, and mutual respect. (It is an open question whether this vision challenges or validates the existing patriarchal order.)

The taint of salaciousness, which may be tied to the fear of women's "ungovernable" sexuality, nevertheless clings mightily to the public image of romance novels—the chaste Harlequins as well as the descriptively erotic "bodice-rippers." One reason, cited by readers, writers, and an editor, may be the cover art that publishing houses choose for romance novels. The covers of bodice-rippers are especially lurid; they usually depict a voluptuous, skimpily-clad woman clutching a sun-tanned, muscular, and often shirtless man. Some readers and writers dislike and are embarrassed by the covers, which they feel misrepresent the genre by stressing sexuality rather than the emotional and narrative elements of the novel. One writer, after expressing her disgust with the covers, said, "It's not just a story about the sweaty clinch. It's a story about the emotional development of a relationship." Many readers and writers would prefer covers adorned with flowers or scenes from the novel, but few romance authors have enough clout to choose their own cover art. Writers and readers know that the salacious covers reflect badly on those who are associated with them; a less erotic, more mainstream cover would protect the reputations of those who read and write the books.[10]

Another woman, a high-school teacher from a large midwestern city and a writer of historical romances, told of a time when she was considered dangerous and polluting because of her identity as a romance writer. An article about her writing had appeared in a local paper, and the parent of one of her students read it. The parent became enraged, contacted the school board, and demanded that the writer be fired—a woman who wrote "trashy" fiction was not considered fit to educate young minds. (Her students, on the other hand, had a new-found respect for her, asked questions about sex and relationships that they were afraid to ask their parents, and started paying attention in class.) When I asked the writer for her own interpretation of the negative image of romance novels, she said, "People sneer at romance because romance touches the heart, and we live in a country where we are based on Puritanism. . . . [But] we don't write sex; we write love stories." For her, as for many romance readers, romance novels are primarily about the emotional component of a sexual relationship—not about the physical act itself. Similarly, Radway's definition of the romance, gleaned from her interviews, stresses emotionality as its fundamental aspect: "To qualify as a romance, the story must chronicle not merely the events of a courtship but what it feels like to be the object of one" (1991:64). Perhaps romances are threatening because they stress the emotional closeness that female sexuality often demands.

A highly successful romance writer, with several best-sellers to her credit, discussed the criticism of romance novels in the following terms:

> It's rather irksome, because men have never had to justify or explain why they like reading Westerns or spy stories or adventure novels, but for some reason a woman has to justify why she would read a romance novel. It's like it's an indication of some kind of deficiency in her make-up, when actually, such is not the case at all. The reason that I write them and the reason that the audience reads them is for entertainment. And that's it. Period.

The implication is clear—romance reading is a leisure-time activity, not the primary purpose of a woman's life. Women who read romance novels also hold down jobs, care for families, participate in volunteer work and a host of other activities, just as a man who watches a football game will eventually get off the couch and do something else. Popular culture studies alerted us to the importance of studying leisure-time activities but should not lead us to believe that there is nothing else in life. Romance novels are so badly stigmatized because they bear a double onus—they are women's work and they are popular culture.

In a way, the denigration of romance fiction—and the concomitant defensiveness on the part of romance scholars and readers—is common to popular culture studies in general. In the face of a contemptuous or unresponsive academy, popular culture theorists came up with an important truth: a cultural product need not be considered artistically great in order to be socially important. Popular culture studies also made us realize that standards of artistic greatness are historically and culturally constructed; these standards are born, not in some Platonic vacuum, but in economic and social relations of dominance. Stuart Hall writes:

> [T]he structuring principle of 'the popular' . . . is the tensions and oppositions between what belongs to the central domain of elite or dominant culture, and the culture of the 'periphery' . . . . For, from

> period to period, the *contents* of each category changes. Popular forms become enhanced in cultural value, go up the cultural escalator—and find themselves on the opposite side. Other things cease to have high cultural value, and are appropriated into the popular, becoming transformed in the process. (1981:234)

Taste, then, is a highly fluid set of standards linked neither to morality, religion, politics, nor law; it is simply a set of culturally-determined rules of aesthetic worth. That these rules are arbitrary does not make them invalid, but it should alert us to their historical embeddedness (as noted by Hall) as well as to their class implications.

Pierre Bourdieu concluded, after massive ethnographic research, that taste is not a "gift of nature" (1984:1), but the result of exposure and instruction in the family and in schools. Taste is a matter of training one's preferences to coincide with those sanctioned (though not necessarily enjoyed) by the ruling classes of a particular culture during a particular historical period. This recognition of the contextuality of taste does not allow us to dismiss it, for all things are contextually anchored. We can still appreciate that some things are done well and others badly, but we cannot ignore or consider neutral the reasoning behind such aesthetic judgment. Bourdieu writes:

> Taste classifies, and it classifies the classifier. Social subjects, classified by their classifications, distinguish themselves by the distinctions they make, between the beautiful and the ugly, the distinguished and the vulgar, in which their position in the objective classifications is expressed or betrayed. (1984:6)

Perhaps the particularly vociferous attacks on romance fiction by female literary critics comes from a desire not to be classified with those women who read and enjoy the material.

Romance readers make distinctions as well; they have very sharply defined and articulated standards of taste. Some novels were heartily recommended to us; others were condemned for a variety of reasons. Romance readers dislike poorly written material and are particularly contemptuous of sloppy and inaccurate books that seem to talk down to them. One of Radway's informants expressed this common sentiment well: "[T]here are well-written books and poorly written books in any group of any kind of reading and we can sift out what we think are the drivel" (1991:115). Another of Radway's informants commented that, "I am whatever is going on in the story. . . . I resent characters in books that are absolutely too naive to be believable, because that way I feel the . . . writer is putting me down" (1991:159). It is also important to remember that the artistic standards held by the romance devotee may not be the same ones held by the scholar. Radway was clearly surprised when her informants discussed "good" and "bad" writing in terms of plot and character, rather than in terms of ingenious or exceptional wording:

> [To Radway's informants], success in writing has nothing to do with elegant phrasing or the quality of perception but is a function of the uniqueness of the characters and events intended by the most familiar of linguistic signs. . . . No matter how often I asked readers to clarify the difference between a well-written book and a poorly written one, I always received an answer dealing with the exceptional nature of a plot or the likeable personality of the heroine or the hero. (1991:189-190)

Thus Radway and her informants express their appreciation of good writing in terms of two somewhat different literary codes.[11]

In terms of content, romance readers have been responsible for a very substantial change—the elimination of rape from the bodice-rippers. In the early 1970s, several romances told the story of a woman who eventually falls in love with a man who has raped her. The rape sagas received such negative response from women readers (and a great many angry letters to publishers) that now most publishers will no longer allow rape to be portrayed as a precursor to romance. An editor from Silhouette said that the romanticized rape is now "totally unacceptable" to her house, and that she hopes that most publishing houses feel the same way. If rape is portrayed, it must be depicted as a violent crime, and the heroine never falls in love with the rapist. Far from passively accepting whatever romance publishers churn out, romance readers were responsible for a profound ideological change.

In listening to the romance writers' and readers' own images of themselves, as opposed to the images drawn by the academy and the general public, one contradiction was particularly striking. Romance readers are expected to be simple-minded ("They expect you to be an idiot!" one romance writer said indignantly); yet, the women to whom we spoke (and the women in Radway's study) consistently portrayed themselves as *readers*, that is, as people involved in an intellectual activity. Most of our informants stressed that romances were not the only books that they read, that they were "always reading something." One woman, a romance writer and former teacher who has many friends in the academic community, said:

> You don't always feel like reading classics, you don't always feel like reading a "worthy" book, an academic book. I mean, I do that, too. But I don't always do. I read mysteries, too, and when I pick up a mystery, I'll pick it up for a particular experience. So I think for any reader, each kind of book you pick up, you pick up for a particular reading experience.

In other words, romance readers do not consider most romance novels "great literature," but they do consider them part and parcel of a generalized intellectualism and a general love of books; even their leisure activities involve reading. One of Radway's informants told her: "The TV doesn't really have that much to offer—nothing that's intellectually stimulating—I mean—at least you learn something when you're reading books" (1991:108). (Consider the professions of some of the women we interviewed: teacher, librarian, writer, editor. All these are traditional careers for female intellectuals.) The women in Radway's study delighted in the historical and geographical knowledge they could glean from romances and were quick to dissociate themselves from housewives who watch soap operas (1991:115). Romance novels emerge as a very curious entity: a form of popular culture slighted by popular culture theorists, a form of women's literature decried by female literary critics, a kind of book mocked by intellectuals.

We do not mean to make any overblown claims for romance novels, nor do we suggest that they are always ideologically pleasing. To the contrary, we find the assumptions in many romance novels disturbing and regressive: the notion that a person is incomplete without a dyadic sexual relationship, for example, or the idea that abortion is immoral. Yet there are ideologically unsettling aspects of virtually every genre, including the works we consider great literature; there is sexism in Wordsworth, anti-Semitism in Dickens, anti-Catholicism in Charlotte Brontë. We must explore and condemn the aspects that are vicious and harmful in any cultural form and any leisure activity, but to ignore or condemn an entire genre because it is flawed is to deny both its merits and its potential for change. As we have seen, romance novels can and do change; and there is no telling how they may change in the future.

Jane Austen's novel *Northanger Abbey* is generally considered a satire on the Gothic novels of her day. While there are many satiric elements in the book, it is well to remember that her sharpest arrows were focussed at those who confuse fiction with everyday life. The naive and immature Catherine Morland expects life to read like a Gothic novel, while the sensible and intelligent Tilneys read Gothics with equal enjoyment, but expect their own stories to be quite different. *Northanger Abbey* is, in fact, one of the most passionate defenses of popular literature *in* popular literature, a nineteenth-century example of the reflexivity and marginalization also common in contemporary women's fiction. Austen, the consummate storyteller, breaks off her narrative for nearly one-and-a-half pages to defend her art:

> Although our productions have afforded more extensive and unaffected pleasure than those of any other literary corporation in the world, no species of composition has been so much decried. From pride, ignorance, or fashion, our foes are almost as many as our readers. . . . [T]here seems almost a general wish of decrying the capacity and undervaluing the labour of the novelist, and of slighting the performances which have only genius, wit, and taste to recommend them. (1972:58)

As Modleski points out, Austen's novels remain the prototype for the domestic romances of today (1990:15, 36). While none of the romance novels that we read contain Austen's greatness, there is no telling what we have missed and what the future might bring.

Concluding Remarks

> Women and fiction might mean, and you may have meant it to mean, women and what they are like; or it might mean women and the fiction that they write; or it might mean women and what is written about them; or it might mean that somehow all three are inextricably mixed together and you want me to consider them in that light. But when I began to consider the subject in this last way,

> which seemed the most interesting, I soon saw that it had one fatal drawback. I should never be able to come to a conclusion.
> —Virginia Woolf (*A Room of One's Own*)

The romance is women's writing, but it is not *all* women's writing. Romance enthusiasts describe the genre's aesthetics and effects in terms very similar to those feminist theorists use to hypothesize an *écriture feminine*—it is a women's genre, a language between women. It is sensual and introspective, private and communal, articulating the divided self from within and eschewing an aesthetic of transcendence from (or ascendance within) this heterogeneity. The genre is about differences of (through, among) identity, sexuality, and language. The longing for a women's language entails a longing for communication among women and specific to women. And the romance has provided many women with a vehicle for both self-expression and community. For every criticism of the romance and every theory about its harmful effects, there are defenses and testimonies from women whose lives have been bettered by the genre. If, in spite of all this, the romance novel still cannot be considered a prescription for liberation and enlightenment, this is because reader response cannot be pre-scripted: despite the definite article, *l'écriture feminine* will not be singular or definite because women are neither singular nor static.

Many feminists today believe that the process of negotiation, the polyvocality that Rita Felski has dubbed the "feminist counter-public sphere," best expresses the female subject (see, for example, Berg and Larsen 1989:xiii; Rabine 1985:13). Just as feminist scholars have used concern about romantic ideals to examine their own theories of gender, members of romance communities have used discussion and authorship of romance novels to create an analogous forum to express and negotiate contradictions embodied in female experience. As in the women's movement more generally, the romance cuts across other lines of affiliation among readers, creating a space for dialogue among them. Since romance fans and more explicitly feminist groups use their forums to discuss similar concerns, rifts between them may not indicate irreconcilable ideologies but differences in expressive and responsive style. In learning to recognize these differences in dialect, we may hope to create another "feminist counter-public sphere" for an interchange of common concerns.

Notes

We would both like to thank the many women at the Indiana Chapter of the Romance Writers of America spring conference in Indianapolis, the 10th Annual Booklovers Convention in Savannah, Bookstores That Care, and *Romantic Times* magazine who gave us their time, ideas, and patience. Special thanks from Clover to Tommye Ring Morton, Shirl Henke, Cathy Hatfield and Sharon Monheit, Chistina Skye, and Kathe Robin. Special thanks from Jean to Lynn Turner, Lucy Hamilton, Jennifer Greene, Allison Knight, Lindsay Longford, Melissa Senate, Sandra Brown, Lori Kring, and Pam Durant for taking the time to talk in Indianapolis, and to Michelle Branigan for help with fieldwork.

1. Louise Rosenblatt rarely receives more than passing reference in works of reader-response theory despite her pioneering and influence in this field. Those interested in reading more about her are referred to a collection of essays entitled *The Experience of Reading: Louise Rosenblatt and Reader-Response Theory*, edited by John Clifford, 1991.

2. All of these statistics can also be found in Williams (in press). Findings often vary somewhat from study to study according to when and where they were conducted, and to what was included under "romance."

3. Mann reported one difference between the average Mills and Boon (a major British publisher of romance novels, similar to Harlequin) reader and the British female population generally: Almost half of the readers surveyed were between twenty-five and forty compared with only one third of the adult women in Britain. This, he points out, dispels stereotypes that readers are either "young factory girls or aged spinsters" (1974:3-4; 1981:13), though Mann's studies have been challenged by Scottish scholar Bridget Fowler (1991), who suggests that he is "massaging" his figures when he claims, for example, that a "fair number of reasonably well-educated women" read the romance. The disagreement, however, seems to be over what can be understood by phrases such as "reasonably well-educated," or "fair number" (and others like "semi-professional") and thus remains moot. See Mann 1974, 1981; and Fowler 1991:216-17.

4. Thurston reports that among romance readers studied in 1982, 31% had had between one and three years of college, and 16.3% held a university degree. This compares with 32% and 16.2% respectively for women generally. This seems to be a conservative estimate, since she mentions one other report claiming that 40% of romance readers are college-educated (1987:135). Of the romance readers who held degrees, 36.3% had earned graduate degrees.

5. Gardiner (1982) follows Chodorow in locating this shifting identification in the mother-daughter relationship. Though we prefer to leave the question of origin open, her theory that women's literature is rich with the ambiguities of female identity seems both reasonable and productive.

6. This objection, also voiced by Bridget Fowler (1991), that by expressing women's dissatisfaction with existing gender relations the romance diffuses protest, thereby reproducing and re-enforcing the structure of dominance, has been raised obliquely about some feminist cultural critique. In an essay on feminist discourse, Jean Bethke Elshtain worries that many descriptive critiques of sexism may "embrace the terms of their own degradation" and asks rhetorically what the effects of internalizing this

view of gender might be (1982:132). If the romance is different than descriptive critique, or even fictionalized "agitation propaganda," it is so only because of the reader's interpretive context. Two assumptions most common to critiques of popular culture—that fiction is either imitated without critical interpretation or that fiction displaces imitative behavior—are not mutually exclusive: these and other modes of reading depend upon the reader. In order to either imitate fiction even subconsciously, or to use it vicariously, the reader must already have made an interpretation of what is being portrayed.

7. There are some gay and lesbian romance novels, and these also negotiate miscommunications between principle characters, problems still largely attributable to internalized structures of sexism and heterosexism.

8. With the exception of Peter Mann's 1981 assurance that Mills and Boon authors at that time were all women, we found no published figures on the percentage of published male romance writers (1981:14). Because of reader preferences, male authors write under female pen names, and while a few have made their gender public others remain hidden because of preference or publishers' contracts. Silhouette Books, for example, protects their sales with the stipulation that male authors keep their identities secret. Tom Huff (who writes romances as Jennifer Wilde) believes that 40% of romance writers are women, though his basis for this estimate is not given and this figure is certainly not reflected in the demographics of romance writers' organizations. Not all romance editors carry male authors, but a few who do report figures roughly between 3% and 20%. The above information is from Guiley 1983:236.

9. As of 1984, when Margaret Ann Jensen's study of Harlequin romance was published, there had never been a woman on Harlequin's board of directors, and only one woman worked at management level in the corporate office. The more diverse Harlequin-Torstar parent conglomerate is little better: of five women in upper-management positions, three have "direct family ownership connections" and the other two had already been in position when their company was acquired by Torstar. But while upper-management theoretically has the final say on publishing policy, in practice key editorial decisions about what and whom to publish are usually handled by editors and other "gatekeeper positions" held by women. It was a woman at Harlequin, Mary Bonnycastle, who first chose to publish romances. A woman, Nancy Coffey at Avon, launched the "bodice-ripper" erotic historical romance, a major departure from previous categories. And *Romantic Times* and other review magazines are run by women whose opinions affect sales more strongly than any publisher can afford to ignore.

10. Some women find the covers "fun," and useful in decoding (from postures and other cues) the degree of sexuality to expect from a prospective book buy. But some also claim that, ironically, the most lurid covers are designed to appeal to the men who serve as buyers for large book chains and distributors. "They're all men. It's the middle-men selling to each other," laughed Kathe Robin, romance reviewer for *Romantic Times*. "They see the breasts, you know, the thighs. Oh, they like that, they *like* that!" (personal communication).

11. Radway's interpretation of the romance reader's taste has been criticized. Many enthusiasts at the Savannah conference (some of whom referred explicitly to Radway's study) told Clover that they care very much about eloquence in both wording and structure. Though both oral commentary and formal reviews of romances focus on plot, they also address writing style. In his discussion of genre fiction generally, Thomas

J. Roberts discusses Radway's conclusion about readers' tastes, countering that, "Even the people who come to [genre fiction] from a learned bookscape talk . . . as though they were only dimly aware of the words themselves, as though they were affected only by the stories they saw through those words. They do not read that simply, though. If they did, they would not be admiring the books and writers they do admire" (1990:205-207). Nor is it a simple matter to write text that appears, as Radway puts it, "a transparent window opening out onto an already existent world" (1991:189). Roberts also points out that although many readers have not been taught a style of commentary adequate to convince genre "allergics" of the richness of their reading experience, this does not mean they are insensitive readers (1990:205-206).

References

Barnhart, Hellene Schellenberg. 1983. *Writing Romance Fiction for Love and Money*. Cincinnati: Writer's Digest Books.

de Beauvoir, Simone. 1989 [1949]. *The Second Sex*. Editor and translator, H.M. Parshley. New York: Vintage Books.

Berg, Temma and Jeanne Larsen. 1989. Introduction. In *Engendering the Word: Feminist Essays in Psychosexual Poetics*, ed. Temma Berg, Anna Shannon Elfenbein, Jeanne Larsen, and Elisa Kay Sparks, pp. xiii-xxv. Urbana and Chicago: University of Illinois Press.

Berger, John. 1973. *Ways of Seeing*. New York: Viking Press.

Bourdieu, Pierre. 1984. *Distinction: A Social Critique of the Judgement of Taste*. Translator, Richard Nice. Cambridge, Massachusetts: Harvard University Press.

Burack, Sylvia K, ed. 1983. *Writing and Selling the Romance Novel*. Boston: The Writer, Inc. Publishers.

Chadorow, Nancy. 1994. *Femininities, Masculinities, Sexualities: Freud and Beyond*. Lexington: University Press of Kentucky.

Christian-Smith, Linda K. 1990. *Becoming a Woman Through Romance*. New York: Routledge.

Clifford, John, ed. 1991. *The Experience of Reading: Louise Rosenblatt and Reader-Response Theory*. Portsmouth, NH: Boynton/Cook Publishers.

Douglas, Ann. 1980. Soft Porn Culture. *New Republic*. August 30:25-29.

Elshtain, Jean Bethke. 1982. Feminist Discourse and Its Discontents: Language, Power, and Meaning. In *Feminist Theory: A Critique of Ideology*, eds. Nannerl O. Keohane, Michelle Z. Rosaldo, and Barbara C. Gelpi, pp. 127-146. Chicago: University of Chicago Press.

Falk, Kathryn. 1989. *Romance Reader's Handbook*. Brooklyn Heights, NY: Romantic Times Books.

_____. 1990 [1983]. *How to Write a Romance and Get It Published*. Reprint with new introduction and statistics. New York: Signet Books.

Fish, Stanley. 1980. *Is There a Text in This Class? The Authority of Interpretive Communities*. Cambridge, Massachusetts: Harvard University Press.

Fowler, Bridget. 1991. *The Alienated Reader: Women and Romantic Literature in the Twentieth Century*. Hertfordshire: Harvester Wheatsheaf.
Gardiner, Judith Kegan. 1982. On Female Identity and Writing by Women. In *Writing and Sexual Difference*, ed. Elizabeth Abel, pp. 177-219. Chicago: University of Chicago Press.
Guiley, Rosemary. 1983. *Love Lines: A Romance Reader's Guide to Printed Pleasures*. New York: Facts on File Publications.
Hall, Stuart. 1981. Notes on Deconstructing "the Popular." In *People's History and Socialist Theory*, ed. Raphael Samuel, pp. 227-240. London: Routledge and Kegan Paul.
Jacobus, Mary. 1986. Men of Maxims and The Mill on the Floss. In *Reading Women: Essays in Feminist Criticism*, ed. Mary Jacobus, pp. 62-79. New York: Columbia University Press.
Jensen, Margaret Ann. 1984. *Love's Sweet Return: The Harlequin Story*. Toronto: The Women's Press.
Kristeva, Julia. 1982. Women's Time. In *Feminist Theory: A Critique of Ideology*, ed. Nannerl O. Keohane, Michelle Z. Rosaldo, and Barbara C. Gelpi, pp. 31-53. Chicago: University of Chicago Press.
Lowery, Marilyn M. 1983. *How to Write Romance Novels That Sell*. New York: Rawson Associates.
Mann, Peter H. 1974. *A New Survey: The Facts About Romance Fiction*. London: Mills and Boon.
_____. 1981. The Romantic Novel and Its Readers. *Journal of Popular Culture* 15(Spring):9-18.
Miller, Jean Baker. 1976. *Toward a New Psychology of Women*. Boston: Beacon Press.
Modleski, Tania. 1990 [1982]. *Loving With a Vengeance: Mass-Produced Fantasies for Women*. New York: Routledge.
Mussell, Kay. 1984. *Fantasy and Reconciliation: Contemporary Formulas of Women's Romance Fiction*. Contributions in Women's Studies 46. Westport, Connecticut: Greenwood Press.
Rabine, Leslie. 1985. *Reading the Romantic Heroine: Text, History, Ideology*. Ann Arbor: University of Michigan Press.
Radford, Jean. 1986. Introduction. In *The Progress of Romance: The Politics of Popular Fiction*, ed. Jean Radford. New York: Virgil Books.
Radway, Janice. 1991 [1984]. *Reading the Romance: Women, Patriarchy, and Popular Literature*. Reprint with new Introduction by the author. Chapel Hill: University of North Carolina Press.
Ramsdell, Kristin. 1987. *Happily Ever After: A Guide to Reading Interests in Romance Fiction*. Littleton, CO: Libraries Unlimited, Inc.
Roberts, Thomas J. 1990. *An Aesthetics of Junk Fiction*. Athens, Georgia: The University of Georgia Press.
Rodenas, Adriana Méndez. 1989. Tradition and Women's Writing: Towards a Poetics of Difference. In *Engendering the Word: Feminist Essays in Psychosexual Poetics*, ed. Temma F. Berg, Anna Shannon Elfenbein, Jeanne Larsen, and Elisa Kay Sparks, pp. 29-50. Urbana and Chicago: University of Illinois Press.

Rosaldo, Michelle Zimbalist and Louise Lamphere eds. 1974. *Woman, Culture, and Society*. Stanford: Stanford University Press.

Rosenblatt, Louise. 1938. *Literature as Exploration*. New York: Appleton-Century.

_____. 1978. *The Reader, the Text, the Poem: The Transactional Theory of Literary Work*. Carbondale, Illinois: Southern Illinois University Press.

Snitow, Ann Barr. 1979. Mass-market Romance: Pornography for Women is Different. *Radical History Review* 20 (Spring/Summer):141-161.

Stephens, Vivian. 1990 [1983]. Stimulating Sensuality. In *How to Write a Romance and Get it Published*, ed. Kathryn Falk, pp. 54-55. Reprint with new introduction and statistics. New York: Signet Books.

Thurston, Carol. 1987. *The Romance Revolution: Erotic Novels for Women and the Quest for a New Sexual Identity*. Urbana, Illinois: University of Illinois Press.

Weigel, Sigrid. 1986 [1985]. Double Focus: On the History of Women's Writing. In *Feminist Aesthetics*, ed. Gisela Ecker, pp. 59-80. Trans. Harriet Anderson. Boston: Beacon Press.

Williams, Clover Nolan. [in press]. Keepers of the Flame: The Romance Novel and its Fans. *Lore and Language*.

Novels Cited

Austen, Jane. 1972 [1818]. *Northanger Abbey*. Harmondsworth, Middlesex, England: Penguin Books.

Winspear, Violet. 1965. *Desert Doctor*. London: Mills and Boon Ltd.

9

Chuck Berry as Postmodern Composer-Performer

Peter Narváez

In pursuing tradition, folklorists accent the significance of repetitive expressive forms and the import of cultural continuity. While a knowledge of folklore is valuable in itself, such knowledge also enables a researcher to discern marked breaks from traditional behavioral patterns, i.e., dramatic cultural change. Thus, Neil V. Rosenberg has demonstrated that the tradition-based sound of bluegrass music, today an acknowledged "genre" of country music, was initiated by Bill Monroe's 1946-48 band (Rosenberg 1985:68-94). Without his knowledge of southern musical traditions, Rosenberg would not have been able to distinguish how innovative this "new" sound really was. Adopting such a folkloristic approach, this presentation will initially examine the artistic exploits of Chuck Berry by citing the role that tradition has played in his music culture. Against this backdrop, a sector of his tradition-based, innovative musical accomplishments will be highlighted; Chuck Berry will be interpreted as a musician-actor who has successfully synthesized specific musical influences into a variety of social roles for different audiences. Rather than viewing his achievements in terms of monolithic style (e.g., "the father of rock 'n' roll"), this analysis will contend that Berry's historic contribution is that, as a postmodern artist, he has been a master of the shifting imagery of method acting. The fact that he has convinced so many that he signifies so much is a testament to his understanding of traditional cultures and his artistic skill in successfully manipulating multifarious masks.

Chuck Berry and African-American Tradition

The threads of folklore that bind the musical achievements of Charles (a.k.a. "Chuck") Edward Anderson Berry (b. 1926) to the cloth of African-American tradition are many and varied. If one considers Chuck Berry's repertoire of songs as a compilation of lyrical–melodic "texts," one may interpret folk blues as being his most obvious traditional tie with African-American folklife (Blumenthal 1991). Like most blues performers, Berry has exhibited varying degrees of emulation and innovation in covering blues songs ("The Things I Used to Do" [Jones 1954]), developing and arranging blues songs ("I Want to Be Your Driver" [Minnie 1941]), and creating blues songs through the use of traditional lingual, thematic and musical formulas ("Wee Wee Hours" [Berry 1955b],"Have Mercy Judge" [Berry 1970]).

Whatever the mainsprings of his songs, however, Berry's musical understanding has been in keeping with the African-American idea that a song's value and meaning derives primarily from a singer's ability to communicate with an audience in performance rather than from an abstract conception of song as isolated lyrical and melodic text (Evans 1974; Evans 1985). While monetary rewards from song writing have been critical to Berry's financial success, ultimately song composition has been secondary to his performances of those songs, for it is through performance that he has won audiences. His belief in songs as means rather than end is illustrated in his forthright, specific citations of models for some of his "original" compositions. "Havana Moon," he maintains, is a re-write of Nat "King" Cole's "Calypso Blues," and his humorous song, "'Jo Jo Gunne,' ... was prepared in fact and phrase from a rather naughty but funny toast ['The Signifying Monkey'] I had heard back in the Algoa [Intermediate Reformatory for Young Men] days" (Berry 1987:161).

Orality and Originality

Any sense of collective creation a black performer may possess, however, necessarily alters when s/he encounters the capitalist values of the mass entertainment industries. A basic tenet of the music business is that lyrics, melodies, and arrangements constitute intellectual property. In his development as a businessman, therefore, Chuck Berry, after long and painful experiences of being economically exploited (Berry 1987:110, 189-90), has learned to protect himself and make sizable financial profits by establishing legal ownership (copyright, publishing rights) of "his" songs. In contrast to this professional necessity, he has recognized that traditional African-American song composition is a process characterized by a melding of conventional as well as innovative elements, many of which have been learned from others in the collective musical culture of one's upbringing and development. In face of the pressures of music critics who search for exact derivations of his music and confront him with linear, literacy-based "sound–as–property" arguments, however, Berry has occasionally judged himself from the European-American perspective of his interviewers as a purloining plagiarist. Thus, while explaining to interviewer Bill Flanagan that Carl Hogan, a guitarist for Louis Jordan, was the source of a guitar riff in "Johnny B. Goode," Berry maintained, "It all comes from somebody else. I've been stealing all these years, man" (Flanagan 1987: 85). This imposed, deprecatory view of self has been shared by other black performers in similar circumstances. Blues singer Big Bill Broonzy might well have felt "guilty" of intellectual "theft" during an interview conducted by Studs Terkel in 1956. Discussing the blues song "Keys to the Highway," Broonzy articulately explained the collective, formulaic nature of the composition and of blues in general.

> Some of the verses he [Charles Segar, pianist–singer] was singing it in the South the same as I sung it in the South. And practically all of blues is just a little change from the way that they was sung when I was a kid.... You take one song and make fifty out of it ... just change it a little bit. (Broonzy and Terkel 1960)

Despite this elucidating description of composition in an oral culture Terkel insisted on assigning proprietary rights to Broonzy, who finally accommodated the interviewer with a compromise in responding to a leading question.

> Terkel: This is your song though. You wrote this one.
> Broonzy: Yeah I wrote it, yeah. *In a way I'll say I wrote it* and Charlie Segar he was in it too. (Broonzy and Terkel 1960, my emphasis)

Intentionality and Folk Performance

But clearly Chuck Berry's recognized artistic achievements do not rest on such collective processes so much as on original genius. His reputation is not that of a great traditional blues artist; rather, he is considered a father of "rock 'n' roll." In this capacity can Chuck Berry be depicted as a neutral conduit in the manner W.T. Lhamon has portrayed Little Richard (Richard Penniman) and his relation to rock?

> Little Richard found rock in its social roots, which he cultivated. Rock was not his invention, Elvis's, or anyone else's. It was a hybridization of pop and folk seeds, for which Richard Penniman was a fruitful medium. (Lhamon 1985:7)

The problem with Lhamon's "performer-as-medium" argument is that it does an injustice to individual talents like Little Richard or Chuck Berry, for it interprets these artists in a simplistic, quasi-deterministic, *highly romantic*, "rock as folk art" manner. Thus, Carl Belz, the well-known advocate of this position, has described Berry as a "folk poet" for his resistance to self-consciousness and because of the ways in which his style "unconsciously expressed the responses of the artist and his audience to the ordinary realities of their world" (Belz 1972:62). Just as Berry's lyrics have represented "the folk artist's unconsciousness of art," Belz has maintained that Berry's guitar style "hardly changed" since "he never felt the need to keep up with stylistic innovations, ... he was never conscious of style itself" (Belz 1972:64-5).

It is unwittingly demeaning, ethnocentric and erroneous to view Chuck Berry simply as a neutral conduit of tradition or an unconscious, naive folk artist. While his artistry clearly draws from a well of musical traditions, it is remarkably unique, the product of a highly creative and very conscious intelligence. Attempts at discovering obvious antecedents to his musical style and his most popular songs inevitably end in frustration. As Tom Wheeler has observed, such research "unearth[s] scattered gems and nuggets, but no mother lode" (Wheeler 1988b:50-54).

What, then, is the nature of Chuck Berry's unique contribution, and what part, if any, has folk process played in his emergence as a father of "rock 'n' roll"? I will argue here that the answer to these queries lies in his union of two de-differentiating roles which blurred boundaries between racial cultures and age cultures. These roles may be viewed as instances of cultural syncretism, i.e., the fusion of similar cultural elements into new forms, but they may also be understood in terms of certain characteristics of postmodern social condition and aesthetic practice, i.e., the playful, promiscuous mixing of codes and styles, the lack of a self-centering identity, the merging of audience and artist, the collapse of cultural hierarchy, a celebration of the immediate and the ordinary, and an emphasis on visual, figurative rather than linear, literary sensibility (Dorst 1988; Featherstone 1988; Lash 1988; Dorst 1989; Workman 1989). The commonplace expectation of popular music audiences today is that celebrities such as Bob Dylan, David Bowie, Michael Jackson, and Madonna will occasionally change their images or "masks" because, like actors, these artists envision differing roles as possessing differing sets of aesthetic possibilities (see Frith 1989; Scobie 1991). The fifties were critical years in the development of such postmodern aesthetic techniques in popular music, and Chuck Berry was a pioneer in this respect.

The Merging of Racial Cultures: "Maybellene"

Beginning in 1951 during his days as the singer-guitarist in Sir John's Trio (later the Chuck Berry Trio) with Johnnie Johnson, piano, and Ebby Hardy, drums, at the Cosmopolitan Club in East St. Louis, Illinois, Chuck Berry cultivated a racially mixed adult audience through the development of a repertoire that juxtaposed blues and rhythm and blues hits alongside country music standards such as "Jambalaya," "Mountain Dew," and "Ida Red" ("favorites of the Cosmo audience" [Berry 1987:143]) and novelty numbers like Harry Belafonte's "Banana Boat Song" and "Jamaica Farewell" (Wheeler 1988a). Berry recalls that initially blacks queried, "Who is that black hillbilly at the Cosmo?" But "after they [the black customers] laughed at me a few times, they began requesting the hillbilly stuff and enjoyed trying to dance to it" (Berry 1987:89). Berry's performances also attracted European-Americans, Berry approximating that sometimes the crowds at the Cosmo were "nearly forty percent ... Caucasian" (Berry 1987:89-90). In juxtaposing songs from differing racial repertoires Berry consciously altered his performance styles. He sang the rhythm and blues trio styles of Charles Brown and Nat "King" Cole with "distinct diction." The influence of Muddy Waters "impelled" Berry "to deliver the down-home blues in the language they come from, Negro dialect" (Berry 1987:90). Finally, Berry recounts that

> When I played hillbilly songs, I stressed my diction so that it was harder and whiter. All in all it was my intention to hold both the black and the white clientele by voicing the different kinds of songs in their customary tongues. (Berry 1987:90-1)

The juxtaposition of musical genres was soon followed by syncretistic song writing. In the Spring of 1955 Berry visited Chicago and was encouraged by Muddy Waters to see record label owner Leonard Chess. Chess encouraged Berry to return in a week with a demonstration tape of original songs. Berry recalls:

> ...I had created many extra verses for other people's songs and I was eager to do an entire creation of my own. The four that I wrote may have been influenced melodically by other songs, but, believe me, the lyrics were solely my own. (Berry 1987:100)

The four songs that Berry recorded for Chess on the demonstration tape included two rhythm and blues pieces, "Wee Wee Hours" and "Together We Will Always Be" (Berry 1955b; Berry 1955d). "Wee Wee Hours" was lyrically suggested by Joe Turner's "Wee Baby Blues" (Turner 1941), and both rhythm and blues songs were strongly influenced by the trio styles and the intimate vocal stances of Charles Brown and Nat "King" Cole. One of the other two songs may have been written in honor of a country music performer. Howard DeWitt has claimed that "Thirty Days" (Berry 1955c) was written "as a tribute to Hank Williams' country music" (DeWitt 1985:14). The final number, "Ida May" combined thematic (cars) and melodic elements from Jackie Brenston's 1951 rhythm and blues hit "Rocket 88" (Brenston 1951), the verbal sentiment (chasing after a woman) and the chord progression of an older jump blues tune "Oh Red" (e.g., Hamfats 1936), and a variation of the tune, rhythm and title of the traditional country song "Ida Red" (e.g., Acuff 1939) (Berry 1987:100, 143-5). Leonard Chess was most impressed by "Ida May." Berry remembers that Chess "couldn't believe that a country tune (he called it a 'hillbilly song') could be written and sung by a black guy" (Berry 1987:100). He wanted, however, a "bigger beat" (Chapple 1977:39; Lydon 1973:10), and at the recording session on May 21, 1955, Chess, or bassist producer Willie Dixon (Flanagan 1987:81), also advised that the title be altered. Berry changed it "on the spot" to "Maybellene," a name of a cow that he recalled from one of his third grade storybooks (Berry 1987:103,145). After thirty-six takes, Chess believed that he had recorded a song that had the potential of being a crossover hit, and shortly thereafter, "Maybellene" (Berry 1955a) reached the number five position on Billboard's popular music chart (Cooper 1980:18; Belasco 1983; Cubitt 1984).

Initial European-American responses to the syncretistic sounds of "Maybellene" were confused as well as enthusiastic. One of Berry's occupational narratives concerns a booking he received in Knoxville[1] for which a backup band was to be provided. Arriving early so that he "could rehearse with the band," he was greeted by a "big guy" who "broke into laughter," saying, "that Chuck Berry was playing there tonight and the show was sold out." After Chuck produced a contract, the attendant said, "It's a country dance and we had no idea that 'Maybellene' was recorded by a niggra man." Although he was paid, Berry was not allowed to play. He finally left the establishment by the "back alley entrance" after hearing "Maybellene" played by a replacement band (Berry 1987:136). Berry has reflected in his biography, "I suppose I was booked in the South many times as a white singer" (Berry 1987:135-6). In a similar vein, Billy Altman has recently observed, it was Berry's "likable, racially ambiguous voice" that spelled his success on the airwaves, for "the fact that he didn't *sound* like a black blues singer undeniably helped him get airplay on mid-Fifties radio stations that were looking for any excuse *not* to program authentic rhythm 'n' blues music" (Altman 1990:5).

Black artists have also recognized the significance of Berry's black-white musical amalgam. Jimmy Witherspoon maintained that "Chuck Berry is a country singer," and Roy Brown remarked, "Chuck Berry ... is a perfect reflection of blending the blues and country music" (DeWitt 1985:14). Given the wide recognition this stylistic union has received, it is surprising that racial attitudes still appear to guide the evaluations of popular music scholars and critics. Thus, "rockabilly," which by 1955 had become a commercial subcategory of country and western, has been enthusiastically interpreted by Greil Marcus as a triumph of white over black. He views it as the "white counterattack" on the "black invasion of white popular culture" that "proved white boys could do it all" (Marcus 1976:165). Other accounts of rockabilly, most notably those of Colin Escott and Martin Hawkins, have defined the music in terms of musical style, song lyrics, and emotional content. Similarly, however, these critics also tend to romanticize and epitomize the cultural blending of the white "rockabilly moment" (Escott and Hawkins 1975;1980). The idea that white and black musics could be *perfectly* fused into syncretisms other than the Memphis rockabilly "sound" of Sam Phillips' Sun Records appears to be beyond the realm of consideration of some critics. Thus Charlie Gillett, refers to Berry's synthesis as the "*nearest* [black] equivalent to rockabilly" (Gillett 1983:30; my emphasis). Michael Bane comments that Berry's "secret was that ... he ... found a way to transcend race. His touchstone was the blending of white country and black blues." Two paragraphs later, however, he maintains, "a fusion had to take place; a white boy had to sing the blues. There had to be an Elvis" (Bane 1982:100-1). More recently, "David P. Szatmary has also interpreted "Maybellene" as "a country song adapted to a boogie woogie beat, which hinted at the marriage between country and R & B that would reach full fruition with the rockabillies" (Szatmary 1987:18). The reason that Szatmary's Maybellene was conceived out of wedlock may be because of the seeming illegitimacy of Chuck Berry's achievement; an African-American's ability to create a racially ambiguous postmodern persona singing a synthetic crossover song, which effectively "fooled" radio stations, may still unconsciously aggravate European-American critics who question the authenticity of a black bluesman playing country, yet who embrace the "full fruition" of a white country singer singing blues, i.e. the "real fusion" of rockabilly.[2]

From a structural perspective, the aesthetic and commercial goals of Chuck Berry and Leonard Chess, and Elvis Presley and Sam Phillips, were at once identical—the creation of new, exciting musical sounds, through the merger of black and white musical forms that would appeal to mass markets (see Reese 1982:31). Given the cultural climate of the time, it is no wonder that in 1955, on more than one occasion, music journalists for *Billboard* and England's *Jazz Journal* "mistakenly" used the term "rockabilly," without racial connotations, to refer to records by black artists (Escott and Hawkins 1980:63). Similarly, the notes to Chuck Berry's first LP describe his music as "rockabilly."[3] What should be remembered is that in 1954 and 1955 two remarkable styles emerged from the syncretism of black and white musics of the South, that of Elvis Presley and that of Chuck Berry. To say that one was a more perfect fusion than the other or to deny the familiarity of racial cultures that went into the reification of these musics is nonsense.

Besides "Thirty Days" and "Maybellene," it should be noted that Berry's continued involvement in country music is demonstrated by his picaresque use of "Wabash Cannonball" (see Narváez 1982) in "Promised Land" (Berry 1964; see Hatch and Millward 1987:17-8), his arrangement of the cowboy folksong "Hell-Bound Train"[4] as "The Downbound Train" (Berry 1955e), his warm liner notes to Jim and Jesse's LP *Berry Picking in the Country* (McReynolds 1965), his characteristic, extensive use of the dominant chord in his melodic progressions, and in terms of text, by his penchant to write songs in narrative form, quite unlike the lyric poetics of blues, rhythm and blues, and most other rock 'n' roll songs.[5]

The Merging of Age Cultures: "School Day"

When Chuck Berry recorded for Chess records in 1955, he was a married twenty-seven year old singer-musician with a family, who had cultivated an adult audience through a varied repertoire. Within a five year period he created and recorded such rock 'n' roll standards as "Maybellene," "No Money Down," "Roll Over Beethoven," "Too Much Monkey Business," "School Day," "Rock and Roll Music," "Sweet Little Sixteen," "Johnny B. Goode," "Carol," "Sweet Little Rock and Roller," "Almost Grown," and "Back in the U.S.A." As Don J. Hibbard and Carol Kaleialoha have observed, these songs, "defined the new teenage environment," and "enveloped the listener in a world of cars, school adolescence, and rock 'n' roll" (Hibbard and Kaleialoha 1983:15). Shaw has asserted that "despite the fact that Berry was a 30-year old man in 1956, there is no songwriter-singer of the period whose songs provide such an in-depth picture of teenage life.... he delineated the world of the teenager in remarkably vivid and entertaining terms" (Shaw 1986:200). At the same time, however, these recorded performances alienated black adults. Nelson George has written that Berry's "white teen records ... cut so deeply to the mood of the moment that Berry has been forever identified by blacks with what they perceived as the silly world of white teenagers" (George 1989:68).[6]

What Berry brought to teenage life, however, was the vitality of adult, black expressive culture, and he brought it with great conviction in performance. Having seen both Bill Haley and the Comets and Chuck Berry play at one of Alan Freed's[7] Times Square Paramount rock 'n' roll shows in New York in 1958, I can honestly echo Jim O'Donnell's judgment that teenage reaction to Bill Haley was that he was "a plain old ordinary family man" (O'Donnell 1975:41; see Swenson 1983). On the other hand, my peers and I never thought of Berry as being anything but dynamic and youthful with a marvelous, athletic stage persona. The racially mixed audience was genuinely committed to his music and to the authenticity of his performance. It is no wonder that Berry himself recalls the surprised reaction of one teenager on hearing his age: "I remember the first time I heard a kid say, 'Thirty-five years old! He's as old as my father!' I went, 'Oh, shit'" (Flanagan 1987:82).

As a "man of words" (see Abrahams 1970), who recognizes that "poetry is my blood flow" (Hackford 1987), one must stress the critical role of Berry's ingenious lyrics in blurring age distinctions, that is, in convincing teenagers that "he is one of us." Berry was obviously close to his own teenage experience, for as he says "I could *remember*" (Flanagan 1987:82). But it was Berry's vernacular conversational tone that first attracted Bruce Springsteen to Berry as a song writing model:

> ... his influence on my own writing came out ... when I wanted to write the way I thought that people talked 'cause that's how I felt, that's how he [Berry] writes. You know if you listen to one of his songs it sounds like somebody's coming in, sitting down in a chair and telling you a story about their aunt or their brother or describing some girl. (Hackford 1987)

The close proximity of performer and audience and the consequent blurring of ages that Berry achieved were accomplished through conversational, vernacular speech but also through first and second person techniques of address that developed a sense of intimacy and immediacy.[8] Berry's songs often sounded very different, therefore, than the songs of artists who sang about similar subjects, but who sang with a greater sense of social and temporal distance. The song topic of school and after school recreation was not new; it had been dealt with by other rhythm and blues artists. Louis Jordan, one of Berry's greatest influences, sang "After School Swing Session" with third person children:

> A B C D E F G H I J K L
> Just listen to them yell,
> School is out you can't you tell,
> When they leave the schoolroom,
> They go to the candy store,
> Turn on the radio,
> And clap their hands,
> While their favorite bands swing out, swing out,
> That's the start of the after school swing session,
> The jump jump jumpin' session ...(Jordan 1940)

In another treatment of this theme, "School Days (When We Were Kids)," Louis Jordan sang nostalgically about his youthful past, from the viewpoint of an adult singer to an adult audience:

> School days, school days, dear old golden rule days,
> Reading and writing and 'rithmetic,
> Taught to the tune of a hickory stick,
> You were my girl in calico,
> And I was your silly bashful beau.
> Mary had a lamb, his fleece was white as snow ...(Jordan 1949)

Bill Haley's "A.B.C. Boogie" not only relegates students to third person status but fantasizes the teacher into some kind of boogie queen:

> Well reading, writing, and 'rithmetic,
> Taught to the tune of a licorice stick,
> No education is ever complete,
> Without a boogie woogie woogie beat! [Band: Well all reat!]
> And when the day is over and it's time to go,
> The children get their books and stand right at the door,
> Teacher is so happy 'cause she's done her bit,
> To educate the kids and make them really fit,

> To say their ABCs with rhythm and ease ...(Haley 1954)

In contrast to these quaint, romanticized, and fantasized depictions of school life, consider the vital, bald realism of Chuck Berry's "School Day":

> Up in the mornin' and out to school,
> The teacher is teachin' the golden rule,
> American history and practical math,
> You're studyin' hard and hopin' to pass,
> Workin' your fingers right down to the bone,
> The guy behind you won't leave you alone.
>
> Ring! Ring! Goes the bell,
> The cook in the lunchroom is ready to sell,
> You're lucky if you can find a seat,
> You're fortunate if you have time to eat,
> Back in the classroom, open your books,
> Even the teacher don't know how mean she looks.
>
> Soon as three o'clock rolls around,
> You finally lay your burden down,
> Close up your books get out of your seat,
> Down the halls and into the street,
> Up to the corner and 'round the bend,
> Right to the juke joint you go in.
>
> Rock the coin right into the slot,
> You've got to hear something that's really hot
> With the one you love you're makin' romance,
> All day long you've been wantin' to dance,
> Feelin' the music from head to toe,
> Round and round and round you go.
>
> Hail! Hail! Rock 'n' roll,
> Deliver me from the days of old,
> Long live rock 'n' roll,
> The beat of the drums loud and bold,
> Rock, rock, rock 'n' roll,
> The feelin' is there body and soul. (Berry 1957)

Like a (Francis James) Child ballad, "School Day" plunges you right into the action, but in this case you are hurled into the tumult of your own daily activities. The teacher, who has no idea how mean she looks, teaches a variety of idealistic (the golden rule), useless subjects as well as practical math. The work is difficult; time is regimented and punctuated by raucous noises. You are ill-fed, conditions are crowded, and there are personal problems ("the guy behind you won't leave you alone"). Whether or not the "burden" of school work will lead to actual achievement seems to be a matter of chance, for even though you are working hard ("your fingers right down to the bone") the best you can do is "hope" to pass. Can there be a better depiction of what Dave Marsh has called, the "energized futility of working-class public high schools" (Marsh 1989:277)?[9] In contrast to that pointless rat race, time after school is one's own. One can freely partake in the activities of a local cultural scene ("juke joint")[10] where romance, music, and dancing to the pulse of rock 'n' roll ("feeling the music from head to toe") predominate. Is there any wonder why the protagonist at the end of this song shouts, "Hail! Hail! rock 'n' roll, deliver me from the days of old"?

Conclusion

Chuck Berry's verbal signifiers have stimulated the visual imagination. As Springsteen has noted about a line from Berry's song, "Nadine," "You know I've never seen a 'coffee-colored Cadillac' but I know exactly what one looks like" (Hackford 1987). As a postmodern artist, Chuck Berry has convincingly communicated such depictions through dramatizing them in various guises. As in the mode of method acting, his persona has been malleable. Black, white, adult, teenager, the raceless, ageless, postmodern persona of Chuck Berry has spoken *directly*. At the most artistically influential portion of his career he spoke to teenagers *as a teenager*, articulating the loci of their conflicts and defining new sites and sources of energy with which they could restructure their everyday social lives.[11] He also communicated to teenagers with the figurative language of a unique musical synthesis that they could call their own, and this empowered them with the antithetical weapon of pleasure. The fact that Berry's music was frowned on or despised by adults only heightened its oppositional role within the larger hegemonic context.

Robert Pattison, author of *The Triumph of Vulgarity*, is representative today of the continuity of this traditional adult role. He loathes Chuck Berry's songs because Berry's

> ... is a universe that pivots on an untranscendent celebration of the energy I can extract from the present moment without recourse to anything but myself. "Go, go" is the imperative of the lyrics, the imperative of fun.
>
> The substitution of fun for joy as the goal of its aesthetic works a transformation throughout rock's Romanticism. The great rock song does not aim for permanence, insight, or rapture. Its virtues are transience, action, and feeling. (Pattison 1987:197-8)

Unfortunately Pattison exhibits a skewed understanding of rock 'n' roll, for far from being the "goal" of rock 'n' roll, "fun" *is rock 'n' roll*, an energy source that fans tap to temporarily transform the social and material elements that oppress them into vehicles of celebration. This, a well-known traditional social function of black folklore, is ultimately Chuck Berry's African-American gift to rock 'n' roll, a gift of process that many "perpetual teenagers" refuse to relinquish under any circumstances, the mature objections of Pattison notwithstanding.[12] Chuck Berry created, donned masks, and crossed barriers of race and age in order to deliver this gift, and we will always be thankful.

Notes

A version of this article was read as a paper at the "Rock and Roll as Social Force, Process, and Tradition" Panel, Annual Meeting of the American Folklore Society, Oakland, California, October 20, 1990. I am grateful for the comments of Jack Santino, Richard Blaustein, and Neil Rosenberg.

1. The city might have been Nashville. See a variant of this personal experience narrative in Flanagan 1987:83.

2. Ironically a reverse racism has been evident in "only-blacks-can-play-blues" criticism. An example of this is Hoffman 1990. For an examination of this phenomenon see Narváez 1993.

3. In recent years, there have been signs that the term "rockabilly" may be returning to the structural openness of early usage. Some critics are employing it in a less restrictive manner. Arnold Shaw has referred to Berry's music as rockabilly without apologies (Shaw 1986:200). David Hatch and Stephen Millward have described Berry's guitar style as being a distinctive "combination of rockabilly and electric blues styles"

(Hatch and Millward 1987:78). For more on Berry's revolutionary guitar style, see Vito 1984.

4. For discussions and variants of "Hell-Bound Train," see Lomax and Lomax 1941:278; Beck 1942:236-8; Lomax 1960:246-7; Laws 1964:393, 402; Fife and Fife 1970:91-4; Randolph, vol. 4, 1980:23-4.

5. For the most part Berry's narrative songs are like African-American narrative folksongs in that they have a strong lyric quality, stressing character, situation and emotion more than events. See Laws 1964:83-94.

6. In contrast, it should also be noted that black bluesmen have often enjoyed Berry's rock 'n' roll songs. Son Seals has said, "Playing Chuck Berry stuff was fun, 'cause he had that blues touch all the time, even though he spoke in rock and roll" (Palmer 1981:271).

7. For accounts of Freed's remarkable career and pivotal role in the history of rock 'n' roll, see Smith 1989:163-219 and Jackson 1991.

8. For a suggestive analysis of lyrics, performance, and social distance, see Laing 1985.

9. See Pichaske 1981:24-5 for a reading of "School Day" as "social protest."

10. Here Berry ingeniously transmutes the meaning of "juke joint"—an African-American roadside establishment for eating, drinking, and dancing—to any ice cream parlor, diner or, luncheon counter that houses a "juke box" (see Shaw 1978:128-9) accessible to teenagers.

11. A more conventional, value-laden interpretation is offered by Bane 1982:101. He argues that Berry simply employed the commercial "gimmick" of the "Eternal Teenager."

12. See the "rock 'n' roll and empowerment" articles of Grossberg 1984; 1987; 1990.

References Cited

Abrahams, Roger. 1970. *Deep Down in the Jungle: Negro Narrative Folklore from the Streets of Philadelphia.* Hawthorne, New York: Aldine.
Acuff, Roy and His Smokey Mountain Boys. 1939. *Ida Red.* Reissued Time Life Records LP TLCW-09.
Altman, Billy. 1990. "Notes," *Chuck Berry—The Chess Box.* Chess MCA Records, CHD3-80,001.
Bane, Michael. 1982. *White Boy Singin' the Blues: The Black Roots of White Rock.* Markham, Ontario: Penguin.
Beck, Earl Clifton. 1942. *Songs of the Michigan Lumberjacks.* Ann Arbor: University of Michigan Press.
Belasco, Warren. 1983. Motivatin' With Chuck Berry and Frederick Jackson Turner. In *The Automobile and American Culture,* ed. David L. Lewis and Laurence Goldstein, pp. 262-79. Ann Arbor: University of Michigan Press.
Belz, Carl. 1972. *The Story of Rock.* New York: Oxford University Press.

Berry, Chuck. 1955a. *Maybellene.* Chess 1604A. Isalee Music Co., BMI.
———. 1955b. *Wee Wee Hours.* Chess 1604B. Isalee Music Co., BMI.
———. 1955c. *Thirty Days.* Chess 1610A. Isalee Music Co., BMI.
———. 1955d. *Together We Will Always Be.* Chess 1610B. Isalee Music Co., BMI.
———. 1955e. *Downbound Train.* Chess 1615B. Isalee Music Co., BMI.
———. 1957. *School Day.* Chess 1653A. Isalee Music Co., BMI.
———. 1964. *Promised Land.* Chess 1916A. Isalee Music Co., BMI.
———. 1970. *Have Mercy Judge.* Chess 2090A. Isalee Music Co., BMI.
———. 1987. *Chuck Berry: The Autobiography.* New York: Harmony Books.
Blumenthal, Bob. 1991. Chuck Berry: Berryland. In *Bluesland: Portraits of Twelve Major American Blues Masters,* ed. Pete Welding and Toby Byron, pp. 238-49. Toronto: Dutton.
Brenston, Jackie. 1951. *Rocket 88.* Reissued, Chess LP CXMP 2002.
Broonzy, Big Bill and Studs Terkel. 1960. *Big Bill Broonzy Interviewed by Studs Terkel.* Folkways LP FG 3586.
Chapple, Steve and Reebee Garofalo. 1977. *Rock 'n' Roll is Here to Pay: The History and Politics of the Music Industry.* Chicago: Nelson Hall.
Cooper, B. Lee. 1980. "Nothin' Outrun My V-8 Ford": Chuck Berry and American Motorcar, 1955-1979. *JEMF Quarterly* 16(57):18-23.
Cubitt, Sean. 1984. "Maybellene": Meaning and the Listening Subject. *Popular Music* 4:207-24.
DeWitt, Howard A. 1985. *Chuck Berry: Rock 'n' Roll Music.* Ann Arbor: Pieran Press.
Dorst, John D. 1988. Postmodernism vs. Postmodernity: Implications for Folklore Studies. *Folklore Forum* 21:216-20.
———. 1989. *The Written Suburb: An American Site, An Ethnographic Dilemma.* Philadelphia: University of Pennsylvania Press.
Escott, Colin and Martin Hawkins. 1980. *Sun Records: The Brief History of the Legendary Record Label.* New York: Omnibus.
———. 1975. *Catalyst: The Sun Records Story.* London: Aquarius Books.
Evans, David. 1974. Techniques of Blues Composition Among Black Folksingers. *Journal of American Folklore* 87:240-49.
———. 1985. *Big Road Blues: Tradition and Creativity in the Folk Blues.* Berkeley: University of California Press.
Featherstone, Mike. 1988. In Pursuit of the Postmodern: An Introduction. *Theory, Culture and Society* 5:2-3:195-215.
Fife, Austin and Alta Fife. 1970. *Heaven on Horseback: Revivalist Songs and Verse in the Cowboy Idiom.* Logan: Utah State University Press.
Flanagan, Bill. 1987. *Written in My Soul: Conversations with Rock's Great Songwriters.* Chicago: Contemporary Books.
Frith, Simon. 1989. Only Dancing: David Bowie Flirts with the Issues. In *Zoot Suits and Second-Hand Dresses: An Anthology of Fashion and Music,* ed. Angela McRobbie, pp. 132-40. Boston: Unwin Hyman.
George, Nelson. 1989. *The Death of Rhythm and Blues.* New York: E.P. Dutton.
Gillett, Charlie. 1983. *The Sound of the City: The Rise of Rock and Roll.* London: Souvenir Press.

Grossberg, Lawrence. 1984. "I'd Rather Feel Bad Than Not Feel Anything at All": Rock and Roll, Pleasure and Power. *Enclitic* 8(1-2):94-110.
———. 1987. Rock and Roll in Search of an Audience. In *Popular Music and Communication*, ed. James Lull, pp. 175-97. Newbury Park, California: SAGE.
———. 1990. Is There Rock After Punk? In *On Record: Rock, Pop, and the Written Word*, ed. Simon Frith and Andrew Goodwin, pp. 111-23. New York: Pantheon.
Hackford, Taylor, filmmaker. 1987. *Chuck Berry: Hail! Hail! Rock 'n' Roll*. Universal City Studios, Inc., Delilah Films Production.
Haley, Bill and His Comets. 1954. *A.B.C. Boogie*. Al Russel and Max Spickel comps. Decca 29204. Publisher unknown.
Hamfats, Harlem. 1936. *Oh, Red*. Reissued Folklyric LP 9029.
Hatch, David and Stephen Millward. 1987. *From Blues to Rock: An Analytical History of Pop Music*. Manchester: Manchester University Press.
Hibbard, Don J. and Carol Kaleialoha. 1983. *The Role of Rock: A Guide to the Social and Political Consequences of Rock Music*. Englewood Cliffs, New Jersey: Prentice-Hall.
Hoffman, Lawrence. August, 1990. Guest Editorial, "At the Crossroads." *Guitar Player* 24:8, 247:18.
Jackson, John A. 1991. *Big Beat Heat: Alan Freed and the Early Years of Rock & Roll*. New York: Schirmer.
Jones, Eddie "Guitar Slim." 1954. *The Things That I Used to Do*. Reissued Specialty LP SPS-2120.
Jordan, Louis. 1949. *School Days (When We Were Kids)*. G. Edwards, W.D. Cobb, comps. Reissued MCA LP MCA2-4079. Mills Music Inc. / Shapiro Bernstein & Co., Inc. ASCAP.
Jordan, Louis and and his Tympany Five. 1940. *After School Swing Session*. Reissued Swingtime LP ST1011. Publisher unknown.
Laing, Dave. 1985. *One Chord Wonders: Power and Meaning in Punk Rock*. Milton Keynes: Open University Press.
Lash, Scott. 1988. Discourse or Figure? Postmodernism as a "Regime of Signification." *Theory, Culture and Society* 5(2-3):311-336.
Laws, G. Malcolm, Jr. 1964. *Native American Balladry*. Bibliographical and Special Series, Vol. 1, Publications of the American Folklore Society. Philadelphia: American Folklore Society.
Lhamon, W. T., Jr. 1985. Little Richard as a Folk Performer. *Studies in Popular Culture* 8(2):7-17.
Lomax, Alan. 1960. *The Folk Songs of North America in the English Language*. Garden City, New York: Doubleday and Co.
Lomax, John A. and Alan Lomax, eds. 1941. *Cowboy Songs and Other Frontier Ballads*. New York: Macmillan.
Lydon, Michael. 1973. *Rock Folk*. New York: Delta.
Marcus, Greil. 1976. *Mystery Train: Images of America in Rock 'n' Roll Music*. New York: E.P. Dutton and Co.
Marsh, Dave. 1989. *The Heart of Rock & Soul*. Markham, Ontario: New American Library.

McReynolds, Jim, Jesse McReynolds and and the Virginia Boys. 1965. *The Great Chuck Berry Songbook: Berry Picking in the Country.* Epic LP LN24176.

Minnie, Memphis. 1941. *Me and My Chauffeur Blues.* Reissued Portrait Masters CD RK 44072.

Narváez, Peter. 1982. "The Wabash Cannonball" Parodic Song Cycle. *Canadian Folk Music Bulletin* 16(4):26.

———. 1993. Living Blues Journal: The Paradoxical Aesthetics of the Blues Revival. In *Transforming Tradition,* ed. Neil V. Rosenberg, pp. 241-257. Urbana: University of Illinois Press.

O'Donnell, Jim. 1975. *The Rock Book.* New York: Pinnacle Books.

Palmer, Robert. 1981. *Deep Blues.* New York: Viking.

Pattison, Robert. 1987. *The Triumph of Vulgarity: Rock Music in The Mirror of Romanticism.* New York: Oxford University Press.

Pichaske, David. 1981. *The Poetry of Rock: The Golden Years.* Peoria, Illinois: Ellis Press.

Randolph, Vance, coll. and ed. 1980. *Ozark Folksongs.* Vols. I-IV. Columbia: University of Missouri Press.

Reese, Krista. 1982. *Chuck Berry: Mr. Rock n' Roll.* London: Proteus Books.

Rosenberg, Neil. 1985. *Bluegrass, A History.* Urbana: University of Illinois Press.

Scobie, Stephen. 1991. *Alias Bob Dylan.* Red Deer, Alberta: Red Deer College Press.

Shaw, Arnold. 1978. *Honkers and Shouters: The Golden Years of Rhythm and Blues.* New York: Collier Books.

Shaw, Arnold. 1986. *Black Popular Music in America.* New York: Schirmer Books.

Smith, Wes. 1989. *The Pied Pipers of Rock 'n' Roll: Radio Deejays of the 50s and 60s.* Marietta, Georgia: Longstreet Press.

Swenson, John. 1983. *Bill Haley.* London: A Star Book.

Szatmary, David P. 1987. *Rockin' in Time: A Social History of Rock and Roll.* Englewood Cliffs, New Jersey: Prentice-Hall.

Turner, Joe. 1941. *Wee Baby Blues.* Decca 8526.

Vito, Rick. 1984. The Chuck Berry Style. *Guitar Player* 18:6(174):72-5.

Wheeler, Tom. 1988a. Chuck Berry: The Interview. *Guitar Player* 22:3(219):56-63.

———. 1988b. Chuck Berry: The Story. *Guitar Player* 22:3(219):50-4.

Workman, Mark E. 1989. Folklore in the Wilderness: Folklore and Postmodernism. *Midwestern Folklore* 15:5-14.

10

Pieces for a Shabby Hut

Lee Haring

Movement of cultural products from one setting to another, or from one audience to another, has become such a commonplace in our time that the notions of setting and audience lose their stability. Even less stable is the notion of authenticity, which motivates much of the interest in folklore. The questions "What is authentic folklore?" and "How can I distinguish it from the inauthentic, the commercialized, or the fabricated?" grow out of dichotomies like *fictional* vs. *factual* writing, whose polarization in our time has been beautifully delineated by Raymond Williams (1977:145-157), but whose antagonism goes back at least to Plato. We tend to see inauthenticity when colorful and attractive elements of traditional dance in, for instance, the Tyrol or East Africa are cultivated for the pleasure of tourists. In folktale collections, inauthenticity is less obvious. But what difference exists between cultivating colorful elements of folklife for tourists and presenting folktales from, say, Madagascar for a European audience? In both cases, artistic behavior leaves one audience and performance context for another; in both cases, some capital gain is expected, either financial or cultural. Printing colonial folktales in French—a microcosm of the folklorization of native cultures (Bouillon 1981:143)—is an instance of Hans Moser's definition of *folklorismus*, "the performance of functionally and traditionally determined elements outside their local or class community" (Moser 1962).

Some call this movement decontextualization. They bewail the extent to which the resultant text, "far from constituting some unified plenitude of meaning, bears inscribed within it the marks of certain determinate absences..." (Eagleton 1978:89-90). They lament the inadequacy of textual representation of presence and seek to mend the breach (Fine 1984). Since folklorism as Moser defined it, however, is the animating principle of contemporary culture (Bausinger 1990), its history demands documentation. Rather than dismiss colonial efforts at collecting, translating, and publishing folktales and myths, one can read into their history the program of Paul de Man (1983), as Wlad Godzich describes it: "to go beyond an inquiry into the validity, or to speak rapidly, into the success or failure of a given methodology, to an elucidation of the relationship of that methodology to its own necessity" (1983:xviii).

What has been the necessity for folklorism in the colonial period in the Western Indian Ocean? Two principles emerging from performance researches point to an answer. One is a certain portability about the words of narratives, identified by Bauman and Briggs (1990), which has declared them available for decontextualization. Narratives about the origins of the cosmos, human beings, or death tend to partake of secret or hidden knowledge that may, however, be less accessible. More than folktales for entertainment, the apparent referent of cosmogonic narratives is "a phenomenologically distinct realm of experience brought to life through word and gesture" (Briggs 1990:216), and not brought to life even then if they are less overtly performed. The other principle is that "performance as a frame intensifies entextualization," the "process of rendering discourse extractable" (Bauman and Briggs 1990:74; Crapanzano 1984). In colonial situations where privileged information is demanded, a decontextualized performance may be the only performance cosmogonic narratives receive. An example of a decontextualized narrative:

> *Zanaharibe*, the great god, had two wives. One day he prepared to give a great feast to celebrate the circumcision of his second wife's son. But his first wife said, "I do not want you to give such a feast for your second wife's son. Only I have a right to that. What's more, I will not stay with you if you keep two wives. Choose the one you want, her or me."
>
> The god kept his first wife and sent the second down to earth, with her son. But from up in the sky the first wife still saw them. She got her husband to exile them beyond the seas. Also, he forbade his second wife's son to be circumcised as the first one had been.
>
> Europeans [*vazaha*] descend from the great god's son and his second wife. That is why they can do many surprising things. They still live beyond the sea where their father exiled them. (Renel 1930:67-68)

This myth of separation comes from a curious collection of five dozen native myths assembled in the first generation after French occupation of Madagascar in 1896. Charles Renel, who was inspector for the colony's schools, directed the teachers under his supervision to find and bring him Malagasy tales. In 1910 he published two volumes of *angano*, tales considered fictional, but the *tantara*—myths, I call them, about the origin of the world and human beings and death and about the acquisition of necessities like rice—remained unpublished until after his death, appearing only in 1930. Publication of this kind exemplifies the new slogan of performance studies, "No decontextualization without recontextualization." The myths now were recontextualized in the alien social context of the French system of literary production, though they carried some of their history with them (Bauman 1990). Elements of recontextualization included reframing into different generic shape, formal transformation, functional shift, and translation. Historical, anthropological, and critical approaches to such material all are concerned to develop the right approach (Godzich, in de Man 1983). What can they tell us?

One might begin to answer this question by focusing on the approach of one formidable figure, Walter Benjamin, while noting that the stimulation that his work provides critics today (for example, Taussig 1993) should not blind them to the preposterous statements he sometimes makes. Much of what Benjamin writes when he imagines the storyteller, in his celebrated essay of that name (in *Illuminations* 1969), can be disproved. The romantic image of the narrator performing in a setting of artisanal work has some reality in central and eastern Europe, but Benjamin's assimilation of *Märchen* to personal experience stories confuses quite distinct kinds of performances (Degh 1968; Stahl 1989). In non-Western societies, a distinction between experience stories and traditional fictions is essential to survival (Jacobs 1964:222). Benjamin also prejudices the listener's relationship to the storyteller as naive, asserting that it "is controlled by his interest in retaining what he is told" (1969:97). Much as the comparative study of literary systems tells us of audience behavior (Peacock 1987, Abrahams 1983, Bauman 1986), none of it portrays listeners to oral performance as aspiring to retain the content unless they are themselves rival performers (Lord 1956). The motivation of audiences is a larger topic: one need only recall the opposed views of Coleridge and Dr. Johnson.

One could as well speculate that most listeners are continually seeking in heard performances images and incidents resembling their early experiences, which they can use as opportunities for rehearsing their past feelings. This search is as greedy as Benjamin's image of the reader of a novel swallowing up "the material as the fire devours logs in the fireplace" (1969:100).

More germane to the study of myth, Benjamin's least convincing statement—to the critic researching the social situations of artistic communication, the relations enacted in performance, the interactive behavior of performers and audiences, and the variety in the world's system of ethnic genres (Ben-Amos 1976)—is a well-known line in the first paragraph of "The Task of the Translator": "In the appreciation of a work of art or an art form, consideration of the receiver never proves fruitful" (1969:69). Reference by a critic to a particular public, whether regarded *en bloc* or as individuals, Benjamin calls misleading. Art, he says, is never concerned with people's response. He ends with an often-quoted line, "No poem is intended for the reader, no picture for the beholder, no symphony for the listener" (1969:69). Taking note of but not deterred by Paul de Man's (1983) attempt to save this affront from its own absurdity, I observe (with Blake) that "the following Contraries to these are True": 1. The criticism of nonwestern verbal art depends on finding and examining the receiver, as much as literary history depends on reconstructing an audience's understanding of genre, precedents, and the peculiarities of literary language. 2. All individual artists, whether "folk," bourgeois, or elite, have been passionately concerned with audience response, which has countless times determined repertoire and the shape of individual performances. 3. Every performance of a folksong, folktale, riddle, or proverb is intended for certain hearers, as much as *The Rape of the Lock* or *Alice's Adventures Underground*.

These propositions are equally true of the productions of ethnographers and folklorists, which aspire through recording, translation, and other recontextualizations to regain the authenticity Benjamin mourns. Criticism of folktale books or folksong records depends on finding and examining what is thought to be the receiver's "horizon of expectations" (as Jauss calls it, 1982) so as to discern how it affected the steps in recontextualization. Anachronistically to attack the Grimm brothers, for example, as failing to live up to standards of fidelity they themselves invented reveals the predicament of the critic who ignores this principle (Ellis 1983). Even when performers of Western Indian Ocean myths are long dead, the life of their art tempts us to reconstruct the moments in which it was asserted and confined.

The study of verbal art as performance (Bauman 1977), even the performances of the dead, performs a service to critical theory by means of its reactionary positions—by taking its inquiry, for instance, to an unfashionable genre like myth and an ignored region like the Western Indian Ocean. In this region, what the west calls myth has no genre attached to it. As in classical antiquity, nothing "warrants attributing to myth a literary genre or a specific type of tale" (Detienne 1986:131), though narratives about the origin of things certainly have been performed, dictated, translated, and published. Thus, in the age of Foucault (1980), one asks how various forms of discourse about folk narrative—myth in this case—come to be materially produced and maintained as authoritative systems. And one couples with that the Platonic question of whether there is a special relation between certain subject matter—cosmogony—and a certain literary form—myth. Local evidence echoes Marcel Detienne's deconstruction of myth in European antiquity: "Does it not cover the ground between the proper name and the epic, the proverb and theogony, the fable and genealogy? . . . [I]ts meaning is at the disposal of everyone who comes along" (1986:130-131). If the subject matter of myth is the creation of the world, the creation of human beings, the origin of death, the acquisition of necessities like rice, and the loss of luxuries like God's presence, then numerous narratives on these subjects have been collected, especially in Madagascar, but they are not usually labeled myths by either Malagasy or Europeans.

Instead of classifying narratives by theme, Malagasy oral critics separate true narratives from fictional ones, at least to begin with. To choose one recent observation, Philippe Beaujard's (1991) excellent ethnography of myth and society among the Tanala of Ikongo shows this group following a long Malagasy tradition of distinguishing narrative genres on the basis of truth (Haring 1980), which many observers have noticed in Africa (Bascom 1984). Tanala distinguish *tantara*—historical traditions, as well as narratives about the origin of creatures and things—from longer *tafasiry*, which deliver some teaching, and shorter, amusing *tafasiry*, which sometimes also have moral content. The notion of *tantara* corresponds, of course, to the European idea of myth (Beaujard 1991:33), but Tanala people, in the spirit of Detienne's remark that the definition of myth is at the disposal of everyone who comes along, tend to blur the terms together. Tales in the ostensibly fictional category, *tafasiry*, are a mixture of what a Westerner would call myth and folktale (1986:41). This category also includes riddles, in conformity again with an African habit of classifying narrative and non-narrative together. A similar ambiguity is seen in the role of Tanala homosexuals: "En fait, il apparaît que de par leur spécificité, des homosexuels trouvaient dans le dit et le chant des *tafasiry* une place sociale, une fonction religieuse de médiateurs, comme chez des peuples indiens d'Amérique du Nord" (Beaujard 1991:39-40). With these people as with many others in Madagascar and the other islands of this region—in Mauritius, for instance, the *séga* can mean a *cante-fable* or a costumed dance in 12/8 time—genre classification is as flexible and variable as the rest of social life and art. Their most sympathetic historians, like Paul Ottino (1986; 1991), emulate their allegorical interpretations.

The European term for these narratives is *myth*, which came into being when certain people agreed to call certain narratives by that name, for ethnocentric political and technical reasons, or advantages, of their own. Some wanted to draw "a boundary at which mythical thought fades away before the rationality of scientists and philosophers." Thus they initiated the opposition between rational thought and myth that has dominated Western thought on the subject ever since (Detienne 1991:10). Others—Beaujard (1991), Ottino (1986; 1991), Jacques Faublée (1947)—take the privilege of naming certain narratives as myths not because of cosmogonic subject matter, but because of their function. They see certain narratives functioning in society to transmit a value system, elaborate a world view, and depict politico-economic tensions and struggles. Such functions, as components of a definition of myth, are part of the Eurocentric equipment and world view the Western-trained anthropologist brings with him to his extensive field experience. Other components of that world view Stanley Fish calls beliefs (1985:443). These beliefs include, for instance, a way of perceiving human and humanlike beings. One assumption has been pointed out by Gregory Schrempp: a fundamental difference, at least for scientific purposes, between our own group—the other scholars for whom we write—and those human or humanlike beings, the storytellers. Collecting and analysis of folktale and myth are most often based, says Schrempp, "on an (implicit or explicit) contrast between two or more groups and their worldviews" (1991:2). Researchers also tend to have beliefs about an impersonal cosmos, notions of the origin of folkloristics during a remote era, images of the major stages in the evolution of their field, and even conceptions about what in it is clean and dirty (Jacobs 1964:370-71). Their belief in "the archival dignity, institutional authority, and patriarchal longevity" of folk narrative scholarship, as Edward Said says of Orientalists, allows these traits to function as a worldview—though with a different political force from the one Said attributes to Orientalism (1989:211).

Though few investigators in the Western Indian Ocean region have used the word *myth*, the concept has clearly been present throughout their discourse since the time of the seventeenth-century French colonist Etienne de Flacourt. The distinct category of origin narratives was well established in European thought by 1648, when Flacourt set foot on Madagascar (which was also the time the Dutch were beginning to exterminate the dodo as part of their occupation of Mauritius). Also part of Sieur de Flacourt's mental equipment were a notion of authenticity and a proto-Malinowskian interpretation of myth as a social charter. Flacourt writes (I preserve his spellings of tribal names):

> I did not want to include in the following history a fable that the nobles of Anossi induce their blacks to believe, in order to abase them. It says that God, having created Adam out of earth, sent him a sleep, during which he drew a woman from his brain. The Roandrian descend from her. Another woman from his neck, from whom the Anacandrian descend. Another from his left shoulder, from whom the Ondzatfi issued. Another from his right side, from whom the great Voadziri, who are black, descend. Another from his thigh, from whom the Lohavohits come. Another from his calf, from whom the Ontsoa come, and the last from the sole of his foot, from whom the slaves issue.

Having classified the fable as inauthentic, hegemonic ruling-class propaganda, Flacourt gives his functionalist interpretation: "The nobles invented this fable to confine each one to his rank and quality. For in that country, a man can never be raised above his birth ..."

(1661:xxi-xxii). The colonist did not need the word *myth* for such useful concepts. Like Jacques Derrida's generic ethnologist, Flacourt accepted "into his discourse the premises of ethnocentrism at the very moment" (1978:282) when he was denouncing them by attributing them to Malagasy nobles.

The concept of myth, or cosmogonic narrative, once deconstructed by Detienne, requires reevaluation, especially in a situation of such cultural convergence. "The quality and the fecundity of a discourse," Derrida suggests, "are perhaps measured by the critical rigor with which [its] relationship to the history of metaphysics and to inherited concepts is thought" (Derrida 1978:282). If this relationship is unclear in the Western Indian Ocean, the materials for thinking about Western Indian Ocean myth are clear enough. They came into existence in the interaction between informants and investigators, who collaborated on a criterion of authenticity. Myth had to be discredited as irrational, but it had also to be authenticated as an indigenous product.

Thus the criterion of authenticity also requires reevaluation. The least to be said about it would be a Richard Rorty (1982) position: the validity of the criterion of authenticity, like any convention, is a function of agreement among members of each group to uphold it. For local informants and European investigators, members of conflicting groups, to agree, they had to enter into that inseparability of attitudes of dominant and oppressed peoples that Mannoni (1964) has demonstrated for Madagascar. The European cultural tradition and practice, exerting its hegemony as Gramsci knew, constructed the domain of Western Indian Ocean folk culture (Williams 1977:111), which incorporated a criterion of authenticity. The next step was for the dominated people, internalizing their oppression, to contemn their cultural products (Haring 1992:102). Today, research looks for the critical role in expressing positive and negative attitudes played by poetics and performance. This role, we now see, was provoked by the colonizers' attempts to capture cosmogonic symbology and thereby relegate superstition to destruction. Neither European colonizers nor Malagasy elders and poets were innocent of ideological pressures or necessarily conservative of ideologies. A principal task for folkloristics today is the study of the relations of transformation that occur when cultures converge. So, bearing in mind the direction of contemporary theorists (Foucault 1980; Eagleton 1978) to seek the forces acting on the groups, we can ask how cosmogonic narratives in Madagascar and elsewhere in this region were transformed when they were performed for Western investigators, as well as how cosmogonic discourse became an authoritative system and gained its new authenticity.

To this Foucauldian question, performance-based researches and a growing body of theory declare their central hypothesis, that performance is constitutive of the domain of myth (Bauman 1984). The particular form of performance behind Renel's myths is dictation by an informant to one of the school inspector's collaborators. What is it in Western Indian Ocean myths that makes them available for dictation in an interview? What contextualization cues can be found in printed texts to "signal which features of the settings are used by interactants in producing interpretive frameworks" (Bauman and Briggs 1990:68)? The novelty in this approach, which I have called folkloric restatement (Haring 1992:12), is its attempt to discover, without directly observing live performance, the extent to which poetically or rhetorically patterned contextualization cues may be visible in Western Indian Ocean performance, and the patterns or links among these cues that may be "creating larger formal and functional patterns" (1992:19).

Where to look? While Beaujard (1991), Noel Gueunier (1991), and other fieldworkers gather narrative texts from present-day storytellers in the islands, I look back to a golden age of collecting in the Western Indian Ocean, which included the nostalgic salvage ethnography of Charles Baissac in Mauritius (1967) and the active collecting and translating of Malagasy tales, proverbs, customs, poetry, and riddles by men of the London Missionary Society. Active collecting continued after French conquest of Madagascar. Renel, profoundly interested in religion and myth, a dedicated comparatist, had studied Vedic, Roman, and Gallic mythology before arriving in Madagascar; subsequently he studied traditional religion there. Reading his posthumous myth texts today, we puzzle over their fragmentary quality. The one cited above is one of the more coherent ones; here is another:

> One day, God's son asked his father's permission to come down here. His father granted his wish. So he left, but when he reached the end of his journey, finding nowhere to set his feet, he had to go back to heaven and tell God his misadventure. When he heard this story,

> God threw forth a large flock of stars. Taking his big knife (the rainbow), he divided this flock. The big pieces formed the mountains, the parts cut by the blade of the big knife formed the valleys, and the rest, broken down into powder, became the plains. That is said to be the origin of the earth. (Renel 1930:136)

It is as if the cosmogony were not narrated but described (Hymes 1975). The narrator uses the word *here* to mean the earth where he and the interviewer are sitting, he annotates the expression *big knife* to mean *rainbow*, and in his last sentence he probably uses the characteristic Malagasy expression *hono*, "it is said," to depersonalize his account. The text is reminiscent of present-day interviews from which the journalist's questions have been deleted to give the impression of a continued speech. How shall this style be interpreted? Does the marked contrast between the smooth, polished narrations of Renel's folktales and the abrupt, inconsequential text of this myth dramatize Renel's sense of the distance between Europeans and Malagasy, the difference between transcription methods in that golden age and transcription methods today, or a reticence on the part of interviewees to reveal sacred matters? All three no doubt, but who was in control?

Doubtless both. Recontextualization was a collaboration. The colonial period in Madagascar was characterized by an unequal exchange of languages (Raison-Jourde 1977). Literacy was introduced as the privilege of Protestant converts and highland courtiers; the orality of villagers furnished raw material for processing by the literate. The texts of Renel's myths come to us from transcriptions by literate persons who were already effecting their own synthesis of Malagasy and European cultures. As a result of Renel's publishing their transcriptions and translations, "phonetic culture claimed," applying Julia Kristeva's words,

> to be a scriptural one.... The temporality of ... text is less a discursive temporality (the narrative sequences are not ordered according to the temporal laws of the verb phrase) than what we might call a *scriptural* temporality (the narrative sequences are oriented towards and rekindled by the very activity of writing). The succession of events (descriptive utterances or citations) obeys the motion of the hand working on the empty page. (cited in Richter 1987:1002)

Kristeva seems to be describing the myth texts I quote above. Their relevance to her theorizing extends farther. Transcriptions, as Kristeva says, were situated in a double space, the authority of writing in the hands of the colonizing power, and the contest with that authority of an informant's words and speech. To what extent did informants embed their assessments of the interview situation in the speech itself? The fragmentary quality of some of Renel's myth texts makes them anti-narratives. Recontextualized into reading matter for the metropole, a *tantara* becomes a folklorized, printed narration of cosmogony and of the colonial encounter. What Frank Lentricchia writes of European developments has stronger parallels in the colonized Indian Ocean: "the refining by literary intellectuals in the late eighteenth century of the concept of the 'literary' to mean 'imaginative writing' becomes an independent service on behalf of the coercive and even totalitarian tendencies of modern society—a way of supervising and containing the 'literary' by keeping it enclosed in its own space, a mode of self-policing, as it were" (1983:54). The refining of the concept of native storytelling to mean translated stories in the multivolume *Collection de contes et chansons populaires*, published in the metropole, kept Western Indian Ocean expression in its own place.

    Texts like the myths I have quoted above are more than grist for the power/knowledge mill. They are also the polite answers of informed but uninterested narrators to the questions of one of Renel's schoolteachers. Is that why they are so uninteresting to read? To what extent does Renel's editorial practice seek to confine a sense of presence? And what were the constraints within which Malagasy narrators operated to begin with? An imaginative anthropology that tried to reconstruct their specific performance context should reveal "an interpretative frame within which the messages being communicated are to be understood" (Bauman 1984:9). Much European folktale research, focusing on the grammar of narrative rather than its rhetoric, has assumed that folk narrators had relatively free choice among specific lexical items so long as the narrative syntax was recognizable (Bremond 1973). That choice, in the circumstances of colonial collecting in Madagascar, should account for the agreement between collector and informant that "these are the words of the myth." But it also accounts, I believe, for why the narrators and transcribers made native culture so uninteresting. The style is a response to the interview.

These texts, untypical of Malagasy storytelling style or of other regional performance styles, result from a process closely analogous to what Hugo Schuchardt (1980) described for language. In the nineteenth century, under the impact of foreign invaders, Malagasy mythology did not keep on gradually developing, but the development was broken off, the mythological system was smashed to pieces by the colonial encounter, and the fragments are what we see in Renel's third volume. It was he, the synthesizer of island cosmology, who tried to put together a new structure, out of the belief that it must once have been coherent.

Another of Schuchardt's metaphors about creolization in language, adapted to creolization in verbal art, puts the local informants into the active role. It was not the foreigners who chipped out single stones from a good, solid building in order to build themselves shabby huts. It was the proprietors themselves, Renel's schoolmasters and their informants, who handed them the pieces for this purpose (Schuchardt 1980:69). The principal force acting on them was the inequality of the exchange. They expressed their sense of that inequality in their narrating style. Like Chicanos in the United States and other marginalized groups who "occupy the periphery of industrial capitalism," these newly colonized artists in the Western Indian Ocean organized their performances of verbal art so as to deconstruct "dominant ideologies and expressive forms" (Bauman and Briggs 1990:66; see also Rosaldo 1982). "The most interesting and difficult part of any cultural analysis," and not only in the complex societies Raymond Williams has in mind, "is that which seeks to grasp the hegemonic in its active and formative but also its transformational processes" (1977:113). As the records of colonial times show, dominated peoples in the Western Indian Ocean region organized their interviews with European investigators towards the same purposes. The speakers, nearly all of whom are anonymous in the sense that their names were kept from us, were partners with the investigators in transactions that imply alternative views of language and social life. They chose the asymmetrical situation of the interview as a place to display not their communicative competence (Bauman and Briggs 1990:72), but their incompetence. Thus they were such skillful, versatile narrators that they embedded their assessments of the interview situation in the speech itself. Renel's myths record the critical role of poetics and performance in a portentous encounter. They are so poor literarily, I believe, first because they are metaperformances, summaries, or paraphrases of ideas. Some of these accounts of the origin of the world, human beings, and death probably had no prior performance context anyway, being unperformed information. The interview with Renel's schoolmaster interpreter, like any interview, "place[d] great constraints on linguistic form, suppresse[d] creativity, and diminishe[d] the importance of reference" (Bauman and Briggs 1990:62). This reductive style, however, "greatly enhance[d] the ability of speakers to bring about a desired" objective, namely giving the alien interviewer, the *vazaha*, what he wanted. This anti-narrative style, a switching of register, "foregrounds the process of extracting discourse from particular speech events," narrowing the broad scope of performance-based study to the restated social setting of the interview.

Rising to the challenge of the bald fragmentariness of the cosmogonic narratives he collected, Renel wrote a coherent study of Malagasy religion; succeeding scholars, such as Jacques Faublee and Paul Ottino, have similarly sought to reconstruct Malagasy mythology. The folk, imagined as the collective author, is displaced on to the European's metatextual account of the mythmaking activity in Ottino's *L'Étrangère intime* (1986), which interprets allegorically some narratives from the classic 1877 collection of the Norwegian missionary Lars Dahle. Now the role of the anthropologist or folklorist is to render an authoritative account of the structure of myths and tales and of "the internal relationships among the various textual strands and levels" (Pease 1990:112).

Myths and folktales from the Western Indian Ocean invite treatment as both a police blotter and a window on artistic communication, through which we discern traces of the deconstructing of dominant ideology. Paul de Man, no fan of myth, in one of his characteristically imperious throwaway lines, revives the ghostly persona of a speaking voice. "Whenever we encounter a text such as [this or any book of myths]"—de Man is writing about Baudelaire—"that is, whenever we read—there always is an infra-text, a hypogram like 'Correspondances' underneath" (1983:262). Is the infra-text the colonial encounter? If the performer's voice has not quite been silenced, the reader seems confined to the New Critical position of being unable to imagine "a text that did not erect its own ghostly persona and speak with the recognizable 'tone' of a single human voice" (Bruss 1982:14). Paradox and ambiguity are thus at the center of Renel's book or any like it. In its folklorismic fashion, it celebrates the life of Western Indian Ocean storytelling and imprisons it at the same time. It honors local artistry by enlarging the audience, while borrowing the power of native culture by appropriating the texts.

Thus, of all the human sciences, the study of performance offers the most vigorous defense of the metaphysics of presence, because it insists on the primacy of the human voice. Writing, in this view, can never replace speaking. The utterly romantic aspiration of performance-based research is to show, in writing, that meaning cannot be put into writing. Knowing that the meaning of a folktale cannot be separated from the words, movements, and accents of the performance, researchers yet undertake to translate, to comment, to interpret, to discuss and debate. Thus among human scientists it is the student of performance who is quickest to support Benjamin's notion of the aura of the work of art. "Even the most perfect reproduction of the work of art," Benjamin writes, "is lacking in one element: its presence in time and space, its unique existence at the place where it happens to be" (1969:220). What fieldworker has not felt keenly the absence of that presence in time and space when translating African or Asian tales for a European audience? Charles Renel doubtless felt it too. The performance-oriented scholar, therefore, will acknowledge from experience the accuracy of Benjamin's remark that what "withers in the age of mechanical reproduction is the aura of the work of art" (1969:221). But that aura draws us on.

References

Abrahams, Roger D. 1983. *The Man-of-words in the West Indies: Performance and the Emergence of Creole Culture*. Baltimore: The Johns Hopkins University Press.

Baissac, C[harles]. 1967 [1888]. *Le Folk-lore de l'Ile Maurice: texte créole et traduction française*. Paris: G.-P. Maisonneuve et Larose.

Bascom, William. 1984 [1965]. The Forms of Folklore: Prose Narratives. In *Sacred Narrative: Readings in the Theory of Myth*, ed. Alan Dundes, pp 5-29. Berkeley: University of California Press.

Bauman, Richard. 1977. *Verbal Art as Performance*. Prospect Heights, IL: Waveland.

_____. 1986. *Story, Performance, and Event: Contextual Studies of Oral Narrative*. Cambridge Studies in Oral and Literate Culture. Cambridge: Cambridge University Press.

_____. 1990. Contextualization, Tradition, and the Dialogue of Genres. In *Rethinking Context*, ed. C. Goodwin and A. Duranti. Cambridge: Cambridge University Press.

_____ and Charles L. Briggs. 1990. Poetics and Performance as Critical Perspectives on Language and Social Life. *Annual Review of Anthropology* 19:59-88.

Bausinger, Hermann. 1990 [1961,1971]. *Folk Culture in a World of Technology*. Trans. by Elke Dettmer. Foreword by Dan Ben-Amos. Bloomington: Indiana University Press.

Beaujard, Philippe. 1991. *Mythe et société à Madagascar (Tanala de L'Ikongo): le Chasseur d'oiseaux et la Princesse du ciel*. Pref. by Georges Condominas. Paris: Editions L'Harmattan.

Ben-Amos, Dan. 1976. Analytic Categories and Ethnic Genres. In *Folklore Genres*, ed. Dan Ben-Amos, pp.215-242. Austin: The University of Texas Press.

Benjamin, Walter. 1969. *Illuminations*, ed. Hannah Arendt. Trans. by Harry Zohn. New York: Schocken.

Bouillon, Antoine. 1981. *Madagascar, le colonisé et son "âme"*. Paris: L'Harmattan.

Bremond, Claude. 1973. *Logique du Récit*. Paris: Seuil.

Briggs, Charles L. 1990. History, Poetics, and Interpretation in the Tale. In *The Lost Gold Mine of Juan Mondragon: A Legend of New Mexico Performed by Melaquias Romero*, ed. Charles L. Briggs and J. J. Vigil, pp. 165-240. Tucson: University of Arizona Press.

Bruss, Elizabeth. 1982. *Beautiful Theories: The Spectacle of Discourse in Contemporary Criticism*. Baltimore: The Johns Hopkins University Press.

Crapanzano, Vincent. 1984. Life Histories. *American Anthropologist* 86:953-60.

Dahle, L[ars]. 1977. *Specimens of Malagasy Folk-lore*. Antananarivo: A. Kingdon.

de Man, Paul. 1982. Introduction. *Toward an Aesthetic of Reception*. By Hans Robert Jauss. Trans. by Timothy Bahti, pp. vii-xxv. Minneapolis: University of Minnesota Press.

_____. 1983 [1971]. *Blindness and Insight: Essays in the Rhetoric of Contemporary Criticism*. Intro. by Wlad Godzich. Theory and History of Literature 7. Minneapolis: University of Minnesota Press.

Degh, Linda. 1968. *Folktales and Society: Storytelling in a Hungarian Peasant Community*. Trans. by Emily M. Schlossberger. Bloomington: Indiana University Press.

Derrida, Jacques. 1978. *Writing and Difference*. Trans. Alan Bass. Chicago: University of Chicago Press.

Detienne, Marcel. 1986. *The Creation of Mythology*. Trans. by Margaret Cook. Chicago: The University of Chicago Press.

_____. 1991. Myth and Writing: The Mythographers. In *Mythologies*. Trans. by Gerald Honigsblum. Comp. by Yves Bonnefoy. Rev. by Wendy Doniger, pp. 10-11. Chicago: University of Chicago Press.

Eagleton, Terry. 1978. *Criticism and Ideology: A Study in Marxist Literary Theory.* London: Verso Editions-NLB.
Ellis, John M. 1983. *One Fairy Story Too Many: The Brothers Grimm and Their Tales.* Chicago: University of Chicago Press.
Faublée, Jacques. 1947. *Récits bara.* Paris: Institut de l'Ethnologie.
Fine, Elizabeth C. 1984. *The Folklore Text, from Performance to Print.* Bloomington: Indiana University Press.
Fish, Stanley. 1985. Consequences. *Critical Inquiry* 11: 433-58.
Flacourt, Sieur [Etienne] de. 1661. *Histoire de la Grande Isle de Madagascar.* Paris: Gervais Clouzier.
Foucault, Michel. 1980. *Power/knowledge: Selected Writings and Other Interviews 1972-1977*, ed. Colin Gordon. Trans. by Colin Gordon, et al. New York: Pantheon.
Gueunier, Noël J. 1990. *La Belle ne se marie point: contes comoriens en dialecte malgache de l'île de Mayotte.* SELAF no. 306. Paris: Peeters.
Haring, Lee. 1980. The Classification of Malagasy Narrative. *Research in African Literatures* 11:342-55.
_____. 1992. *Verbal Arts in Madagascar: Performance in Historical Perspective.* Publications of the American Folklore Society. Philadelphia: University of Pennsylvania Press.
Hymes, Dell. 1975. Breakthrough Into Performance. In *Folklore: Performance and Communication*, ed. Dan Ben-Amos, and Kenneth S. Goldstein, pp. 11-74. The Hague: Mouton.
Jacobs, Melville. 1964. *Pattern in Cultural Anthropology.* Homewood, IL: Dorsey.
_____ and Bernhard J. Stern. 1952 [1947]. *General Anthropology.* College Outline Series. New York: Barnes and Noble.
Jauss, Hans Robert. 1982. *Toward an Aesthetic of Reception.* Trans. by Timothy Bahti. Minneapolis: University of Minnesota Press.
Lentricchia, Frank. 1983. *Criticism and Social Change.* Chicago: University of Chicago Press.
Lord, Albert Bates. 1956. Avdo Mededovic, Guslar. *Journal of American Folklore* 69:320-30.
Malinowski, Bronislaw. 1948. *Magic, Science and Religion and Other Essays.* Introd. by Robert Redfiled. Garden City, NY: Doubleday-Doubleday.
Mannoni, O[ctave]. 1964. *Prospero and Caliban: The Psychology of Colonization.* Trans. by Pamela Powesland. New York: Frederick A. Praeger.
Moser, Hans. 1962. Vom Folklorismus in unserer Zeit. *Zeitschrift für Volkskunde* 58:177-209.
Ottino, Paul. 1986. *L'Etrangére intime: essai d'anthropologie de la civilisation de l'ancien Madagascar.* Paris: Editions Des Archives Contemporaines.
_____. 1991. The Mythology of the Highlands of Madagascar and the Political Cycle of the Andriambahoaka. In *Mythologies: A Restructured Translation of Dictionnaire des mythologies et des religions des sociétés traditionnelles et du monde antique*, Vol. 2, ed. Yves Bonnefoy, pp. 961-976. Chicago: The University of Chicago Press.

Peacock, James. 1987 [1968]. *Rites of Modernization: Symbolic and Social Aspects of Indonesian Proletarian Drama*. Chicago: The University of Chicago Press.
Pease, Donald E. 1990. Author. In *Critical Terms for Literary Study*, ed. Frank Lentricchia and Thomas McLaughlin. Chicago: University of Chicago Press.
Raison-Jourde, Francoise. 1977. L'échange inegal de la langue: la pénétration des techniques linguistiques dans une civilisation de l'oral (Imerina, début du XIXe Siecle). *Annales Economies, Sociétés, Civilisations* 32.4:639-69.
Renel, Charles. 1910. *Contes de Madagascar*. 2 vols. Paris: Ernest Leroux.
———. 1923. *Ancêtres et dieux*. Bulletin de l'Académie Malgache. Antananarivo: Academie Malgache.
———. 1930. *Contes de Madagascar*. Paris: Ernest Leroux.
Richter, David H., ed. 1982. *The Critical Tradition: Classic Texts and Contemporary Trends*. A Bedford Book. New York: St. Martin's.
Rorty, Richard. 1982. *Consequences of Pragmatism (essays: 1972-1980)*. Minneapolis: University of Minnesota Press.
Rosaldo, Michelle Zimbalist. 1982. The Things We Do with Words: Ilongot Speech Acts and Speech Act Theory in Philosophy. *Language in Society* 11:203-35.
Said, Edward W. 1989. Representing the Colonized: Anthropology's Interlocutors. *Critical Inquiry* 15.2:205-25.
Schrempp, Gregory. 1991. Dimensions of Worldview: Worldview as an Organizing Concept in Ethnographic and Narrative Research. Unpublished paper distributed in advance to participants in 1992 Congress of the International Society for Folk Narrative Research.
Schuchardt, Hugo. 1980. The Language of the Saramacca Negroes in Surinam. In *Pidgin and Creole Languages, Selected Essays*, ed. Glenn G. Gilbert. Cambridge: Cambridge University Press.
———. 1980. *Pidgin and Creole Languages: Selected Essays by Hugo Schuchardt*, ed. Glenn G. Gilbert. Cambridge: Cambridge University Press.
Stahl, Sandra Dolby. 1989. *Literary Folkloristics and the Personal Narrative*. Bloomington: Indiana University Press.
Taussig, Michael. 1993. *Mimesis and Alterity: A Particular History of the Senses*. New York: Routledge.
Williams, Raymond. 1977. *Marxism and Literature*. Oxford: Oxford University Press.

11

Slave Spirituals: Allegories of the Recovery from Pain

Laura O'Connor

In a brilliant and harrowing study, *The Body in Pain* (1985), Elaine Scarry describes death (the cessation of sentience) and pain (the grotesque overload of sentience) as the most extreme forms of self-negation. She juxtaposes the self which she locates in the voice, with the body, or mere sentience. She analyses torture as an extreme process of self-negation until torture victims experience themselves exclusively in terms of sentience or the body, and the torturer sees himself exclusively in terms of self-extension or the voice. I contend that the conditions of antebellum slaves were analogous to torture, since slavery was a concerted effort by white masters to usurp the slaves' voice and reduce them to mere sentience. The slaves' pain had a private and public dimension: private insofar as all suffering is deeply isolating and incommunicable, and public since it was the common experience of African-American people. Recovery from pain, therefore, had to serve personal and public needs by healing both the individual and the communal psyche. I will first examine the structure of spiritual performances to show that they are determined by a movement towards integrating the body and voice and lending communal support to individual leadership. Later, I will consider how allegory was used to form continuities with an African past, to encode clandestine liberation messages, and to project journeys to freedom.

The master deconstructed the slave into sentience by fictionalising blackness as absence and whiteness as presence, the voice of representation. The voice of the master explained master/slave roles as a function of white/black skin colour. The slaves' blackness was presented as the reason why the rewards of work, or bodily extension upon the world, were denied them and why their children were taken from them as commodities and sold into slavery. Their blackness was the "reason" why their youth, strength, fertility, and beauty was dehumanised into a market exchange value. It was purportedly why they lived under the constant threat and frequent practice of torture and, should they attempt to escape, it was their blackness that would betray their fugitive status to the world. The sense that "my body's hurting me" (see Scarry 1985:47) was intensified for slaves in a macabre manner as their skin was experienced as the agent of imprisonment from which there was no escape.

The first essential step towards rejecting the master's attempt to displace his culpability onto the fiction of blackness as absence is the repossession of the voice. Voicing pain, as opposed to emitting cries or groans of pain, is already a triumph over pain. Nor was the voice asserted by negating the body, since spiritual performance integrated the use of body and voice in a manner unparalleled by the comparatively disembodied use of the voice in Western music. In a performance, group and leader parts could overlap with murmurs, shifts in vocal timbre and complex patterns of counterrhythms. With "Swing low, sweet chariot," for example, it is possible to imagine the chorus providing a swell of rhythmic intonation, like the rolling Jordan itself, over which the solo voice would soar, glide, slur and swoop as his/her voice changed from open, ringing tones to strong nasalization to powerful rasp, from falsetto coo to bass grunt. The virtuosic use of the voice was a striking antidote to the process of voice deconstruction in torture, or to the "silence" that is considered to be a characteristic of all oppressed or "voiceless" groups (see Scarry 1985:207).

The rhythmic complexity of African and African-American music is an acknowledged greatness. Regularity of pulse acts as a basic framework against which a series of rhythms are syncopated. Head swaying, torso swaying, thigh slapping, foot stamping and hand clapping could amplify these syncopated rhythms by turning the body into an elaborate percussive instrument, each part playing a different rhythm pattern. The close relationship between African music and dance was maintained in African-American culture, and many camp meetings would have culminated with a ring shout, when a ring dance pounded out or chanted the basic unit of spirituals, the repeated one line or ground motif. Thus the voice set the pattern that was developed by greater bodily participation, achieving maximal integration of voice and body. Rhythm can be imagined as an externalisation of the heart beat which reminds participants in a powerful, unconscious way that they are indeed alive and surviving. By projecting beat and soul into an independent existence in the world, the form of spirituals was evidence that, despite the odds, the hearts, souls and bodies of the performers had somehow managed to survive intact.

The return to, or repetition with variation, of the one-line unit creates the "structural effect" that Fineman isolates as the key feature of allegory (1981:33). One-line structure requires the concentration of as much meaning into as few words as possible, without contextual detail. Such contextual explanation was unnecessary since spirituals, unlike the slave narratives whose polemic audience was the oppressor, were acts of self and communal expression in a shared idiom and context. Successful one lines satisfy people as "saying it all" and the most significant mobilising ideas in history are expressed in rallying one lines.

The one lines are notably extrovert and positive and attention is directed away from the dreadful circumstances of slavery, which are downplayed in understatements like "de trouble I've seen" or "unfriendly worl'" (Bontemps and Hughes 1958:294, 287). This accords with shamanistic healing practices in oral cultures throughout the world which draw upon the power of the word to fix attention away from pain towards hope and recovery. Blinderman describes Yoruba healing as a call-response interchange between healer and patient so that healing is effected by "compulsion through orderly repetition" (1985:43). The most famous spiritual one line, "we shall overcome," similarly directs the will to triumph.

Good one lines beg repetition and there is a natural inclination to repeat them in varying contexts. The implications of "No more!" are teased out in "No more auction block for me" variously as "no more peck of corn for me," "no more driver's lash for me," or whatever substitution would have been considered appropriate by the singers (Bontemps and Hughes 1958:291-292). The paratactic structure facilitates substitution for different performances, and by foregrounding words against the foil of the underlying shape, it enables individuals to substitute personal meanings for general terms. "No more auction block for me" follows a counting pattern of undoing that negates the averse conditions in the incremental rebuilding that is so characteristic of spirituals.

One lines usually form the response in the call and response structure of the spirituals. A leader initiating the spiritual with a call of "Swing low, sweet chariot," for example, evokes the one line response "Comin for to carry me home," followed by variations, "I looked over Jordan, and what did I see?" (Bontemps and Hughes 1958:295). Whoever initiates the lyric—a gifted performer, a respected leader, or perhaps a wronged individual—takes leadership, which alternates between members of the group, even within the duration of a performance. The call of each individual is responded to and endorsed by the group, destroying the sense of isolation inflicted by pain. Spirituals are fundamentally improvisational and are structured about "spaces" that a group fills according to their need, prowess or individual personalities. The creative making and use of spaces by group members reflects the non-hierarchical, mutually-supportive nature of relations between them. It enhances the representative power of the voice, by creating a multivocal "one voice" that emphasises, rather than elides, distinctive individual voices. The highly sophisticated, sensitive nature of improvisation reinforces and reinvigorates the social structure between them that slavery sought to erase. By strengthening solidarity and nurturing leadership, spiritual performance could heal the body politic of the group.

Many of these generalizations about the structure of spirituals can be observed in a single lyric, "There's a man goin' roun' takin' names." The commonplace occurrence of a man taking names is one loaded with malignity in an African-American context. Families were routinely separated and slaves were re-named by masters to designate them as their property. The name motif is central in African-American literature, especially in slave narratives where slaves typically celebrate their freedom by re-naming themselves. Here the word "take" signifies the appropriation and plunder of a name as drastic as the taking of a life. "Taking" conflates blasphemy with the master-language, writing, and highlights its debasement into an abuse of power. The man's register is like a cattle census, the naming of commodities that will be listed in an auction catalogue.

> There's a man goin' roun' takin' names,
> There's a man goin' roun' takin' names,
> He has taken my father's name,
> And he's left my heart in pain,

> There's a man goin' roun' takin' names,
>
> O death is that man takin' names,
> O death is that man takin['] names,
> He has taken my mother's name,
> And he has left my heart in pain,
> O death is that man takin' names,
>
> (Fisher 1926:28-29)

The lyric reappropriates the taken names. The half-rhyme of name and pain accentuates the essential purpose in the lyric of naming pain in order to overcome it. "My father" (or my mother, brother, sister, aunt....) disavows proper names in favour of emphasis upon familial relationships, the possessive "my" usurping the master's claim to ownership. In successive verses the lyric lists family members in an act that re-assembles or rebuilds the now separated family. The register of loss translates the man's inhumane list into human terms, substituting a litany of love for his auction catalogue.

The line "O death is that man taking names" names the man as death, for he is not only a harbinger of death but a personification of it, since humanity is dead in him. His name taking is a brutal form of subtraction. The simplest fact about the body, whether it is present or absent, is most commonly registered by the act of counting (see Scarry on body count in war, 1985:116-117). In the family/community census constituted within the lyric, the subtraction is converted into making those actually absent present through invocation. It is an elegiac counting that restores the human dignity that was taken by the commodity census. Two key features of spirituals, naming and listing, are a verbal substantiation that is parallelled by a restoration of community. The materiality of counting is crucial, for its absolute referentiality directs attention away from unnameable pain and annihilating sentience outwards towards the world and human relationships. Thus, the undoing of the community or reduction into sentience that is the purpose and practice of slavery is resisted.

There is a possible interpretation of my argument that spirituals are allegories for the recovery from pain that would support what Scarry argues is the principle aim of torture, that is, the conversion of pain into a fiction of power. Thus, as a white literary critic, I can argue (with the support of shamanistic therapy) that singing a song makes one feel better, or alternately, (citing examples from literary history) that the torsion of pain creates intensity of utterance and great art. However, to argue that this alone represents "recovery" would be to conform closely to the viewpoint of the white master, who approved of spirituals as a means of increasing the slave's productivity and as a form of renewal that enabled him/her to further endure "life." As a temporary respite from pain, spirituals served as a safety valve in the interests of white masters by effectively increasing the slave's endurance for pain and thereby prolonging it. Recovery that was nothing more than such readjustment would be self-defeating.

The temporary respite from pain afforded by spiritual performance allowed slaves to concentrate on the wish expressed in the one line, and by constant return to the original conceit of the allegory, they could will it into being. The wish to be elsewhere, or to be "home," is the most common wish in extant spirituals. Home was where slave families could be reunited and live as freed people, which geographically could be anywhere but which historically must often have seemed to the slaves to be nowhere. Allegory was used to project spatially the journey "home" and to create an imaginative geography of this Utopia. Home was imagined as the antithesis of here: "Dere's no rain to wet you, / O yes I want to go home. / Dere's no sun to burn you, / O yes I want to go home" (Allen et al. 1940:91). The persistence of the not here/elsewhere motif helped performers to resist accepting "here" as a norm or as an inevitable fate.

Life was imagined by the slave as a journey, and many of the spirituals feature modes of transportation—a chariot, a boat, a train—which could carry them home. The sense of mobility achieved through imaginative travel broke the cycle in slavery of bodily confinement in a proscribed place. Spirituals feature the trying but ultimately successful passage through the wilderness, the lonesome valley, across the river or the mountain top. These songs imaginatively prepared the slave intending to escape for the difficulties he/she would encounter in his/her bid for freedom. Spirituals also encoded clandestine escape messages in "underground railroad songs" that were transmitted along the "grapevine telegraph." The "railroad" led fugitive slaves north through a pathway of sanctuaries ("stations") with the aid of "conductors" (Mansur 1967:143). Among the popular underground railroad songs were "Steal Away to Jesus," "Good News, de Chariot's Coming," and "Follow the Drinkin' Gourd" which directed fugitives to follow the Big Dipper to go North. Allegory is an ideal vehicle for saying the unsayable, for as Frederick Douglass observes: "A keen observer might have detected in our repeated singing of 'O Canaan, sweet Canaan, / I am bound for the land of Canaan' something more than a hope of reaching heaven. We meant to reach the *north*—and the north was our Canaan" (Douglass 1987:170).

The theme of "home" suggests an originary place of safety, and spirituals provided a cultural link with Africa, supporting Fineman's argument that allegory attempts to recuperate the past: "It is as though allegory were precisely that mode that makes up for that distance, or heals the gap, between the present and a disappearing past, which, without interpretation, would be otherwise irretrievable and foreclosed" (1981:29). Keeping African musical traditions alive in spirituals was an important connection with an otherwise brutally sundered past heritage, and cemented an ethnic bond among African-Americans.

That "home" may have signified heaven, and the journey man's spiritual progress, are obvious allegorical interpretations for these motifs, since it is as devotional methodist or baptist hymns and conversion songs that spirituals would have held most significance for many performers. Rather than entering the debate of whether the spirituals were primarily otherworldly or this-worldly, and hence how politically motivated they were, I'd like to address the selectivity of Biblical borrowings, which scholars agree are mostly from the Books of Exodus and Revelations. The theme of Moses, Daniel or Joshua as deliverers of an exiled people into the Promised Land, that "the God that lived in Moses' time is jus' de same today" (Johnson 1940:80-81) has obvious appeal, as does the idea that the white masters' hierarchy and moral order would be overthrown. Blacks, not whites, were imagined as the chosen people, and the claim that the master would be humbled and the slave exalted found frequent expression, together with thinly veiled threats like "Ev'ry body talkin' about heaben ain' gwine der" (Johnson 1940:71).

What is less easily decoded is the predominance of apocalyptic imagery. Apocalyptic spirituals abound in images of blood and fire and identify God with retribution and violence:

> Jacob's ladder deep an' long,
> See God's angel comin' down,
> Comin down in a sheet of blood,

> Sheet of blood all mingled wid fire.
> (Johnson 1940:153)

The concern with apocalypse may just reflect the contemporary influence of popular millennial revivalism, or it could be a register of what Frantz Fanon diagnosed a century later as a common reactionary psychosis among colonised peoples to "the firm impression . . . of being caught up in a veritable Apocalypse" (1963:251). Nevertheless, it remains anomalous with the refusal to dwell upon pain or the masters' violence discussed above, and this may suggest that the imagining of apocalyptic violence in spirituals has an aggressive, and not a fatalistic, role.

The constant repetition of apocalyptic themes functions like a mantra of violence, a means of readying performers for the violence that would inevitably accompany (or so it must have seemed) that moment when the humble would be exalted and the exalted humbled. A parallel is drawn between Christ's crucifixion and the fate of the individual at the moment of reckoning:

> Dey whipp'd Him up an dey whipp'd Him down,
> What yo' gwine to do when yo' lamp burn down?
> Dey whipp'd dat man all ovah town
> What yo' gwine do when yo' lamp burn down?
> (Johnson 1940:170-171)

Since such sacrifice would mean annihilation, apocalyptic spirituals seem to reverse the movement towards holism and recovery that I suggest subtends them. On the other hand, René Girard argues in *Violence and the Sacred* (1977) that religions developed around the idea of sacrifice, or ritual scapegoating, and the sanctification of that ritual in order to immunize the community against violence. Bakan supports Girard's theory of immunization through sacrifice in his theory of recovery from amputation. He argues that the amputee re-imagines his limb, which heretofore has been "me," as something which is "not me" and that that "not me" is sacrificed in order that "I" might continue to live. A possible explanation for the predominance of apocalyptic imagery in spirituals, therefore, is that they project the awaited cataclysm as a necessary bloodletting where parts of the community might have to be sacrificed in order to ensure the survival of the rest of the community.

The structure of spirituals is deeply representative. Each voice speaks for a common pain, and the communal voice endorses, supports and elaborates the voice of the individual. Naming, listing, and community censuses reconstitute the presences of community members. The rhythmic use of the body to harmonise with the voice and to create "one voice" chorus-effects asserts the embodiedness of the voice that slavery attempted to destroy. Folk memory and the Bible provide memorable one-lines which survive in folk memory today and recur constantly in political speeches and rallying-cries, songs and book titles. The materiality of these techniques re-present the self, a social self validated by the community, with ever-increasing insistence, making denial of that selfhood impossible.

Parallel to self-extension through vocal representation, spirituals map the slaves' bodily extension upon the world by projecting journeys away from their presently proscribed place and by imagining "home." This movement towards sanctuary elsewhere is the prime movement in spirituals, and maps out the path to recovery as the community wills itself towards that goal. A return to the organizing allegorical structure of this paper lends the insight that "allegory seems by its nature to be incompleteable, never quite fulfilling its grand design" (Fineman 1981:22). To suggest that spiritual performance could ever undo the barbaric effects of slavery would be absurd, but nonetheless, the fact that such a grand design could be conceived and re-conceived under the pressure of intolerable conditions is ground for hope.

References

Allen, William Francis, Charles Pickard Ware and Lucy McKim Garrison, eds. 1940. *American Negro Songs*. New York: Howell, Soskin & Co.
Bakan, David. 1968. *Disease, Pain and Sacrifice*. Chicago: Chicago University Press.
Blinderman, Abraham. 1985 [1973]. Shamans, Witchdoctors, Medicine Men and Poetry. In *Poetry as Healer*, ed. Jack J. Leedy. New York: Vanguard Press.
Bontemps, Arna and Langston Hughes, eds. 1958. *The Book of Negro Folklore*. New York: Dodd Mead & Co.
Douglass, Frederick. 1987. *My Bondage and My Freedom*. Chicago: University of Illinois Press.
Fanon, Frantz. 1963. *The Wretched of the Earth*. New York: Grove Press.

Fineman, Joel. 1981. The Structure of Allegorical Desire. In *Allegory and Representation*, ed. Stephen Greenblatt, pp. 26-60. Baltimore: Johns Hopkins University Press.
Fisher, William Arms, comp. 1926. *Seventy Negro Spirituals*. Boston: Oliver Ditson Co.
Girard, René. 1977. *Violence and the Sacred*. Baltimore: Johns Hopkins University Press.
Johnson, J. W. and J. R., comps. 1940. *The Books of American Negro Spirituals*. New York: Viking Press.
Mansur, A. 1967. *Let My People Go*. Galt, California: The Author.
Scarry, Elaine. 1985. *The Body in Pain*. Oxford: Oxford University Press.

12

Re-presentations of (Im)moral Behavior in the Middle English Non-Cycle Play "Mankind"[1]

Michael J. Preston

How to understand the Middle English morality play, *Mankind*, written c.1466, has presented various problems for academics throughout the nineteenth and twentieth centuries because of its mix of religion and bawdry, and early editors who printed the text expurgated it. David Bevington's influential book, *From "Mankind" to Marlowe* (1962), has convinced many that *Mankind* is the earliest surviving evidence of professional players. A recent thought-provoking essay on *Mankind* is that of Anthony Gash (1986), "Carnival against Lent: The Ambivalence of Medieval Drama." I have various reservations about much that has been written about *Mankind*, which I will detail below, but I want to avoid the common rhetorical practice of beating up on the stimulating work of others in order to further one's own project. Instead, I offer correctives and alternatives, these from the perspective of an academic Catholic, however wavering, whose class-identity and life-experiences suggest an alternative approach as well as make the critical question of considerable interest. My approach, as critical of Bakhtin's *Rabelais and His World* (1968) as of Gash's application of it because I do not see in the play the degree of social protest which breaks open whole systems, is intended to open up a more wide-ranging discussion of *Mankind* and Early English drama generally.

For the non-medievalist reader of this essay, *Mankind* should be understood to be a brief play (914 lines survive) which begins with a speech by the character Mercy, represented as a priest, whose goal is to encourage the central character Mankind to live a proper life and thereby save his soul. Mercy is opposed in this effort by Mischief and three fashionable young men, New Guise, Nowadays, and Nought. The comic devil Titivillus makes an appearance later in the play in order to make Mankind's attempt to lead a good life all the more difficult. Mankind, however, returns to virtue by the end of the play.

Mankind may have been something of a problem long before modern scholars became aware of its existence, because the second leaf in the manuscript is missing, and it would have been on that leaf that New Guise, Nowadays, and Nought made their initial appearances. Although accidents to manuscripts certainly have happened, it is my experience with medieval manuscripts that there was much censoring of them after the Reformation, both official censorship as well as the private acts of individuals. This practice is readily demonstrated with surviving illuminations of manuscripts, such as the representation of Christ healing a demoniac in the ninth-century Stuttgart Gospels, in which the female's "private parts" have been erased (reproduced in Russell 1989:46), thus documenting the distance between what presumably was appropriate in the ninth century and what was considered "seemly" in a later era. In addition, it is easily understood that the Catholic worldview of medieval texts was often not acceptable in post-Reformation England. Indeed, the thesis of *Mysteries' End: An Investigation of the Last Days of the Medieval Religious Stage* (Gardiner 1967 [1946]) is that an entire dramatic tradition was destroyed because of religious differences.

In this essay, I attempt to re-situate *Mankind* so that it might be better understood over all. I explore some of the popular and learned traditions which its author may have made use of in its composition, such as "folk-plays," balancing an evaluation of modern (mis)understandings of such traditions against an evaluation of twentieth-century objections to what is represented in the play. My methodology is eclectic.

An overview of *Mankind* is that it is a dramatic representation of the psychomachia, the battle between good and evil for the souls of all members of the human race, but, as Gash has rightly observed,

> It is more usefully seen as compounding two genres, one official, the other unofficial, by punning between the morality play structure (the fall, repentance and salvation of mankind) and a festive structure (the battle between the licence of Christmas and the prohibitions of Lent). (1986:82)

Built upon the medieval tradition of allegory, *Mankind*'s cast of characters are presented as moral abstractions, but represented "as recognisable social types" (Gash 1986:94). This is the tradition that, one hundred thirty years later, was one basis for Shakespeare's *Henry IV, Part 1*, in which Prince Hal describes Falstaff as "...an old fat man....that reverent Vice, that grey Iniquity..." (II.iv.448-454). In the late twentieth-century, that tradition continues in popular cartoons in which an angry Donald Duck is sometimes depicted with an angelic duck on one shoulder and a demonic duck on the other, both giving him advice. In *Henry IV*, Prince Hal is likewise pressured by his father (the good duck) to improve his behavior and not act like Falstaff (the bad duck). Indeed, Hal explicates his situation in "festive" terms, strikingly like what Gash argues for *Mankind*:

> If all the year were playing holidays,
> To sport would be as tedious as to work;
> But when they seldom come, they wish'd for come,
> And nothing pleaseth but rare accidents.
> So when this loose behavior I throw off
> And pay the debt I never promised,
> By how much better than my word I am,
> By so much shall I falsify men's hopes,
> And like bright metal on a sullen ground,
> My reformation, glitt'ring o'er my fault,
> Shall show more goodly and attract more eyes
> Than that which hath no foil to set it off.
> (I.ii.204-215)

Prince Hal's mention of "holiday" is germane, but it should not be taken too literally, because Hal is not acting as he acts so much because of the time of the year, such as Shrovetide, but rather—more generally—because of the time in his life: as heir apparent he had time to play, to "sport," before shouldering the responsibilities he would have as king. Nonetheless, he was judged by his father and those around him as a less-than-worthy heir. Hal, like Mankind, talks the talk appropriate to his various activities, whether that of play or of the serious work of the monarchy.

Shakespeare's *Henry IV* makes a clear distinction between manners and morals—indeed, it is built upon that distinction—, and yet our society often conflates the two, as did Shakespeare's character,

Henry IV. This conflation is illustrated by Laura Kipnis's Cultural Studies essay, "(Male) Desire and (Female) Disgust: Reading *Hustler*" (1992). Kipnis's argument that "anti-porn feminism lapses into bourgeois reformism" is important in demonstrating the conflation of gender and class concerns in academic discourse and perhaps more generally. The same kind of conflation or confusion of the one with the other is my concern with our cultural tendency to confuse manners with morals, and that, we shall see, is relevant to a consideration of *Mankind*.

The Church as Context

Before proceeding, I need to discuss certain issues, because they lie at the heart of (mis)understandings of any medieval text. First of all, the medieval Church was not as much a single entity as Gash seems to assume; its voice was often polyphonic, even though in many particular places and at many particular times an official "party line" was harshly enforced. It seems that it was more often at the higher level of international politics, secular interests wrapped up in religious arguments, sometimes compounded by cross-cultural misunderstandings—the justification for the invasion of Ireland by Henry II is a good example—that the perspective of the Church can be seen as enforcing a narrow orthodoxy. In America today, parts of this diversity in the Church have been thoroughly documented by Andrew M. Greeley in *The Catholic Myth* (1990). Non-Catholics today see sameness where Catholics experience diversity. As a remedy, we should re-read William Jansen's aging essay, "The Esoteric-Exoteric Factor in Folklore" (1965 [1959]), and recognize that members of a group understand their behavior in a way different from what non-members understand, and both parties' understandings of the others' understandings differ analogously. In-group humor is the basis for such popular books as *What's So Funny About Being Catholic? An Uproarious Collection of Blasphemous Facts, Unholy Jokes, Irreverent Folklore, and More* (Warner 1994). In the example of *Mankind*, I argue that it has been read variously by those outside of the Church as well as those within from post-Reformation and post-Counter-Reformation perspectives, rather than from inside the pre-Reformation Church, which was the fact of life in the mid-fifteenth century, however "unorthodox" an individual or group may have been considered or thought they were, and that in-group humor of various kinds characterizes the play.

For a modern reader, the medieval Church might be compared with benefit to the U. S. Armed Services. I make this comparison because of, rather in spite of, the faults that those outside of the military, such as myself, have long seen in "the military establishment." Setting that criticism aside and looking at the military itself reveals certain traditional rivalries, such as that between the Army and the Marines, which, to an outsider, might appear as negative criticism, hostility, or petty back-biting—depending upon how it is expressed—rather than a rivalry. Indeed, I think that this might well serve as a useful paradigm for understanding the various religious orders of the Church, and the civilian population of the U.S. might well serve as a paradigm for those not in religious orders in the Middle Ages. The Church and the military, of course, have similar hierarchical structures.

Authorship and Audience

If we bring the idea of a differentiated medieval religious society to bear on *Mankind*, a number of questions arise about authorship, performers, and audience(s) which Gash did not consider. About authorship, Gash wrote:

> It seems likely...that the play resulted from a professional collaboration of learned Cambridge clerics and professional actors, taking the play on tour to East Anglian villages. It indicates that the small professional touring companies...were important agents of the cross-fertilisation of clerical and popular culture, and of the subtle subversion of homiletic forms from within." (1986:83)

To me Gash's view seems to be suspiciously modern in that it accords Cambridge the intellectual dominance of the region and supposes an unspecified collaboration with professional actors. Gail McMurray Gibson has a very different suggestion, that the *Mankind* manuscript is connected to the Benedictine abbey of Bury St. Edmonds in Suffolk and that "the money-collecting speech in *Mankind*...is acknowledgement not of a professional traveling troupe, but of the real fundraising motive behind the play's performance—to raise money for Christ's church" (1989:111). Gash's essentializing of "the Church" as well as his hostility to it—"oppressive institution" (1986:88), "punitive, castrating patriarchy" (1986:90)—seem to blind him to distinctions, such as when he writes that "the compilation of the individual guild plays into a centralised 'register' [of the York Plays] may be regarded as itself an implicit act of censorship by the Church and the civic authorities" (Gash 1986:75). This statement may be true, but it certainly is misleading because, as Richard Beadle informs us, the register was compiled over a period of time somewhere between 1463 and 1477. "Rather than being a relatively short and continuous stint, the process of copying was probably an extended and (to the scribe) an unusual task, involving the collection of a large number of exemplars in different handwritings, and different states of preservation" (Beadle 1982:11). Citing dates from 1501 to 1554, Beadle continues:

> The expression ["keep the Register"] is generally taken to mean that the surviving manuscript was used to check what was taking place in performance, and many of the numerous annotations in it by later hands, such as those alluding to stage business or to plays having been revised or rewritten, are likely to have derived from this activity.
>
> Though the Register was intended to be a full record of the text of the cycle, it was never completed....The manuscript is last heard of in its official capacity in 1579....(Beadle 1982:12)

I find it astounding, considering the religious turmoil in England between 1463 and 1579, that Gash refers to "the Church" as if "it" were a single stable entity and that he can attribute to "it" a constant "implicit act of censorship" (Gash 1986:75). Indeed, what might have been undertaken in a spirit of local pride, a kind of antiquarianism, does seem to have culminated in censorship in the sixteenth century, but, here as elsewhere, Gash paints with so wide a brush that it seems to limit his thinking about what members of the clergy could do.

Let us assume that Gail McMurray Gibson is correct and that *Mankind* was written by a Benedictine monk at Bury St. Edmonds. That, at the least, would provide the basis for a gloss on "demonycall frayry" (153), punning between "demonical" and "Dominican," thus resolving different understandings of that word and recognizing the rivalry between different orders. Much in *Mankind* would be understood very differently if it were performed by a group of (presumably) young monks at Bury St. Edmonds, and yet differently if they performed it elsewhere in the region. Gash's narrow view of "the Church," witness his misplaced emphasis on the Bible when he writes about other medieval plays which contain "Biblically unauthorised figures" and "Noah's cantankerous wife" whose "rebellious and anarchic behavior is unauthorized by the Bible" (1986:78), is misleading concerning what clergy could write about. The Bible, as we conceive it now, was certainly an important set of texts in the Middle Ages, but there were other important texts and other traditions, such as saints' legends, from which even the most orthodox of clergy could draw, but then, as now, clergy were not always, or even usually, restricted to narrowly "religious" topics in their reading and writing, however their religious perspectives may have affected their understandings.

At the monastery at Bury St. Edmonds, there would certainly have been an esoteric recognition of exoteric perspectives about what monks did, particularly in hard-to-fathom areas such as celibacy. Thus it would be particularly appropriate for an in-group audience of monks to hear New Guise say that "There are but sex dedly synnes, lechery is non" (706) and to mention "þe comyn tapster of Bury" (274). Sexual exploitation of parishioners is an important topic, and it is today the subject of numerous newspaper articles, whether or not the clergyman was a supposed celibate. Certainly, the sexual behavior of priests has been a much speculated-about subject, as in the exposé written by Jeremiah J. Crowley, *Romanism: A Menace to the Nation* (1912). Such popular books document anti-clerical and anti-religious sentiments which can be traced throughout the Middle Ages. Like many such "contemporary legends," there probably were bases for it, whether particular sexual acts preceded and therefore were the bases for legend-formation, or whether particular sexual acts were acting the legends out. A modern example of an analogous "legend" is recounted in Jeffrey Victor's *Satanic Panic: The Creation of a Contemporary Legend* (1993) and *The Satanism Scare* (Richardson *et al*.: 1991). Stories and songs about randy monks would almost of necessity be known, or known about, in a large monastery—whatever an individual monk's sexual life may have been—, and at a time of carnival the exploitation of such themes, although certain to be considered "vulgarities" (Coogan 1947:77), would not be "sins" of a grave nature.

Although *Mankind* represents a distinctly male perspective, we should not forget the otherwise unrecorded reality of the "comyn tapster of Bury." Here I shift again to modern evidence to state that an informant of mine has told me in graphic detail about her room-mates at a college in Maryland in the 1960's who took it as a challenge to seduce seminarians at a nearby Catholic seminary. My point is not to minimize any exploitation of local women by the clergy at Bury St. Edmonds, but rather to point to sexual contact's sometimes being a two-way street, and perhaps a greater subject of speculation than reality. Nonetheless, as a common topic of conversation in such a context, this theme finds its appropriate place in a local play, meaning perhaps one thing to an audience of clergy and something quite different if a group of monks performed the play in neighboring towns. Indeed, the setting of the play at Shrovetide with its "raucous gaity" (Coogan 1947:8) might well be distinguished from when the play was actually performed, the licence of the Shrovetide setting perhaps allowing the play to be performed successfully on a greater number of days than Shrovetide itself.[2]

"An Outspoken Age"

Sister Coogan made the important point that the fifteenth century was "an outspoken age," and, arguing for "rural or village audiences," she describes the humor of the play as "a realistic adaptation for dramatic purposes of the language of most of the audience in their moments of relaxation" (1947:95). I disagree with Sister Coogan's town-*versus*-country assumption as being perhaps too modern, in part because almost no one in the fifteenth century could have been unaware of the physicality of the animals with which they were surrounded: animals defecated and urinated in city streets as well as in fields out of sight; then as now mares and cows came visibly into heat, and bulls and stallions had notable erections. We should, I think, extend Sister Coogan's necessarily restrained comment by considering the recent work of Malcolm Jones (1993-1994). His extended essay discusses a variety of artifacts, but I quote here at length from his discussion of a generally unknown kind of "little lead badges or broaches":

> In recent years an extraordinary series of artefacts which, to our modern sensibilities, at least cannot help but seem bizarre, has emerged from the villages of Holland's Scheldt estuary in particular (inundated in the early decades of the 16th century), and from riverine deposits throughout Europe [including the Thames foreshore]. These little lead badges or broaches provide a fascinating opportunity to examine a class of personal ornament which was cheap enough to be afforded by even the poorest peasant, and this very fact gives them a disporportionate, and still to be fully explored importance. It is hardly surprising that the Kolner Kunstgewerbemuseum has miscatalogued two of these flimsy flying phalluses as Roman....So too—for unless one has seen enough of this frequently bizarre material it is sometimes difficult to believe one's eyes—-the same cataloguer of a 15thC. badge found in France must be forgiven for describing the gigantic penis which rears up to confront the little man with the dog on his shoulder, as "ein nicht identifizierbarer Gegenstand"! ...I believe we are entitled to conclude that some of this badge-imagery is intentionally comic...where we see a ship "crewed" by phalli, it is "emptily" humorous, having no ulterior purpose beyond that of raising a laugh...but in other examples the humor seems to me clearly *satiric* in intent....The most drastic example I have yet come across of such a presumably satiric intention, which must, I believe, belong to the polemics of the reformation, is a badge...: three phalli walking on human legs are carrying a sort of litter on which rides a vulva crowned with three more miniature phalli. I suggest this may be seen as a Protestant attack on a Catholic procession in honor of the Virgin Mary, whose image, perhaps in the form of a crowned statue of the Queen of Heaven, and surrounded by a rayed "glory" or mandorla—a vulvate shape, of course—was paraded through the streets on her feast-days. (Jones: 1993-1994:193-194)

How far Jones's account—even the limited excerpt above—differs from what most of us have thought went on in the fifteenth and sixteenth centuries should make us pause. One need invoke the title only of David Lowenthal's *The Past Is a Foreign Country* (1990 [1985]) to make us realize that a complete understanding of any text from a remote period may be impossible, and yet the patient accumulation of evidence and the stripping away of biased perspectives may make possible a "better" or "fuller" understanding; a new theoretical perspective may also be of use.

What is fresh—and good—about Gash's essay is that, through the use of Bakhtin's theorizing of carnival and the grotesque, he strips away calcified commentary. I see the class-values of Victorian academics in bourgeois reformism, and even more so in J. Q. Adams's carping about *Mankind*:

> The moral element is reduced to a minimum, and even the sole representation of good, Mercy, is deliberately made fun of with his ponderous Latinate diction and his saccharine talk; the humor becomes at times exceedingly vulgar; and the literary skill of the writer is unusually poor. (1924:304)

Mark Eccles, although more modern in his language, continues the tradition:

> the speeches of Mercy are tedious, but moralizing must be expected in a moral play....The play is amusing to read and would probably be even funnier when acted. (1969:xlv)

In approaching *Mankind* it is necessary to keep in mind how little we know about everyday medieval culture—"folklife," in my vocabulary—, not just because so little record was kept of it, but because much of the academic enterprise has been rooted in the concerns of the privileged classes. Adams's use of the word "vulgar" applies equally to subject-matter and to what he might, like our conservatives today, call the "underclass," and even though Eccles may have sniggered in his study, he was not about to defend the vulgarity of *Mankind*. That both Eccles and Adams fell back on a charge of "bad writing" is significant—they don't like it—, but what they don't like about it—and why—they do not explain in detail, thereby implying that their good taste is an absolute standard. N. F. Blake, however, states that "The humour comes from the incongruity of the different linguistic levels and to some extent from the vulgarisms present" (1981:68), all in "an East Midlands dialect" (1981:66). Blake's observations are, without a doubt, correct, but how one understands them in terms of the word-by-word arrangement of a text such as *Mankind* remains a problem. As Thomas W. Ross begins an essay:

> When Chaucer wrote "pisse" would his audience have been shocked or titillated? or would they have considered the word innocent enough? Was it in fact a neutral term? Or was it the kind of locution, albeit reprehensible, that one would expect from the Wife of Bath, rather than the pompous, Latinate "purgacioun of uryne" which she uses at one point? (1984:177)

Removed more than five hundred years from the composition of *Mankind*, how can we understand the effect of any word—"magnyfyede" (2) or "schytyth" (337)—or the specific meaning of any phrase—"Be medyacyon of Owr Lady" (22), "I com wyth my leggys wnder me" (454), and "a deull wey" (158)? Blake weasels somewhat when he writes of "levels" and "vulgarisms" as different conceptual categories in the same sentence.

It is with such problems in mind that, early in my career, I began to produce concordances (M. Preston 1975) in order to bring together, not just similar words, but similar locutions in context. I went beyond producing lexical concordances of the usual sort, developing a system whereby the parts of a particular speaker could be removed from the rest of the text and concorded separately in order to highlight verbal idiosyncrasies (See M. Preston and Pfleiderer 1982:337-408); other formal segments of texts, such as stanzas containing particular words or phrases, could also be retrieved for closer study (See C. Preston 1989). That project remains to be completed, due to the vagaries of an academic career, but it remains suggestive of how computer-technology might help resolve basic problems of understanding by recreating the contexts for words and phrases that were in the memory of every native speaker of, for example, *Mankind*'s specific East Anglian dialect. Without such "futuristic" resources, the active reader of a text such as *Mankind* must look closely at the words of the text as well as remember where else such words and phrases occurred. Thus one builds up a context for understanding the differences between one level of diction and another. That, whether a purely human or computer-assisted activity, is the only way to resolve the basic problem with which Ross (1984) was concerned. On the other hand, more general issues—whether Latinate English is good or bad—can be argued to their culturally appropriate conclusions.

In the instance of *Mankind*, though, one must also consider the influence of John Lygate, the monk of Bury, whose reputation must have saturated every crevice of the monastery at Bury St. Edmonds. If *Mankind* was a product of that monastery, and it was written not long after the death of Lydgate, then his "aureate" diction might itself have been subject to criticism. This is not necessarily Gash's "clerical scriptwriter, with unorthodox views" (1986:76), assuming from Gash's language that "unorthodox" meant one out of step with "the Church," but rather a clerical playwright who, based on his own sensitivity to language-use, dramatizes and criticizes the language-excesses he encountered daily in living at Bury St. Edmonds, in reading but perhaps also in speech. Today we might, together with Gash, read such criticism of language as "allowing the actors to woo the audience's approval for controversial social comments" (1986:76) because aureate diction does signify, not just a refined language register, but also the cultural imperialism of both the Church and the Latin tradition. But if we are concerned with what *Mankind*'s author might have intended, I do not think we can attribute to him revolutionary motives but rather lower-level objections to verbal pomposity, or, more probably, the social hypocrisy of public-*versus*-private language practices.

> It is human nature to be amused at minor embarrassment of a person in authority. Only a completely humorless person can see in such amusement the flouting of all authority, or even disrespect for the individual who is the object of the laughter. Quite law-abiding citizens have been known to enjoy a joke on a traffic officer. A clerical author would probably take more liberties in the fun he allows the evil characters to have at Mercy's expense than a lay person would, simply because of the special immunities of his position. There are pleasant possibilities of humor in such a situation, particularly if the audience knows the author. (Coogan 1947:97)

I think that *Mankind* is, at least in part, a play about language, just as Gibson argued that "latinate language is the real focus" of the N-Town "Mary in the Temple" play (1989:133), not "language" in the sense of a dialect removed from social issues, but rather in the sense of "refined language" which signifies a set of cultural values in opposition to the more common cultural values adhered to by those who spoke the local dialect. As a result, Mercy, who is represented more commonly as a woman, might in *Mankind* be seen as a priest so effeminate, considering outsiders' speculation about what went on in monasteries, that an audience might question the nature of his sexuality, this in contrast to the hearty heterosexuality elsewhere in the play.

Although the sometimes-earthy language of *Mankind* has bothered some readers, Erich Auerbach (1965) provides a paradigm based on St. Augustine for both the practice of the author of *Mankind* as well as the negative judgement of those who write too crudely. According to Auerbach, Augustine "cautions the student against introducing the lofty style too abruptly or using it at excessive length; he recommends frequent use of the lowly style" (1965:34), which should be "unadorned but neither slovenly nor uncouth" (1965:33). I do not want to put too much emphasis on St. Augustine's statements here, but an awareness of different levels of style was in the conscious level of medieval thinking about writing, religious or not, however differently inflected by geography and time. In the history of commentary on *Mankind*, I note two major critical objections: the "boring" language of Mercy (i.e., aureate language) and the "vulgarity" when Mercy is not in control of the play. Although the first of these objections is probably an anachronistic romantic reaction against "artificiality" and the second the effect of our middle-class's increasingly refined language behavior, as if this is not equally artificial, there may well have been linguistic turmoil in the region at the time which resulted in hard-and-fast moral judgments made based on how one spoke.

The Influence of the Continent

I want to argue multiple considerations here. First, middle-class English language has been strongly influenced by our Puritan ancestors who can be traced back to what I call the "proto-Puritan" strain in medieval culture, in which East Anglia played a major part. In support of this, Gibson writes that "latent Puritanism existed in English culture long before it had a name" (1989:108) and that East Anglia quickly became a "Puritan stronghold" (1989:22).

Secondly, there has been much discussion of East Anglia's connections with the continent, usually concerning trade, but there were other areas in which these connections were significant. In her description of Hengrave Hall, Gibson notes that "the windows are quite

Flemish in style although household accounts of the 1520s and 1530s record payments for the windows to a glazier named Robert Wryght from Bury St. Edmunds" (1989:113). I read this as signifying that a local craftsman was making "Flemish" windows. This continental influence—which may have been seen as a relatively new phenomenon, hence the use of the characters "Nowadays" and "New Guise" in *Mankind*—is in a long line of a variety of English objections to the culture of the continent. For example, in Shakespeare's *Richard II*, John of Gaunt and and the Duke of York open Act II, bewailing the behavior of Richard. Gaunt wishes that his "death's sad tale may yet undeaf his ear." York replies:

> No, it is stopped with other flattering sounds,
> * * * * *
> Lascivious metres, to whose venom sound
> The open ear of youth doth always listen;
> Report of fashions in proud Italy,
> Whose manners still our tardy, apish nation
> Limps after in base imitation.
> Where doth the world thrust forth a vanity—
> So it be new, there's no respect how vile—
> That is not quickly buzz'd into his ears?
> (II.i.16-26)

Xenophobia is often part of the rhetoric of nationalism, as here, and usually glazed with moral judgement. If the reader remembers the "little lead badges or broaches" which were "cheap enough to be afforded by even the poorest peasant" (Jones 1993-1994:193), one might suspect that more was imported than the knowledge of how to make Flemish windows. This suggests to my folklorist persona that we consider Alan Dundes's controversial book, *Life Is Like a Chicken Coop Ladder: A Portrait of German Culture through Folklore*, in which he argues:

> In German folklore, one finds an inordinate number of texts concerned with anality. Scheisse (shit), Drek (dirt), Mist (manure), Arsch (ass), and similar locutions are commonplace. Folksongs, folktales, proverbs, riddles, folk speech—all attest to the Germans' longstanding special interest in this area of human activity. I am not claiming that other peoples in the world do not also express a healthy concern for this area, but rather that the Germans appear to be preoccupied with such themes. (1984:9)

If this is a cultural characteristic of, if not the German nation as Dundes argues narrowly, but rather Germanic peoples, then a continental influence on East Anglia most probably resulted in a reinforcement of the use of such native "earthy" speech, as we see in *Mankind*, and this would have grated on the ears of the privileged (such as mine) which were more attuned to French and Latin. Aureate language, much like our own learned use of latinate clinical terms for body parts and body functions, is a logical alternative, and it could have become a public ideal in certain circles, the clergy for one, because of its distance from so-called "Anglo-Saxon four-letter words" and, implicitly, the people who spoke them.

Even though our idea of "class" differs from general social distinctions in the fifteenth century, nonetheless I want to suggest, based on Kipnis's essay and the hierarchical structure of the Church, that we have something akin to class-based language uses represented in *Mankind*, something that is conflated with traditional concerns with post-lapsarian humanity. From the perspective of the person-on-the-street, such issues are behavioral rather than moral, and one learns early on, as today, that certain words are not to be used in certain contexts. Examples of such different perspectives are not difficult to locate in *Mankind*. I point here to:

> Ey, ey! yowr body ys full of Englysch Laten.
> * * * * *
> I prey yow hertyly, worschyppul clerke,
> To haue þis Englysch mad in Laten:
> 'I haue etun a dyschfull of curdys,
> Ande I haue schetun yowr mowth full of turdys.'
> (124, 129-32)

This scatalogical reply to Mercy's having rhymed "denomynacyon" and "communycacyon" in lines 122 and 123, thereby having emphasized their use, reflects more antagonism to a competing behavior than a theoretically informed opposition. This is, to carry along my references, much like Larry Flynt's *Hustler*-response to modern middle-class proprieties. This attitude is conveyed forcefully in "Osculare fundamentum" (142)—and in Latin, to boot!—, a wide-spread retort of all Germanic peoples and the one phrase (in Swedish) which I inherited from my Swedish maternal grandfather whom I never met. Here we have, in the fifteenth century, the same metaphor discussed by Kipnis—the body is a metaphor for society, and the middle-class and upper-class gaze is directed above the waist and the lower-class gaze is directed below the waist:

> Lo, master, lo, here ys a pardon bely-mett.
> Yt ys grawntyde of Pope Pokett,
> Yf 3e wyll putt yowr nose in hys wyffys sokett,
> 3e xall haue forty days of pardon.
> (143-146)

This introduces the concept of variable human behavior: that sometimes we may read *Hustler* or we may gaze below the waist (i.e., act like a lower-class person) or—to use the alternative paradigm—gaze according to our lower (baser) desires; at other times we may gaze above the waist, ideally above the shoulders. This may be more Rabelaissean than Bakhtinean, because Nicolaisen (1980), in discussing "cultural registers," argues convincingly that we all vary in our behaviors, but not all in the same range, thus undercutting notions of homogeneous behavior on the part of the individuals of any class. Stanley Kahrl noted, with customary discretion, our different behavior at different times: "Nought, New Guise, and Nowadays enter dancing, opting for mirth, and singing funny scatological songs of the type we associate with an evening of beery gaiety after a good dinner" (1974:117). I have already cited Coogan for writing about "the language of most of the audience in their moments of relaxation" (1947:95). In *Mankind* this is expressed overtly: "I kan not bere it ewynly þat Mankynde ys so flexybull" (741). Indeed, the entire play is concerned with Mankind's flexibility.

The tradition of man as a "stynkyng dungehyll" (204) is a gloss on the uses of traditional similes in the play. When Mankind is under the influence of Mercy, he uses the proper simile "swetere þen hony" (225), but Nought says that his purse is "as clen as a byrdys ars" (489). The split between these similies may be explained by Cathy M. Orr's—now Cathy Lynn Preston's—1976 study of "Folk Comparisons from Colorado." "Sweeter than honey" remains in proper discourse while "clean as a bird's ass" remains a rough male locution.

English Cultural Traditions

I am intrigued by Gash's understanding of the English "folk-play" tradition in East Anglia, which is important in his discussion of "carnival." He makes use of this tradition many times (1986:76, 77, 78, 84, 89, 92, and 94), and yet he references just Tiddy (1923) and Chambers (1933) and (1903). A new era in the study of British traditional drama was launched with the publication of *English Ritual Drama* (Cawte et al. 1967), in which we find very few references to folk plays in all of East Anglia. Smart (1917) could not have known about this paucity of evidence, but a modern scholar should. The compilers of *English Ritual Drama*, despite the service that the book has been, were essentially ham-strung by their belief in a ritual origin of English traditional drama. As a result they did not include customs which served similar purposes, such as The Derby Tup, and which were regionally dominant. One effect of that appears in the map which plots the "Distribution of the *Ceremony* [my emphasis] in Great Britain:" there is empty space in northern Derbyshire, northwest Nottinghamshire, and extreme southern Yorkshire where the "ceremony" had not been recorded (1967:32).

Recently E.C. Cawte, after reading Joseph Fontenrose's *The Ritual Theory of Myth* (1971) in which Fentenrose considers systematically the fragile evidence in support of such theories and discredits most of it, published "It's an Ancient Custom—but How Ancient?" In it he writes of Fontenrose's book: "The inconsistencies of the arguments put forward by Frazer and his followers were reviewed more than twenty years ago in a work that does not seem to have been drawn to the attention of students of traditional custom until now" (Cawte 1993:38). Despite the volume of published material on the antiquity of various customs in Britain, most of it is similarly flawed and should be used with discretion.

Received ideas die hard, and research which contradicts them is often not accorded the resepect it should have. In the area of traditional drama, I note the important work of the historian M. W. Barley (1953), which was treated shabbily by English folklorists at the time. In terms of folklore generally, the best work in Britain is done by Professor J. D. A. Widdowson and those associated with his Centre for English Cultural Traditions and Language at Sheffield. The work at

CECTAL must be taken into account by those interested in Early English drama and all others concerned with English cultural traditions.

Over the years I have acquired virtually all known recordings of traditional drama in England—perhaps 3,500 texts and 7,500 fragments, descriptions, and allusions—, and I still cannot fill in the blank of East Anglia. If this tradition was ever common there, it disappeared without significant record. I do think, however, that the tradition of the house-visit by bands of disguised individuals was common enough. Winter-time visits by bands of disguised individuals, singing, dancing, and displaying themselves in exchange for food and drink (and later money), was a wide-spread tradition in northern Europe. (See M. Preston 1971, despite its unfortunate use of the term "ritual luck-visit," and Halpert and Story 1969.) In terms of *Mankind*, if one could connect it to the house-visit tradition, it could be played any time that such house-visits occurred in East Anglia—the first three weeks of November in Cheshire, the same amount of time in the spring in areas of Lancashire, and three weeks or more following Christmas or New Year's Day throughout much of the rest of English-speaking Britain.

Surviving evidence suggests that a play, as we understand the term, was a latter-day add-on, one more kind of possible entertainment that might be put on to increase the cash-reward at the end. (See M. Preston 1976 and M. Preston and Smith 1996 forthcoming.) As a result, I read into Gash's essay perhaps more than he intended. He writes that "Where folklorists and anthropologists used to be interested in the pagan origins of medieval festive practices, more recent historians and anthropologists have considered their social functions...." (1986:80). Later he writes about "the pagan past" (1986:94), which bothers me because it might suggest to some readers the existence of a pagan pre-Christian "merrie England," whereas surviving evidence about pre-Christian religions points to rather gloomy outlooks. As a medievalist-folklorist, I'm concerned with studying meaning in the here and now, both for itself, but also in order to construct "mental models" by which we might come to understand better the necessarily fragmentary record of the past.

Medieval Studies is both cursed and blessed with just studying that which survives, largely the record of privileged people, with the record of the other, the little people as well as those cast out silently, having been too often erased from our consciousnesses; there are no informants to interview. It is for that reason that I have spent twenty-five years studying folklore, by which I mean the unofficial and private sides of our lives (as opposed to quaint calendar customs and old tales which is the amusingly Victorian view that most inhabitants of English departments have of folklore). That there are no recorded folk plays from Norfolk or Suffolk in *English Ritual Drama* (Cawte *et al.* 1967) may be the result of the way such things have been collected. Peter Millington, in a private communication, demonstrated that, if one plots the density of the places at which folk-plays are recorded in *ERD* to have been performed, the places of the greatest density pin-point the residences of the major collectors of folk-plays. This is no more than what a critic of the enterprise might suppose—that the collected information is not a representative sample. On the other hand, I think that the lack of information from Norfolk and Suffolk may reflect the complete local victory of either the proto-Puritans or the Puritans who dominated the area later—I can't guess which it was—, and it leaves medievalists who would deal with such traditions out on a very fragile limb: either they must posit a uniform "merrie England," or they must wade through the records of flesh-and-blood people—reading omissions as well as entries—to explain what did, or did not, exist in a particular area. I know that Richard Beadle (1991), among others, is concerned with the literary geography of medieval Norfolk as a phenomenon distinct from other areas. It would be only logical to suspect that other cultural traditions might be similarly geographically based.

As I approach closure, I point to a gracefully-aging essay of Roger Abrahams (1970) about traditional drama in the British West Indies in which he points out the "strange contradiction" between the tendency of English folklorists to hold to a monolithic "life-cycle" theory about the origins of traditional drama which control their thinking while carrying out rigorously empirical research into those traditions. (This, by the way, is also a *caveat* for those who use the Records of Early English Drama volumes.) According to Abrahams, for most of the "peasant communities" in recorded history, little is cyclic in our larger sense of that word in that seasons are celebrated—and coped with—as they are encountered, individually, not as parts of some greater whole. Indeed, the larger schemes that we talk about seem to be more the product of the needs of Victorian and later city-dwellers, represented in the past by those who lived by Ecclesiastical or other formal calendars. I let Abrahams say this himself:

> To regard the "original life-cycle play" as a total statement of the cycle is to place folk religious practice into the sophisticated and abstract frame of reference of philosophical religion. The folk are concerned primarily with the problems posed by specific seasons; but from the vantage of the city, where the longer view can be taken, this seasonal frame of reference is interpreted as concern with the total interpenetration of life-and-death. It is this sophisticated vision which is responsible for the collection and discussion of folklore in the first place, for it is the intellectual superstructure of the antiquarian movement. But it is misleading to attribute to peasant society such an intellectualized perspective on the nature of their festivals. (1970:242)

Abrahams may not have been totally correct—his twenty-five-years-ago use of terms such as "folk" and "peasant" grate on my more democratic ears—, and yet what he wrote bears out the objections of Fontenrose (1971) to ritual theory: that there is very little evidence in favor of it. It seems, more than anything, to fade into a kind of convenience for those who keep the books, a way to keep the complicated world more orderly. Here, too, the ghosts of our gentlemanly Victorian academic predecessors continue to haunt Medieval and Renaissance Studies.

I have, as the reader may have noted, totally avoided any specific consideration of traditional drama and its influence on *Mankind*, despite Smart's much-cited essay (1917). I have done so because the "classic" folk drama allusion in *Mankind*, Mischief's description of Mercy—"Yowr wytt is lytyll, yowr hede is mekyll" (47)—, is no more than an echo of Big Head's part. Big Head, in the form of John Finney, said at Lower Heyford, Oxfordshire:

> Here comes I now that haven't been yet,
> with my great head and little wit.
> Though my head is so big and my wit so small,
> I can play a tune that will please you all.
> (Tiddy: 1923:221)

At Headington Quarry, also Oxfordshire, it was Fidler who said:

> In comes I, as 'ant bin hit
> With my big head and little wit:
> My head's so big and my wit's so small
> So I've brought my fiddle to please you all.
> (Coppock and Hill 1933:58)

At Ducklington, Oxfordshire, according to the Bodleian Library MS.Eng.Poet.C.17, Jack Finney said in 1884:

> In comes I that aint been it
> with my great head and little wit
> my head so big my wit so small
> I do endeavour to please you all.

I cited three versions of Big Head's speech from a very small region to demonstrate both the characteristic variation in the text and the variation of the speaker. I'll concede that Big Head's speech, perhaps the most widely distributed speech in all of traditional drama, *may well be* echoed in *Mankind*, but what such an echo signifies has been totally ignored; certainly we may assume that the author of *Mankind* was not an anthropologist or an antiquarian, and so such an echo would have to have significance beyond an allusion to a local tradition. Was it a simple quatrain spoken or sung at a house-visit, perhaps followed up by a fiddle-tune, or, in other versions, a dance? (This is what I think.) And what did Big head look like? Or was Big Head, as in the plays from Oxfordshire, merely a "supernumerary" of a folk-play troupe, introduced after the significant action for some kind of added comic effect? Whichever, what may shed light on this probable use of a local custom, while being directly relevant to the play's theme and its presumed acting circumstances, is the song:

> Yt ys wretyn wyth a coll,
> He þat schytyth wyth hys hoyll,
> But he wyppe hys ars clen,
> On hys breche yt xall be sen.
> *Cantant omnes.* Hoylyke, holyke, holyke!
> (335-343)

This may be a parody of the "Sanctus" from the Mass—"holy, holy, holy" is close enough to "hole lick, hole lick, hole lick" in Middle English—, but if it is a parody (as I think it is), it is not a direct representation. Therefore the employment of the Big Head line may be an invocation of its cultural register, that of the rough and rowdy house-visitation which involved the use of disguise, but it must certainly have been more than that. (Remember that this line introduced Titivillus, perhaps played by the actor who also played Mercy.) Thus, to have the actor, who played a linguistically effeminate priest, double as Titivillus and enter *in disguise*—the less representational the better—and also use alliteration which was understood to mark the antithesis with the Latin tradition, would probably have been funnier in performance than even the stage effects for this comic devil. As a result, I think that Smart's basic assumptions were invalid and that, rather than a "folk-play" allusion in *Mankind*, there was use made of a disguising tradition, that of the house-visit.

Here I want to introduce (only) a larger argument about song and dance. That Titivillus says that he blesses with his left hand is little more than what I call "stage devilry," i.e., the inversion of what is right and proper. That is the stereotypical view of "otherness," that there is an evil black in opposition to our white, and if we do not know what it is, we create it by inversion. That was the history of interrogations for witchcraft, Lolladry, and unorthodoxy generally, the most grotesque forms of which occurred after the Reformation. In order to understand some of this, I argue that we need to think about more than the highly romanticized "mumming" tradition; such traditions as those discussed by E. P. Thompson in "Rough Music Reconsidered" (1992)—Riding the Stang, Skimmity Riding, etc.—are an important part of the social cacaphony of Mischief and his friends. In Thompson's words: "rough music is a vocabulary which brushes the carnival at one extreme and the gallows at the other" (1992:13). I have attempted to introduce the idea of "rough language," and I advocate our considering "rough dance" as well as "rough music."

Conclusions

The culture of East Anglia was problably more complex than many imagine, but contemporary scholarship and politics makes it possible to understand plays such as *Mankind* better than we have. The notion that *Mankind* was probably performed inside a pub clearly reflects the class-judgments of Academe and that *Mankind* was understood only in terms of its overt structure suggests that that Victorian gentleman either was not very "flexible," or—more probably—he was very "flexible," but didn't dare admit it in public.

This investigation of *Mankind* suggests, beyond specific details that may have been mentioned, the following changes in our understanding of the play:

1. *Mankind* was probably written by a monk at the monastery in Bury St. Edmonds as Gibson has suggested.

2. Although it probably was performed within the monastery, its primary audience was outside, but within the cultural sphere of the monastery. Gibson suggested a fundraising motive.

3. Although its setting was Shrovetide, I can conceive of its having been performed on almost any day after Christmas and before Easter.

4. The play demonstrates a confounding of manners and morals similar to that which marks modern American and academic cultures.

5. The part of Mercy suggests that aureate language was not widely appreciated.

6. Speculation about the sexual activities of monks at Bury was a part of local culture.

7. The "culture-collision" between native and continental traditions continued, perhaps intensified because of increasing direct contact with the continent as well as recent religious controversies.

8. Relatively modern or regional traditions, such as that of "folk-plays," cannot be assumed to have been a part of the culture of East Anglia, nor can we assume that traditional drama generally is a latter-day manifestation of "age-old" ritual behavior. Other "rough" traditions more probably influenced *Mankind*.

Notes

1. A version of this essay was presented at the 1992 British Studies Conference in Boulder, Colorado. I acknowledge my indebtednesses to the late Professor Edward Peter Nolan who heard that version and commented most helpfully, Professor Gerald B. Kinneavy who read a later draft, and Professor Emeritus D. C. Baker with whom I first studied Early English drama and for whom I wrote the very first version of this paper in 1968. It has been my pleasure and to my considerable benefit to have them as colleagues and friends.

2. Douglas Caskey, who had been a graduate student in my medieval drama seminar in 1987, produced a somewhat modernized version of *Mankind* for his Master of Arts project in Theatre in 1990. Out of season and out of its cultural context, the play was well received.

References

Abrahams, Roger. 1970. British West Indian Folk Drama and the "Life Cycle" Problem. *Folklore* 81:265.

Adams, J. Q., ed. 1924. *Chief Pre-Shakespearean Drama*. Boston: Houghton Mifflin.

Auerbach, Erich. 1965. *Literary Language and Its Public in Late Antiquity and in the Middle Ages*. Translated by Ralph Manheim. Bollingen Series, no. 25, Princeton: Princeton University Press.

Bakhtin, Mikhail. 1984. *Rabelais and His World*. Translated by Hélène Iswolsky. Bloomington: Indiana University Press.

Barley, M. W. 1953. Plough Plays in the East Midlands. *Journal of the English Folk Dance and Song Society* 7:68-95.

Beadle, Richard, ed. 1982. *The York Plays*. London: Edward Arnold (Publishers), Ltd.

_____. 1991. Prolegomena to a Literary Geography of Later Medieval Norfolk. In *Regionalism in Late Medieval Manuscripts and Texts: Essays celebrating the publication of "A Linguistic Atlas of Late Mediaeval English"*, ed. Felicity Riddy, pp. 89-108. Cambridge: Boydell & Brewer, Ltd.

Bevington, David. 1962. *From "Mankind" to Marlowe: Growth of Structure in the Popular Drama of Tudor England*. Cambridge MA: Harvard University Press.

Blake, N. F. 1981. *Non-standard Language in English Literature*. London: André 37 Deutsch, Ltd.

Cawte, E. C. 1993. It's an Ancient Custom—But How Ancient? *Aspects of British Calendar Customs*, ed. Theresa Buckland and Juliette Wood, pp. 37-56. Sheffield: Shieffield Academic Press, Ltd.

_____, Alex Helm, and N. Peacock. 1967. *English Ritual Drama: A Geographical Index*. London: Publications of the Folk-Lore Society, no. 127.

Chambers, E. K. 1903. *The Mediaeval Stage*. Oxford: Oxford University Press.

_____. 1933. *The English Folk-Play*. Oxford: Oxford University Press.

Coogan, Sister Mary Philippa. 1947. *An Interpretation of the Moral Play, "Mankind"*. Washington, D.C.: The Catholic University of America Press.

Coppock, G. A. and B. M. Hill. 1933. *Headington Quarry and Shotover*. Oxford: Oxford University Press.
Crowley, Jeremiah J. 1912. *Romanism: A Menace to the Nation*. Aurora, Missouri: The Menace Publishing Co.
Dundes, Alan. 1984. *Life Is Like a Chicken Coop Ladder: A Portrait of German Culture Through Folklore*. New York: Columbia University Press.
Eccles, Mark, ed. 1969. *The Macro Plays*. Oxford: The Early English Text Society, No. 262.
Fontenrose, Joseph. 1971. *The Ritual Theory of Myth*. Berkeley: University of California Press.
Gardiner, Harold C., S.J. 1967 (repr. 1946). *Mysteries' End: An Investigation of the Last Days of the Medieval Religious Stage*. n.p.: Archon Books.
Gash, Anthony. 1986. Carnival against Lent: The Ambivalence of Medieval Drama. In *Medieval Literature: Criticism, Ideology & History*, ed. David Aers, pp. 74-98. New York: St. Martin's Press.
Gibson, Gail McMurray. 1989. *The Theater of Devotion: East Anglian Drama and Society in the Late Middle Ages*. Chicago: University of Chicago Press.
Greely, Andrew M. 1990. *The Catholic Myth: The Behavior and Beliefs of American Catholics*. New York: Macmillan Publishing Company.
Halpert, Herbert, and G. M. Storey, eds. 1969. *Christmas Mumming in Newfoundland: Essays in Anthropology, Folklore, and History*. Toronto: Published for Memorial University of Newfoundland by University of Toronto Press.
Janson, Wm. Hugh. 1965 (repr. 1959). The Esoteric-Exoteric Factor in Folklore. In *The Study of Folklore*, ed. Alan Dundes, pp. 44-51. Englewood-Cliffs, N.J.: Prentice-Hall, Inc.
Jones, Malcolm. 1993-1994. Sex and Sexuality in Late Medieval and Early Modern Art. *Privatisierung der Triebe*, ed. D. Erlach, M. Reisenleitner *et al.*, pp. 304. Bern: Frühe Neuzeitstudien 1.
Kahrl, Stanley J. 1974. *Traditions of Medieval English Drama*. London: Hutchinson & Co., Ltd.
Kipnis, Laura. 1992. (Male) Desire and (Female) Disgust: Reading *Hustler*. In *Cultural Studies*, ed. Lawrence Grossberg *et al.*, pp. 373-391. London: Routledge.
Lowenthal, David. 1990 (repr. 1985). *The Past Is a Foreign Country*. Cambridge: Cambridge University Press.
Nicolaison, W. F. H. 1980. Variant, Dialect, and Region: An Exploration of the Geography of Tradition. *New York Folklore* 6:137-149
Orr, Cathy M. 1976. Folk Comparisons from Colorado. *Western Folklore* 35:175-208.
Preston, Cathy Lynn. 1989. The Way Stylized Language Means: Pattern Matching in the Child Ballads. *Computers and the Humanities* 23: 323-332.
Preston, Michael J. 1971. The British Folk-Play: A Ritual Luck-Visit? *Western Folklore* 30:45-48.
———. 1975. *A Concordance to the Middle English Shorter Poem*. COMPENDIA Series, No. 6, Pts. 1-2., gen. ed., R. A. Wisbey. Leeds: W. S. Maney & Son, Ltd.
———. 1976. The Robin Hood Plays of South-Central England. *Comparative Drama* 10:91-100.

_____ and Jean D. Pfleiderer. 1982. *A KWIC Concordance to the Plays of the Wakefield Master*. Contextual Concordances. New York: Garland Publishing, Inc.

_____ and Paul Smith. 1996 forthcoming. 'See Sirs, See Here....': Two Quack Doctor Songs and Traditional Drama in England. In *Folk Drama: Contemporary Perspectives*, ed. Thomas A. Green and Paul Smith. New York: Garland Publishing, Inc.

Richardson, James T., Joel Best, and David G. Bromley. 1991. *The Satanism Scare*. New York: Aldine de Gruyter.

Ross, Thomas W. 1984. Taboo-Words in Fifteenth-Century English. In *Fifteenth-Century Studies: Recent Essays*, ed. Robert F. Yeager, pp. 137-160. Hamden, Conn.: Shoe String Press, Inc.

Russell, Jeffrey Burton. 1989. *The Prince of Darkness: Radical Evil and the Power of Good in History*. London: Thames and Hudson, Ltd.

Smart, Walter K. 1917. Mankind and the Mumming Plays. *MLN* 22:21-25.

Thompson, E. P. 1992. Rough Music Reconsidered. *Folklore* 103:3-26.

Tiddy, R. J. E. 1923. *The Mummers' Play*. Oxford: Oxford University Press.

Victor, Jeffrey S. 1993. *Satanic Panic: The Creation of a Contemporary Legend*. Chicago: Open Court.

Warner, Karen. 1994. *What's So Funny about Being Catholic? An Uproarious Collection of Blasphemous Facts, Unholy Jokes, Irreverent Folklore, and More*. New York: Harper Collins Publishers.

13

Oralities [and Literacies]: Comments on the Relationships of Contemporary Folkloristics and Literary Studies

Eric L. Montenyohl

The history of (American) language and literary studies is a long and complex one, and far too large to deal with adequately here.[1] However, it is worth pointing out that what began as language and literary studies has produced a large number of offspring, mostly during the last century. These include linguistics (and its subdisciplines), comparative literature, folkloristics, popular culture, rhetoric, and a host of specific literatures (African, Afro-American, Women's, American, English, etc.) as well as different groupings (children's literature, gay and lesbian literature, Southern literature). There are specializations (e.g., literary history) and approaches (e.g., Marxism, feminism) and many combinations and subspecializations. This fracturing of the original field has led to sometimes inspired and exciting developments, as developing disciplines created new theories, methodologies, terms, and standards. And yet this explosion of interests has caused considerable unease, even anxiety, in our postmodern world. Have we (both as a culture and as a profession) completely lost our focus? Have we wholly lost sight of texts and performances, distracted by theoretical wrangling over what a text is, how it can mean, how gender affects reading, etc.?

At times it seems that the modern—and especially postmodern—development of language and literature is somewhat like the Big Bang theory of the creation of the universe: enormous, empowering, violent, and extremely rapid. Further, once all of these new fields have been generated they seem to move farther and farther away from one another. Each develops its own arguments for existence and persistence, its own language and terminology, its own kind of publications, and its own standards for assessing contributions. Are all these fields, once parts of a relatively unified field of language and literary studies and now apparently wholly independent of each other, sailing off into a scholarly cosmos and putting more and more distance between one another?

One hopes that this comparison to the Big Bang theory is not entirely accurate. New disciplines do not necessarily travel farther and farther away from others. In fact, there are times, areas of research, and theories which seem actually to attract groups and build new interdisciplinary areas and new approaches to common or related areas. Orality seems to be an example of just such a recent nexus.

Scholars may be a bit surprised to hear that orality, a relatively new area of study, has been one of the fastest-growing fields of research over the last generation.[2] To be sure, language and literature studies (including, but not limited to, the activities of the Modern Language Association of America) have always had some interest in oral forms and folklore.[3] And yet orality is not precisely the same as folkloristics or any other field. At first glance, the term orality seems to cover concerns from fields as diverse as linguistics, Biblical studies, communications, psychology, education, rhetoric, anthropology, comparative literature, literary studies and theory, history, political science, and even criminal justice. As a result, an electronic search of the scholarship on orality can quickly become bewildering. And yet, after eliminating a few conceptions of orality which share the name but are based in rather different issues, there appears to be a real nexus among these fields and many of the individual scholars. Scholarship from criminal justice, in which orality seems to refer to kinds of crimes such as fellatio can pretty safely be set aside as different and unrelated. Some education and political science statements which are really arguments to promote the expansion of literacy can also be put aside (e. g., *Louisiana Literacy Forum* 1990). These may be based upon some research on orality, but their agenda is wholly political, not scholarly. The resulting corpus of scholarship remains large, encompassing works from a wide variety of disciplines, and it is growing at a pace far faster than most other areas of the humanities.

That folkloristics should belong in this group seems self-evident. After all, one of the fundamental characteristics of folklore has been its recording and study of face-to-face communication, which has usually meant oral/aural performance. Yet one of the disciplines relatively untouched by this recent explosion of interest is folkloristics. Somehow it seems amazing that a discipline which has collected and analyzed perhaps more oral data *per se* than any other discipline has mostly remained outside of the scholarship devoted to orality. How then has the study of orality come about? Why has folkloristics not been much of a factor? Is there a common goal such that orality becomes a critical intersection for a wide range of disciplines? What can folklorists contribute to this field?

The origins of recent research on orality are only approximately one generation old, dating back to the early 1960s. The interest in orality came from a number of disciplinary directions at about the same time. Slavics scholar [and folklorist] Albert B. Lord's *The Singer of Tales* (1960) documented a living tradition of oral epic performance in Yugoslavia. His study of oral performance demonstrated the methods by which members of the community learned the tradition, practiced it, and maintained it. Lord's book (based on his own fieldwork, as well as earlier work by Milman Parry) helped generate the oral-formulaic theory and relate it to the Homeric epics and other works around the world.[4] Eric A. Havelock, another scholar interested in classical languages and literatures, produced *Preface to Plato* in 1963. In that work, he argues that Plato is a key figure in the history of poetry since the Hellenic culture was in the process of moving from an orally-based culture to one which was writing-based. Plato reflects and comments upon this as no one else does. And finally, communications theorist Marshall McLuhan's *The Gutenberg Galaxy* was published in 1962. In that work he argues that "a message does not reduce to its obvious content but carries with it a latent content constituted by the medium that transmits it" (Zumthor 1990:24). He traces the technology of communications and tries to relate that form (e. g., orality, literacy) to the mental and psychological characteristics of cultures. These contributions from three different fields within several years all focused attention in one way or another on orality and helped spark scholarly research on orality, from many different disciplines and directions.

The figure whom many scholars now turn to as the authority on orality is Fr. Walter J. Ong, S. J. He has written a number of works dealing with orality, including *The Presence of the Word* (1967), *Interfaces of the Word* (1977) and *Orality and Literacy* (1982). These have become standard works for scholars just entering the study of orality. Ong's books allow researchers to get a substantial taste of the scholarship on orality as well as seeing a bit of the theory in the area.[5] Yet after studying Ong's works folklorists may have a number of problems relating to these studies, and may well decide not to pursue orality—or at least this orality. There are a number of reasons for concluding that the scholarship from language and literary studies (e.g., Fr. Ong) and that from folkloristics has generated two very different oralities. And this, then, says a good deal about the contemporary relationships between folkloristics and language and literary studies.

Fr. Ong's work on orality is based heavily on the communications works of Marshall McLuhan in which McLuhan sees an evolution in cultures of the communications technology from oral face-to-face communication to writing and print [lumped together as literacy] and finally to a range of electronic media (radio, television, telephones, computers, etc.). Among other things, Ong's work argues that "Each of the various media—oral, chirographic, typographic, electronic—determines differently the constitution of the thought it communicates" (Ong 1977:118). That is, the technology of communication determines not just *how* and *how far* something can be spread, but also *what kinds of things* can be thought and communicated. In general, the different kinds/stages of communications technology (orality, literacy, secondary orality) cause a host of different characteristics: "To store and retrieve its knowledge, an oral culture must think in heavily patterned forms facilitating recall—antitheses, epithets, assertive rhythms, proverbs, and other formulas of many sorts" (Ong 1977:191).[6] Ong refines this scheme a little, describing a tripartite evolution of cultures' communications technology from orality to literacy to "secondary orality."[7] This view of culture based on the history of communications technology seems straightforward and fairly reasonable. However, there are several problems with it.

First, a description of the [communications technology] history of one culture [mostly Greece] is hardly grounds for the assertion/premise that the same pattern will necessarily hold true for all other cultures, no matter how familiar this pattern may seem to the reader. Ong sees all cultures changing as western European cultures have, moving gradually from orality to literacy toward secondary orality in a linear evolutionary progression. In fact, folklorists and anthropologists will recognize a remarkable relationship between Ong's division of cultures based on their communications technology and that of English anthropologist E. B. Tylor more than a century ago in which he divided cultures into "primitive, barbarian, and civilized" societies. Tylor's theory, heavily influenced by Darwin and others writing about evolution, also argued for a universal cultural progression, although his criteria for categorizing cultures were not limited only to the communications technology in place. The criticisms of Tylor's scheme, including the charge that those evaluating other cultures frequently demonstrate their own ethnocentrism in the classification schemes of different cultures is no less pertinent for the communications work of McLuhan and Ong. Communications technology is not separable from historical, social and religious factors. Thus, the introduction of writing or electronic media may normally be bound to specific national and cultural factors (religion, nationalism, ethnicity, etc.) and not be independent as McLuhan and Ong seem to believe. Technology (communications or other) is neither "pure" nor independent. Even now, writing is several thousands of years old—but has not yet spread to all cultures and language-groups around the world. Further, there are now some cases of individuals and cultures leaping (if one can pardon the choice of terms) directly from orality to "secondary orality." The Cajuns of South Louisiana are an excellent example of a culture adapting to many kinds of electronic media—telephones, radio, television, recording media, etc.—long before worrying about how to write down something in Cajun French. As a result, there is now seventy-five years of "secondary orality" for the Cajuns—but still no written corpus.[8] Thus, the linearity of the model—and perhaps the entire notion of "technological progress"—needs to be revised.

In Ong's work orality is basically synonymous with preliteracy. It is variously a stage of culture or state of mind/mental development, and refers to a time when the culture is not aware of writing and literacy. Literacy (including both writing and print) then develops over many centuries, and Ong identifies and analyzes some of the "oral residue" in literate cultures, from Renaissance England to contemporary Africa and America.[9]

Within folklore, on the other hand, orality refers primarily to the means of transmission—the medium through which communication is carried. Thus, folklorists concern themselves with the collection, transcription, and analysis of (orally performed) texts, the variation among and between tellings, and repertoire analysis. The matter of *pre*literacy or *il*literacy of informants or cultures has not been an issue in folkloristics with rare exceptions. That is, folklorists have been interested in what has been preserved in oral tradition whatever the level of literacy involved with an informant and his/her culture. In this sense, oral performance is a significant choice, no matter the level of literacy for any particular person.

Further, literacy's impact on oral traditions is hardly a simple or linear matter. Many oral genres and traditional performances continue long into periods of literacy—but this seems to be a question unique to each culture and its history. It also seems to involve more than the issue of technology of communication. Changes in a culture's social events and in their relative value may lead to fewer oral performances, a change or decline in oral genres, etc. This is a complex issue, one rooted in the relationships of orality and literacy *within* a particular culture. Generalizations across cultures about the impact of literacy on oral cultures or performers are more difficult.

One study which did consider literacy is Albert Lord's *The Singer of Tales* (1960), in which he asserted that oral epics survived in Yugoslavia at least partly because of the illiteracy (and *not* preliteracy) of the singers. Whether he was arguing that literacy would have a tremendous impact on the oral culture because of the mental and psychological constraints or whether he was just acknowledging that reading and writing might well dramatically change the social and cultural events of the community, including those in which the epics were performed, is not entirely clear. However, few later works by folklorists have dealt with or thoroughly tested connections between oral performance and the informants' level of literacy.

Ong's argument that the medium is the single, and indeed only, important factor is crucial here. English folklorists (Andrew Lang, George Laurence Gomme, Edwin Sidney Hartland, and others) a century ago debated why the Scottish tradition of *Märchen* died out in the nineteenth century. One theory blamed the Church for suppressing imagination and the narrative traditions which may have predated Christianity. Another theory was that formal schooling caused the decline of this particular folk form. To some extent, both of these point to the impact of literacy on a traditional oral art form. And yet neither argument by itself is sufficient to deal with the changes in the culture.

After all, the nineteenth century was also the age of industrialization, an age which radically changed the lifestyles of many peoples, including many of those in Scotland. The decline of the *Märchen* tradition during this period probably has no one simple cause, whether it be the spread of print/literacy, formal religion, or sociocultural changes related to industrialization. To argue, as Ong and McLuhan do, that literacy does make such differences seems overly simplistic.

Another problem is that folklorists may well dispute a number of assertions about orality and oral cultures found in Father Ong's works. For example, Ong argues that language is inherently oral:

> Human beings communicate in countless ways, making use of all their senses, touch, taste, smell, and especially sight, as well as hearing.... Some non-oral communication is exceedingly rich—gesture, for example. Yet in a deep sense language, articulated sound, is paramount. Not only communication, but thought itself relates in an altogether special way to sound.... Wherever human beings exist they have a language, and in every instance a language that exists basically as spoken and heard, in the world of sound. Despite the richness of gesture, elaborated sign languages are substitutes for speech and dependent on oral speech systems, even when used by the congenitally deaf. (Ong 1982:7)

Some of these comments about sign languages seem to be inaccurate—or at least debatable. Scholars have already documented children of deaf parents "babbling" in signs. To be sure, the members of any culture must learn language through imitation. But how much sign languages are dependent upon specific oral speech systems is still under study. Indeed, linguists, anthropologists, sociologists, and others have recently made convincing arguments for (American) sign language to be a separate language based on a unique culture. They have questioned the traditional view that all language is necessarily based on oral speech systems.

A second assumption about orality which folklorists might well question is its uniformity. In *Interfaces of the Word*, Ong describes orality as a (pretty much) uniform stage of culture (cross-culturally), and in *Orality and Literacy*, he proceeds to enumerate and describe the "psychodynamics" of orality (1982:31-77). In so doing, Ong seems to give little consideration to variation in forms of communication within or between cultures—that is, that communication is affected by many social and cultural as well as psychological factors. Ong ignores a rich vein of ethnographic data from linguistic and social anthropologists (Goody 1968, 1986, 1987; Finnegan et al. 1977, 1988) indicating that cultures can use language differently. Thus orality may not be nearly as uniform (and abstract) as Ong's description indicates.

Further, Ong generates his "psychodynamics of orality" by analysis of such data as the Homeric epics (or the work of Parry and Lord on them). Thus, for example, he asserts that oral cultures are fundamentally additive rather than subordinate, aggregative rather than analytic, redundant, conservative, agonistically toned, homeostatic, situational, etc. While some of these characteristics may be valid in characterizing oral cultures, Ong doesn't seem fully to appreciate that what he has selected for his data are examples of oral *performance*. That is, he has picked data that have peculiar qualities (due to the way in which they must be generated and performed).[10] Indeed, Ong tries to use the qualities of oral performances to draw conclusions about how oral peoples think, even how they are: "One can go further: oral cultures not only express themselves in formulas but also think in formulas." (Ong 1977:103). And Ong argues that these qualities of oral performance generalize and are valid for all of oral culture(s)—a "psychic unity" of all cultures characterized by orality? That is, *all* oral peoples (not just the skilled performers of ballads or epics) think in formulas, etc. Here he doesn't seem to appreciate the discoveries and distinctions made by scholars such as Dell Hymes (1975), Gary Gossen (1977), Richard Bauman (1977), and others about verbal art in performance. Somehow it seems bizarre even to consider *everyone* in any oral culture thinking and speaking like Homeric poems (in formulas, etc.). And yet Ong's *Orality and Literacy* (1982) is substantially a characterization of orality (in general) by listing and describing the characteristics of Homer's performances. To his credit, Ong describes other examples of oral cultures in his research—in *Interfaces of the Word*, for example, he includes a chapter on African drum talk. He argues there that drum talk is absolutely representative of oral cultures—thus, it is formulaic, stylized, etc. It makes little difference that these forms are examples of oral performance and have special markers of that distinction within their culture. To generalize (even about one culture) seems wrong, and to attempt to universalize about orality in this way seems ludicrous.

Finally, folklorists might well be repelled by the fact that Ong, a past-president of the Modern Language Association, views orality as a stage of cultural development—and one which is *de facto* dead. What is left for us is the "residue" in various texts as different peoples and cultures became increasingly literate and even shift into "secondary orality." This view belies Ong's own explanation that

> ...of all the many thousands of languages—possibly tens of thousands—spoken in the course of human history only around 106 have ever been committed to writing to a degree sufficient to have produced literature, and most have never been written at all. Of the some 3000 languages spoken that exist today only some 78 have a literature.... Even now hundreds of languages in active use are never written at all: no one has worked out an effective way to write them. (Ong 1982:7)

Despite these statistics, Ong seems to hold that orality is dying or already dead. This would seem to turn folkloristics into something like linguistic archaeology—or a dead or dying field as well. Perhaps folkloristics in America has not changed so very much from when the American Folklore Society was founded over a century ago—to collect the "fast-vanishing remains" of oral traditions?[11]

Language and literature scholars and folklorists have basically been looking at very different oralities. Language scholars have held that their orality (*pre*literacy) is largely dead. Thus the appropriate way to study it now is archaeologically. As a result, these scholars study products: printed texts, in an effort to uncover the "oral residue." Thus, we have highly literate scholars studying (written and printed) texts in order to deduce something about the prehistory of the culture which produced them—while at the same time asserting that oral cultures have fundamentally different "psychodynamics" and thus even think differently from literate cultures.

Folklorists (and anthropologists) are less convinced that orality is necessarily dead. Their focus is on the communicative process: how verbal art (whether epic, ballad, proverb, joke, or legend) is created, performed, transmitted, reshaped and retold within and between cultures. Their attention is on the choice of the technological medium, the issues involved in the performance, etc.—not whether this medium is the only one possible. It is ironic that folklorists have not been as active contributing to the study of orality as they might have been.

However, orality remains a research field which can and should generate a cross-disciplinary nexus of scholarship. If scholars can place orality within its larger realm of language and literature studies, then the researchers can draw upon methods from a number of disciplines. Folklore and folklorists can make significant contributions to this broader study of orality and oral performance. How, and in what ways?

First, folklorists and anthropologists can provide the data to test the validity of the claims about orality (or oral cultures) versus literacy (or print cultures) made by communications theorists (McLuhan, Ong, et al) and others. Scholars from a wide range of disciplines have begun to reconsider orality and oral performance. Folklorists and anthropologists have written about the distinctive features that distinguish oral performance—and thus verbal art—from everyday speech. Ong and other literary theorists would generalize from the markers of verbal art to argue that oral cultures in general are limited in some way to this kind and form of thought. A further examination of oral cultures and oral performance is justified. And while folklorists do not generally seek out or study preliterate cultures, their scholarly training would make them aware of how and where to lay their hands on representations of, if not actual recordings of, verbal performances of preliterate, illiterate, *and* literate cultures.

In so doing, folklorists might well come to support the conclusions of a number of social anthropologists (Finnegan 1977; Goody 1986, 1987) who argue that while communications technology indeed is important, it in and of itself is unlikely to cause the same effects cross-culturally. Instead, language use and performance, social events and relations, etc.—a number of factors—come into play. In essence, cultures are finely-tuned *systems* of relations, each culture finding a balance of those relations in its own way. A change in any one aspect, even one as vital and far-reaching as communications technology, does not necessarily impact each culture in the same way. What it does seem to do is change the system's balance and forces it to reestablish a new kind of equilibrium.

Second, folklorists can continue to pursue productively the study of verbal performance and bring that research to the attention of scholars working on orality. Clearly it is important to analyze verbal art and its characteristics, and many different scholars have made contributions in this area. This research is especially important because it challenges the leap that Ong makes in claiming that the performance characteristics of oral art are valid for *all* of oral culture. Indeed, scholars in performance studies have asserted that verbal art is clearly framed and marked *as* a performance—in order *not* to confuse its audience about what it is.[12]

Third, folklorists can and must contribute to a *full* ethnography of communication—both speaking and writing. Folklorists have historically focused on the oral medium and then only part of that—the traditional artistic performances in that medium. If folklorists (and anthropologists) are willing to expand their scope, they may well learn a great deal by studying performance and communication in its broadest respect. When and why are particular oral forms/strategies selected? If one medium (oral, written, or electronic) is chosen, what forms (traditional or not) are used, and why? What changes are made by informants within a culture when moving from one communications technology to another? What is it about culturally-sanctioned forms which makes an individual or culture persist in using traditional genres? Folklorists, linguistic anthropologists, linguists, and others have all pursued parts of these questions. And yet there is much more work to be done. Professors Richard Bauman and Joel Sherzer's 1975 essay provides a wealth of sources on the ethnography of speaking, and Wallace Chafe and Deborah Tannen's 1987 essay does the same for scholarship on the relationships between written and oral speech. Both essays point to areas for further research. Keith Basso's brief essay (1989) proposing an ethnography of writing points out how little we really know about a communication medium which has become the standard in Western cultures.

Fourth, some scholars have questioned the focus of the study of orality and whether conclusions can be drawn about it cross-culturally. Changes in the communications media of cultures is often dependent upon or related to significantly different elements, including religion (Sweden), nationalism (Finland), and ethnic identity (parts of America and Africa). To disregard or subordinate these historical forces seems to place far too much emphasis on the medium alone and ignore the cultural and historical context. Folklorists, anthropologists, historians, and linguists may be able to demonstrate the importance of linguistic and cultural history to the issue of orality.

Finally, folklorists and anthropologists can reexamine and refine the definitions of orality and literacy. If orality is to mean only preliteracy and a complete unawareness of written communications of any kind (as it seems to do for Ong), then orality may well be dead. But most peoples worldwide speak one language (their mother tongue) and read or write a different one (a father tongue). Is it so evident that literacy in *one* language changes the communications, worldview, etc. of the individual even in his/her mother tongue—which may still have never been written down? (I draw here on my personal experience in southern Louisiana with Cajun French, which continues to be an oral form and has moved into secondary orality [via recordings, television, and radio] long before any real interest in writing it down was expressed.) Or are Ong, McLuhan and others seeing as the norm those who become literate in their mother tongue? And even in English and the major European languages, just how much impact has literacy made on oral traditions? To be sure, McLuhan and Ong argue persuasively that literacy changes the way that a culture sees itself and its communications. But there may be a wide spectrum of oralities and literacies in different cultures.

The study of orality, including orally-based literatures, oral performance, language use, etc. will certainly go on with contributions from a wide range of scholars and fields. Folklorists clearly need to be a part of this group. Folkloristics has a great deal to offer—in data, experience, and perspective. And orality has begun to draw together scholarship from many disciplines in order to address important questions and issues, including the relationships between language and culture, the role and impact of the medium of transmission, and the connections between oral literatures and written literatures. Folklorists have the opportunity, and indeed the responsibility, to participate, even to become leaders in this field—and in so doing they likely will demonstrate the significance of collecting and studying oral traditions.

Language and literary studies in our postmodern era will certainly continue to produce new bursts of energy and excitement in the generation and division of specific theories, areas and even new disciplines. This may well continue to generate some anxiety about the size and scope of the field. And yet this growth of scholarship in language and literature is not necessarily comparable to the primal Big Bang. Issues and areas such as orality have the potential to bring scholars from many diverse fields together to focus on it, and in so doing to put the entire study of language and literature back into its broader perspective. For how can we truly know about the development of literatures (Afro-American, Women's, English, French, etc.) if we have not studied the relationship of oralities *and* literacies in their social and cultural contexts?[13]

As literary scholars shift (inevitably) from defining literature ethnocentrically and from an etic standpoint to an emic viewpoint, the significance of oral traditions and verbal art will grow. The prospects for a continuing multidisciplinary study of oralities and their relationships to literacies are quite good. While the disciplinary boundaries have grown enormously, the fundamental issues in language and literature study have the power to attract scholars from across many subdisciplines. If these scholars can truly learn about and from one another's research, then the future is bright.

Notes

1. A useful survey of American humanistic studies is Graff 1987. However, it does not deal specifically with the relationships between folkloristics (as it developed in America) and other humanistic studies. For those interested in the relationship of folkloristics to this humanistic tradition in America, see Zumwalt 1988 and Bronner 1986. For a history of European folklore studies, especially in relation to the contemporary humanistic traditions, see Cocchiara 1981.

2. One can measure this growth either by the increase in publication of scholarship or in the number of scholars contributing to the area. For a record of this growth, see Foley 1985 and the annual updates in the journal *Oral Tradition*. For a history of orality—or parts of it—see Foley 1988.

3. See Montenyohl 1991 for some of the connections between folklore studies and language and literature studies in general.

4. Part I of Lord's study is the study of the living epic tradition and his theory of how it works. Part II is entitled "The Application" and involves the relationships Lord draws to Homer as an oral poet, the *Odyssey* and the *Iliad*, and medieval epics. Scholarship since then has expanded the use of Lord's ground-breaking work much further. See, for example, Foley 1985, the contents of the journal, *Oral Tradition*, and Foley 1990.

5. Folklorists might well appreciate, however, perusing Foley 1985, 1988, and 1990 for his surveys of scholarship and history of the field.

6. Fr. Ong admits his debt to Marshall McLuhan. McLuhan, however, did not originate all of these ideas about communications technology and their impact. See especially *The Presence of the Word* 1967:7-9.

7. Ong uses the term secondary orality to refer to communication using electronic media (radio, television, telegraph). These forms of communication have some characteristics which are similar to oral, face-to-face communication. And yet they are also profoundly different from traditional oral or written communication. Ong's schema closely follows that explained by McLuhan in *The Gutenberg Galaxy* (1962).

8. Recent attempts over the last decade have produced a Cajun dictionary and some first collections of Cajun "literature." Ironically, traditional verbal forms valued by the culture (i.e., folklore) have been generally collected and then translated for presentation in English because of the wider American reading audience. Many forms, from tall tales to proverbs, jokes to songs still have not yet been accurately transcribed and published. This says a good deal about Cajun culture and its ability to maintain its verbal artistic forms, especially in the face of an overwhelming English-language culture. However, it also says something about *printed* Cajun works—in what sense do they accurately reflect the culture?

9. Ong uses the term residue in both Ong 1965 and Ong 1967.

10. And this has been part of the point of folkloristic research since Lord and through Bauman et al.

11. See W. W. Newell's opening essay in the first issue of the *Journal of American Folklore* 1 (1888).

12. This is the point to Bauman's section on "The Keying of Performance" in Bauman 1977, in which he points to special codes, figurative language, parallelism, special paralinguistic features, special formulae, appeals to tradition, and even disclaimers of performance.

13. Already there are signs that literary scholars have begun to recognize this. See the recent Modern Language Association publication, Ruoff & Ward 1990, which includes an entire section on "Oral Dimensions of American Literature."

References

Abrahams, Roger D. 1977. Toward an Enactment-Centered Theory of Folklore. In *Frontiers of Folklore*, ed. William R. Bascom, pp. 79-120. Boulder: Westview Press.

———. 1983. *The Man-of-Words in the West Indies: Performance and the Emergence of Creole Culture*. Johns Hopkins Studies in Atlantic History and Culture. Baltimore: Johns Hopkins University Press.

Basso, Keith. 1980. Review of *The Domestication of the Savage Mind*, by Jack Goody. *Language in Society* 9:72-80.

———. 1989. The Ethnography of Writing. In *Explorations in the Ethnography of Speaking*, ed. Richard Bauman and Joel Sherzer. Second edition. Cambridge: Cambridge University Press.

Bauman, Richard. 1977. *Verbal Art as Performance*. Prospect Heights, Ill.: Waveland Press.

———. 1986. *Story, Performance, and Event*. Cambridge: Cambridge University Press.

_____. 1989. *Explorations in the Ethnography of Speaking*. Second edition. Studies in the Social and Cultural Foundations of Language. Cambridge: Cambridge University Press.

_____ and Sherzer, Joel. 1975. The Ethnography of Speaking. *Annual Review of Anthropology* 4:95-119.

Biebuyck, Daniel, ed. and trans. 1969. *The Mwindo Epic from the Banyanga (Congo Republic)*. Berkeley: University of California Press.

Bleich, David. 1974. *Subjective Criticism*. Baltimore: Johns Hopkins University Press.

_____. 1988. *The Double Perspective: Language, Literacy, and Social Relations*. New York: Oxford University Press.

Bowden, Betsy. 1982. *Performed Literature*. Bloomington: Indiana University Press.

Bowra, C. M. 1962. *Primitive Song*. Cleveland: World Publishing Company.

Briggs, Charles. 1988. *Competence in Performance*. Philadelphia: University of Pennsylvania Press.

Bright, William. 1984. *American Indian Linguistics and Literature*. New York: Mouton.

Bronner, Simon J. 1986. *American Folklore Studies: An Intellectual History*. Lawrence: University Press of Kansas.

Bruns, Gerald L. 1982. *Inventions: Writing, Textuality, and Understanding in Literary History*. New Haven: Yale University Press.

Chafe, Wallace and Tannen, Deborah. 1987. The Relation Between Written and Spoken Language. *Annual Review of Anthropology* 16: 383-407.

Clifford, James. 1988. *The Predicament of Culture: Twentieth-Century Ethnography, Literature, and Art*. Cambridge: Harvard University Press.

_____ and George E. Marcus, eds. 1986. *Writing Culture: The Poetics and Politics of Ethnography*. A School of American Research Advanced Seminar. Berkeley: University of California Press.

Cocchiara, Giuseppe. 1981. *The History of Folklore in Europe*. Translated by John N. McDaniel. Philadelphia: ISHI.

Finnegan, Ruth. 1970. *Oral Literature in Africa*. Oxford: Clarendon Press.

_____. 1977. *Oral Poetry: Its Nature, Significance, and Social Context*. Cambridge: Cambridge University Press.

_____. 1988. *Literacy and Orality: Studies in the Technology of Communication*. New York: Basil Blackwell.

Fish, Stanley. 1980. *Is There a Text in this Class? The Authority of Interpretive Communities*. Cambridge: Harvard University Press.

Foley, John Miles. 1985. *Oral-Formulaic Theory and Research: An Introduction and Annotated Bibliography*. New York: Garland Press.

_____. 1986. *Oral Tradition in Literature: Interpretation in Context*. Columbia: University of Missouri Press.

_____. 1987a. *Comparative Research on Oral Traditions: A Memorial for Milman Parry*. Columbus: Slavica Publishers.

_____. 1987b. A Festschrift for Walter J. Ong. *Oral Tradition* 2:1.

_____. 1988. *The Theory of Oral Composition: History and Methodology*. Bloomington: Indiana University Press.

_____. 1990. *Oral-Formulaic Theory: A Folklore Casebook*. New York: Garland Press.

Gelb, I. J. 1952. *A Study of Writing; The Foundations of Grammatology*. Chicago: University of Chicago Press.
Goody, Jack, ed. 1968. *Literacy in Traditional Societies*. Cambridge: Cambridge University Press.
_____. 1986. *The Logic of Writing and the Organization of Society*. Studies in Literacy, Family, Culture and the State. Cambridge: Cambridge University Press.
_____. 1987. *The Interface Between the Written and the Oral*. Studies in Literacy, Family, Culture and the State. Cambridge: Cambridge University Press.
Gossen, Gary H. 1977, *Verbal Art as Performance*. Prospect Heights, Illinois: Waveland Press.
Graff, Gerald. 1987. *Professing Literature: An Institutional History*. Chicago: University of Chicago Press.
Harris, William V. 1989. *Ancient Literacy*. Cambridge: Harvard University Press.
Havelock, Eric A. 1963. *Preface to Plato*. Cambridge: Belknap Press.
Heath, Shirley Brice. 1985. *Ways With Words: Language, Life, and Work in Communities and Classrooms*. Cambridge: Cambridge University Press.
Horowitz, Rosalind and Samuels, S. Jay. 1987. Comprehending Oral and Written Language: Critical Contrasts for Literacy and Schooling. In *Comprehending Oral and Written Language*, eds. Rosalind Horowitz and S. Jay Samuels, pp. 1-52. San Diego: Academic Press.
Horton, Robin. 1967. African Traditional Thought and Western Science. *Africa: Journal of the International African Institute* XXXVII: 50-71, 155-87.
Hymes, Dell. 1975. Breakthrough into Performance. In *Folklore: Performance and Communication*, eds. Dan Ben-Amos and Kenneth S. Goldstein, pp. 11-74. The Hague: Mouton.
_____. 1981. *"In Vain I Tried to Tell You": Essays in Native American Ethnopoetics*. Philadelphia: University of Pennsylvania Press.
Iser, Wolfgang. 1974. *The Implied Reader: Patterns of Communication in Prose Fiction from Bunyan to Beckett*. Baltimore: Johns Hopkins University Press.
Jousse, Marcel. 1990. *The Oral Style*. Albert Bates Lord Studies in Oral Tradition. New York: Garland Press.
Kintgen, Eugene R., Barry M. Kroll, and Mike Rose (eds.). 1988. *Perspectives on Literacy*. Carbondale and Edwardsville: Southern Illinois University Press.
Lord, Albert Bates. 1960. *The Singer of Tales*. Cambridge: Harvard University Press.
Louisiana Literacy Forum. 1990. Baton Rouge: Louisiana Endowment for the Humanities.
Lunsford, Andrea A., Helene Moglen, and James Slevin, eds. 1990. *The Right to Literacy*. New York: Modern Language Association.
McDermott, Ray P. 1977. The Ethnography of Speaking and Reading. In *Linguistic Theory: What can it say about reading?*, ed. Roger W. Shuy, pp. 153-85. Newark, Delaware: International Reading Association.
McLuhan, Marshall. 1962. *The Gutenberg Galaxy: The Making of Typographic Man*. Toronto: University of Toronto Press.
Miller, Joseph C. 1980. *The African Past Speaks: Essays on Oral Tradition and History*. Hamden, Connecticut: Archon Books.

Montenyohl, Eric L. 1991. Folklore Studies and the Modern Language Association. *Midwestern Folklore* 17(2):110-124.

Nystrand, Martin. 1987. The Role of Context in Written Communication. In *Comprehending Oral and Written Language*, eds. Rosalind Horowitz and S. Jay Samuels, pp. 197-214. San Diego: Academic Press.

Okpewho, Isidore. 1979. *The Epic in Africa: Toward a Poetics of the Oral Performance*. New York: Columbia University Press.

Olson, David R., Nancy Torrance, and Angela Hildyard, eds. 1985. *Literacy, Language, and Learning: The Nature and Consequences of Reading and Writing*. Cambridge: Cambridge University Press.

Ong, Walter J. 1965. Oral Residue in Tudor Prose Style. *PMLA* 80:145-54.

——. 1967. *The Presence of the Word: Some Prolegomena for Cultural and Religious History*. Minneapolis: University of Minnesota Press.

——. 1977. *Interfaces of the Word: Studies in the Evolution of Consciousness and Culture*. Ithaca: Cornell University Press.

——. 1982. *Orality and Literacy: The Technologizing of the Word*. New Accents. London and New York: Methuen.

——. 1988. Before Textuality: Orality and Interpretation. *Oral Tradition* 3(3):259-69.

Pattison, Robert. 1982. *On Literacy: The Politics of the Word from Homer to the Age of Rock*. Oxford and New York: Oxford University Press.

Ruoff, A. LaVonne Brown and Jerry W. Ward. 1990. *Redefining American Literary History*. New York: Modern Language Association.

Sampson, Geoffrey. 1985. *Writing Systems: A Linguistic Introduction*. Stanford: Stanford University Press.

Scheub, Harold. 1977. Performance of Oral Narrative. In *Frontiers of Folklore*, ed. William R. Bascom, pp. 54-78. Boulder: Westview Press.

Sherzer, Joel. 1977. The Ethnography of Speaking. In *Linguistic Theory: What can it say about reading?*, ed. Roger W. Shuy, pp. 144-52. Newark, Delaware: International Reading Association.

Stock, Brian. 1983. *The Implications of Literacy: Written Language and Models of Interpretation in the Eleventh and Twelfth Centuries*. Princeton: Princeton University Press.

Tompkins, Jane P. 1980. *Reader-Response Criticism: From Formalism to Post-Structuralism*. Baltimore: Johns Hopkins University Press.

Watson, Rita and David R. Olson. 1987. From Meaning to Definition: A Literate Bias on the Structure of Word Meaning. In *Comprehending Oral and Written Language*, eds. Rosalind Horowitz and S. Jay Samuels, pp. 329-53. San Diego: Academic Press.

Zumthor, Paul. 1990. *Oral Poetry: An Introduction*. Theory and History of Literature, Volume 70. Minneapolis: University of Minnesota Press.

Zumwalt, Rosemary Lévy. 1988. *American Folklore Scholarship: A Dialogue of Dissent*. Bloomington: Indiana University Press.

Notes on Contributors

Cristina Bacchilega is Associate Professor of English at the University of Hawai'i at Mānoa. Her work on folk narrative, contemporary fiction, and feminist theory has appeared in *Textual Practice, Journal of Folklore Research, Fabula, La ricerca folklorica, New York Folklore, boundary 2*, and other journals. Recent articles include "The Fruit of the Womb: Creative Uses of a Natualizing Tradition in Folktales" in *Creativity and Tradition in Folklore* (1992). She is the editor of *La narrativa postmoderna in America: testi e contesti* (1986) and the co-editor of a *Western Folklore* special issue on the "Innocent Persecuted Heroine" Fairy Tale (1993); she is currently finishing a book on gender and narrativity in contemporary revisions of classic fairy tales.

John D. Dorst is Associate Professor in the American Studies Program at the University of Wyoming. He is the author of *The Written Suburb: An American Site, An Ethnographic Dilemma* (1989) and various essays including, "Postmodernism vs. Postmodernity: Implications for Folklore Studies" in *Folklore Forum* (1988) and "Tags and Burners, Cycles and Networks: Folklore in the Telectronic Age" in the *Journal of Folklore Research* (1990). He is currently working on a study of display environments in the American West (museums, folk art environments, living history exercises, theme parks), with the intention of identifying a discourse of looking, through which this region constructs itself.

Jean R. Freedman is a Ph. D. candidate in Folklore and Ethnomusicology at Indiana University. She has previously written about representations of women and female sexuality in Scottish traditional ballads, an example of which is her article, "With Child: Illegitimate Pregnancy in Scottish Traditional Ballads" in *Folklore Forum* (1991). Her Ph. D. dissertation will focus on the interaction between expressive culture and political ideology in wartime London.

Alesia García is a Ph. D. candidate in Literature at the University of Arizona. Her research focuses on Chicana feminist theories and

Chicano, Native American, and African American folklore as it intersects with "canonical" nineteenth and twentieth century American literatures. She is also interested in exploring how literary theory can be transformed into a profession that encourages bridging theory and practice.

Lee Haring is Professor of English at Brooklyn College of the City University of New York. His research in African and Western Indian Ocean folklore has been published in articles in the *Journal of American Folklore, Research in African Literature,* and *Fabula.* He is author of *Malagasy Tale Index* (1982) and *Verbal Arts in Madagascar* (1992).

Eric L. Montenyohl was a faculty member in the English Department at the University of Southwestern Louisiana from 1986 until quite recently when he moved to North Carolina. His research interests include historiography, contemporary folklore, and the relationships of folklore and literature. He has published essays in a number of publications, including *Folklore Forum, Western Folklore, Southern Folklore,* and *Motif,* as well as contributed to a number of reference works, including *Notable Women in American Folklore, The Mark Twain Encyclopedia,* and MLA's *Literary Research Guide.*

Peter Narváez is an Associate Professor of Folklore at Memorial University of Newfoundland. A past president of the Folklore Studies Association of Canada and the Association for the Study of Canadian Radio and Television, he has published many articles in academic journals on a wide variety of topics including Newfoundland folklore, African-American blues, vernacular song, folk narrative, folk belief, occupational folklife, and popular culture. In addition, he has edited *Media Sense: The Folklore-Popular Culture Continuum* (with Martin Laba) and *The Good People: New Fairylore Essays.*

Laura O'Connor is a graduate student at Columbia University. She is writing her dissertation on Celticism in modern poetry. The poets who feature in her work include Matthew Arnold, Gerard Manley Hopkins, W. B. Yeats, Marianne Moore, Hugh MacDiarmid, Nuala Ni Dhomhnaill, and Medbh McGuckian.

Notes on Contributors

Cathy Lynn Preston teaches at the University of Colorado at Boulder. Her research interests focus on socio-cultural constructions of gender, class, and sexuality. She is the editor of *A KWIC Concordance to Thomas Hardy's "Tess of the d'Urbervilles"* (1989), co-editor of two volumes of *Urban Folklore from Colorado* (1976), and has published articles on folk and vernacular culture, most recently "'The Tying of the Garter': Representations of the Female Rural Laborer in 17th-, 18th-, and 19th-Century English Bawdy Songs" in the *Journal of American Folklore* (1992) and "Cinderella as a Dirty Joke: Gender, Multivocality, and the Polysemic Text" in *Western Folklore* (1994). She is co-editor of a forthcoming collection of essays entitled, *The Other Print Tradition: Chapbooks, Broadsides, and Related Ephemera*.

Michael J. Preston is Associate Professor of English at the University of Colorado at Boulder where he was Director of the Center for Computer Research in the Humanities for fourteen years. He has edited a dozen concordances, including *A Concordance to the Middle English Shorter Poem* (1974) and *A KWIC Concordance to the Plays of the Wakefield Master* (1982), co-authored *Chapbooks and Traditional Drama* (1977), and co-edited two volumes of *Urban Folklore from Colorado* (1976). His work is published broadly in such journals as *Computers and the Humanities, Comparative Drama, The Bibliothech, Herpetological Review, Keystone Folklore, Journal of American Folklore*, a most recent example of which is "Traditional Humor from the Fax Machine" in *Western Folklore* (1994). He is co-editor of a forthcoming collection of essays entitled, *The Other Print Tradition: Chapbooks, Broadsides, and Related Ephemera*.

Danielle M. Roemer is Associate Professor of folklore and literature in the Literature and Language Department at Northern Kentucky University. She has published articles in the fields of children's folklore, bodylore, and folklore and literature, recent examples of which are "The Personal Narrative and Salinger's *Catcher in the Rye*" in *Western Folklore* (1992) and "Photocopy Lore and the Naturalization of the Corporate Body" in the *Journal of American Folklore* (1994). She is co-editor of a *Western Folklore* special issue on "The Personal Narrative in Literature" (1992). Her current research interests are in the intertextual relations of written literature, folk legend, and *marchen*.

María Herrera-Sobek is Director of the Chicano/Latino Studies Program and Associate Professor of Spanish at the University of California at Irvine. She is the author of several articles and books, including *The Bracero Experience: Elitelore versus Folklore* (1979), *Beyond Stereotypes: The Critical Analysis of Chicana Literature* (1985), *The Mexican Corrido: A Feminist Analysis* (1990), and "*Corridos* and *Canciones* of *Mica, Migra* and *Coyotes*: A Commentary on Undocumented Immigration" in *Creative Ethnicity: Symbols and Strategies of Contemporary Ethnic Life* (1991). She has also co-authored *Chicana Creativity and Criticism: Charting New Frontiers in American Literature* (1988).

Clover Williams is a doctoral candidate in Folklore at Indiana University. She has published articles on various aspects of women's culture, including quilting, sex-industry work, and romance novel reading, recent examples of which are "The Bachelor's Transgression: Identity and Difference in the Bachelor Party" in the *Journal of American Folklore* (1994) and "Keepers of the Flame: The Romance Novel and its Fans" (forthcoming) in *Lore and Language*. Her dissertation fieldwork is on long-distance truck driving.

Mark E. Workman is Professor of literature and folklore and Chair of the Language and Literature Department at the University of North Florida at Jacksonville. His research centers on various aspects of the relationship between oral and written literature. His recent publications include an article on beginnings, entitled "Foreplay," which appeared in *SubStance* (1991), an article on "Narratable and Unnarratable Lives" in *Western Folklore* (1992), and an article on metaphor, entitled "Tropes, Hopes, and Dopes," which appeared in the *Journal of American Folklore* (1993).

NEW PERSPECTIVES IN FOLKLORE
CARL LINDAHL AND MARGARET MILLS, *Series Editors*

FINNISH FOLK POETRY
AND THE *Kalevala*
Thomas A. DuBois

FOLKLORE, LITERATURE,
AND CULTURAL THEORY
Collected Essays
edited by Cathy Lynn Preston

THE OTHER PRINT TRADITION
*Essays on Chapbooks, Broadsides,
and Related Ephemera*
edited by Cathy Lynn Preston
and Michael J. Preston